S

is a former stock-ma
plier-turned-public s
banned from America
was forced to reappra me, reading over a thousand books in just under six years. He credits books as
being the lifeblood of his rehabilitation.

Shaun's writing, smuggled out of jail, attracted international media attention to the human rights violations
he witnessed. He now tells his story to schools and on
online platforms to put young people off a life of drugs
and crime. He campaigns against injustice via his books
and blog, and has appeared on major television outlets
in over forty countries talking about issues affecting
prisoners' rights.

You can find him at www.shaunattwood.com, where
he'd love to hear from you.

Also by Shaun Attwood

Sitdowns with Gangsters
Sitdowns with Female Gangsters

SITDOWNS WITH SERIAL KILLERS & MURDERERS

Shaun Attwood

SEVEN DIALS

First published in Great Britain in 2025 by Seven Dials,
an imprint of The Orion Publishing Group Ltd
Carmelite House, 50 Victoria Embankment
London EC4Y 0DZ

An Hachette UK Company

The authorised representative in the EEA is Hachette Ireland, 8 Castlecourt
Centre, Dublin 15, D15 XTP3, Ireland (email: info@hbgi.ie)

1 3 5 7 9 10 8 6 4 2

A CIP catalogue record for this book is
available from the British Library.

ISBN (Mass Market Paperback) 9781399607216
ISBN (Ebook) 9781399607223
ISBN (Audio) 9781399607230

Typeset by Born Group
Printed and bound in Great Britain by Clays Ltd, Elcograf S.p.A.

MIX
Paper | Supporting
responsible forestry
FSC   FSC® C104740
www.fsc.org

www.orionbooks.co.uk

To Ron, Dan and Baby Nova

Contents

Introduction

Desensitised from interviewing so many people with dark stories, I was surprised by the disturbed sleep I experienced after doing a podcast episode with Dellmus Colvin – a serial killer serving multiple life sentences who claims to have murdered more than fifty women. Even more surprising was how I was drawn to re-listen to the podcast (something I never do) when I woke unsettled the following morning. Perhaps it was the manner in which Colvin transitioned from warm greetings and prison banter to then casually describing his time as a long-haul truck driver. He would give the truck-stop sex workers one chance and if they pestered him further, he would invite them into his vehicle, snap their necks and sling their bodies in the back.

Colvin described the chilling details of his actions with the pride of someone more accustomed to cleaning up the streets. Equally disturbing was how easy he found it to commit these murders, while living a double life with his girlfriend, enjoying barbecues on the weekends.

For the next week, I couldn't get Dellmus Colvin out of my head and, even now, a small part of him remains, which is why this book should probably come with a warning: be careful what you put into your own mind! In comparison to the hard-hitting stories in my previous books, *Sitdowns with Gangsters* (2023) and *Sitdowns with Female Gangsters* (2025), the stories in this book are extreme. In those earlier books, redemption was a strong feature of many story arcs, but when dealing with serial killers and murderers, redemption is absent in many cases. If Colvin hadn't been caught, or if he were released tomorrow, I can only imagine the scale of the horrors he would be orchestrating.

After reading the chapter on Dellmus Colvin, you might conclude that he is far removed from the 'serial-killer stereotype' we often see on TV or films or read about. Indeed, murderers come in all shapes and sizes, and from my own experience of six years of incarceration, meeting and living alongside many murderers, I quickly learned about the range of crimes committed: from the family man with a thriving business who comes home to find his wife in bed with a lover and shoots them both dead in a crime of passion to the Aryan Brotherhood (AB) gang member who murders to rise up in the gang and proudly displays tattoos that enable those in the know to recognise his deadly achievements. The crime-of-passion prisoners were some of the most remorseful and well behaved, whereas the prison gang members were running huge drug conspiracies which periodically required acts of extreme violence and murder to keep everyone in line – which brings us to the world of former Aryan Brotherhood prison gang leader Michael Thompson, also featured in this book.

When it comes to murder, the Aryan Brotherhood, according to the Federal Bureau of Investigation (FBI), is responsible for a disproportionate number of murders in the US prison system. Presently, it is classified as a neo-Nazi gang and organised crime syndicate with an estimated 20,000 members, both inside and outside prison. Michael Thompson became a leader of the gang by default. Incarcerated for forty-five years for a double homicide he told me that he didn't commit, he ascended the ranks, noted for his remarkable fighting skills whereby he dominated and excelled in endless fights, even though he was stabbed and shot multiple times. As a feared leader, he gave the orders, outsmarted the prison administration's security protocols to get weapons smuggled in (using, among others, the infamous Charles Manson's female visitors) and helped to build a criminal empire worth millions. But when his associates voted to assassinate relatives of gang drop-outs, it crossed a line in his moral universe and he dropped out. In the following decades, he survived numerous attempts on his life by gang members – and prison guards!

In the notorious California State Prison, Corcoran, the guards formed their own gang and held gladiator games, whereby inmates were forced to fight, sometimes to their deaths, and some who refused were executed. I'll never forget Michael Thompson telling me that he had to work out sufficiently to grow his muscles to a size that would absorb the guard's bullets and be able to fight a few extra seconds against his knife-wielding opponents. The staff placed bets on who would win, ambulances were standing by and death reports written up in advance. The death rate went up so high that the FBI were called in to investigate the prison. Another punishment inflicted by the guards was to put Rudy the Brute in your cell – a murderer, serial rapist and prison enforcer who received special treatment from the staff in return for sodomising prisoners.

Another class of murderer featured in this book is Mafia killers. For Two Tonys, the first convicted killer I interviewed at length, breaking bones, burying bodies and planting bombs became second nature while working as an associate for the Bonanno Italian-American crime family. I'll never forget him describing the fine mist that filled a hotel room as he executed a man with a shot that disintegrated a section of his opponent's skull. Formerly in the Navy, Two Tonys compared killing in the Mafia to killing in the army, whereby you sign up to kill or be killed if you break the code. Under the old-school traditions, killing women and children was prohibited. The chapter on Anthony Ruggiano Jr., a former proposed member of the Gambino family, reads like a scene out of *The Godfather*, when he tricks his own renegade and abusive brother-in-law into attending a meeting where his fate awaits him.

The men in this book have committed the most serious crimes I have ever heard about and many of them, such as Two Tonys, have done so unapologetically. Interviewing them was a real eye-opener to the scope and range of motivations for murder. It is my hope that in entering the minds of these killers, we gain a greater understanding of the dangers that lurk in society. Dellmus Colvin may be behind bars for life, but he claims there are other serial killers out there, just like him.

1

John Hilton

'We live on the outskirts of society'

The man waits under the lorry with his shotgun lying next to him and hopes the target will arrive soon.

The damp from the drizzly London evening is working its way slowly into his clothes and the cold, hard ground is becoming uncomfortable to lie on. He mutters a curse and hopes the target will hurry up. Minutes tick by and the lights of a car flash down the road. The vehicle pulls in behind the lorry and the man grabs his shotgun in anticipation. Peering out from under the vehicle, he recognises the target's car: a maroon-coloured Daimler.

It's on.

From his hiding place, he watches his target as he crosses the tree-lined avenue in the rich North London suburb of Golders Green. He is wearing an unbuttoned dark overcoat and carrying a black bag in his left hand. This is the prize: a bag containing £400,000 worth of diamonds. As he watches, another man dressed in dark clothing emerges from the shadows behind the target and rushes up to him.

That's the cue. Clutching his shotgun, he emerges from under the lorry and rushes across the road to join the fray. The man in dark clothes – his partner, Alan – is attacking the target with a

5

truncheon, much like the police use, but it's having little effect. The man won't let go of his bag and is protecting himself against the baton, using his briefcase as a shield. The man tries to escape and starts shouting in Hebrew, presumably calling for help.

He curses under his breath; he had told Alan the truncheon would be useless. But no time for regrets now, he has to make a quick decision. There is only one thing for it. He barks out a quick warning to his partner to get out of the way, then fires the shotgun, aiming at the target's leg. But just as he fires, the two men spin around in their struggle. Instead of hitting the target, the shot strikes Alan in his left thigh. Alan goes down on one knee, but immediately gets back up. Meanwhile, the target is escaping with the bag. He raises the shotgun and fires, hitting the man squarely in the lower back, causing him to fly through the air before landing in a heap, face down on the ground. For a minute, he marvels at how shooting someone really is just like in the films, then snaps back into action. He grabs the bag with one hand and his partner Alan with the other, then rushes back to their getaway car.

After helping Alan into the backseat, he throws the bag in after him. He flings the shotgun onto the passenger seat then gets into the driver's seat, turns on the ignition and races off, taking several sharp turns until he's out of the immediate vicinity of the robbery. When he's far enough away to relax a little, he takes a look at Alan in the rear-view mirror and asks how he's doing.

Alan's face is pale as he clutches his leg. 'I'm in trouble,' he gasps.

He stares grimly at the road in front and wonders whether these diamonds were worth all the trouble. This must be what they mean by blood diamonds, he thinks wryly, as he wonders what to do about his dying partner.

*

The shooter was John Hilton, a notorious armed robber who wasn't afraid to use his gun. Convicted of two murders, and involved in four other shootings, in 1963 he was sentenced to a total of three life sentences, spending forty-five years in prison. He is the longest-serving UK prisoner I have ever interviewed, a man who has spent time in every prison in the UK. Now in his mid-nineties, Hilton is still going strong and as energetic as ever, telling the story of his life with a twinkle in his eye and an incredible memory for detail.

Born in 1929, in Brixton, South London, some of Hilton's earliest memories were of the bombs falling on London during the Blitz. 'I used to lie in my room listening to the shrapnel rattling down,' he told me, 'and the guns going off, bombs falling down . . . Every morning at school, we'd say prayers for the kids that were killed the night before.'

Most of the children in London had the opportunity to evacuate to the countryside, where they were temporarily housed by families living in safer areas. Hilton's family had their own chance of escape when his parents found a new house in Harrow, a town on the north-west outskirts of London. The family moved into a row of terraced houses where, in the war-time spirit of camaraderie, everyone looked out for each other. A twelve-year-old Hilton was enamoured by the war and would spend his free time exploring bomb craters and collecting empty shell and ammunition cases.

But the conflict would soon become more than a game. Hilton woke up one night to find himself choking on dust and covered in rubble. 'I remember shouting and screaming, "Mother! Mother! Mother!"' he told me. 'And I heard someone shouting, "Alright, we're coming!" And I went unconscious.'

He woke up in Harrow Hospital with a depressed fracture to the skull. But the news was far worse than his injuries. A stick of bombs had fallen on Hilton's row of houses, demolishing all five of them and killing everyone inside, including his parents and his two older sisters. He was the only person left alive.

Hilton spent some time recuperating in hospital, where the nurses mothered him. One of the Irish women told him, 'God must have kept you alive for a reason.'

Hilton recovered swiftly and one day he was surprised to find he had a visitor, an attractive woman who stared at him with an odd intensity. He was even more surprised when she told him that she was his biological mother. It was only then he discovered that he had been fostered. His biological mother had got rid of him at birth, but now, hearing of his plight, she had come to take him back home with her.

Hilton returned with his mother to her flat in Belgravia but his dreams of having someone to care for him were soon shattered. His mum didn't seem to want to have anything to do with him. She hated him hanging around and soon he spent most of his time trying to avoid her. She got her wish to be rid of him again when he was evacuated to a village near Derby to escape the Blitz, but he was swiftly sent back after he stole a bike and hid it behind a church. In the meantime, his mother had found a new house in Hove, a town on the South Coast.

Hilton's new home was expansive and lavish with a grand piano and a balcony overlooking the sea, but it was also devoid of love. The young boy spent most of his free time tinkering with his bike, changing the gears and making other alterations. He soon found that his ability to modify the bike was limited by his small set of tools so, one day, he ventured to a nearby shop, where he spotted the adjustable spanner he needed. The temptation to steal was too strong and Hilton slipped the tool into his pocket.

Unfortunately, he was spotted and collared by the eagle-eyed shopkeeper, who called the police. Hilton was sent to Hove Juvenile Court, where he was fined a mere two shillings. The magistrate was about to release him with the fine and a stern talking-to when his mother stood up and requested to speak. To Hilton's stunned amazement, instead of putting in a good word for her son, she told the judge that she thought he would benefit from a period of discipline. The surprised judge agreed to her request and sentenced Hilton to an eighteen-month stint in an approved school, a residential institution for children with behavioural issues.

At the approved school in Redhill, Surrey, Hilton tried to keep his head down and stay out of trouble. One day, one of the older boys started bullying him, trying to make him do his work for him. Hilton refused to back down and as the argument escalated, more boys gathered round, egging them on to fight. Taking the lead, Hilton stepped forward and punched the bigger boy three times in the face, stunning him and causing him to drop to the floor. Realising that he was now in for a severe beating from the boy and his gang, he then turned and ran across the fields and out of the grounds. He made it to the train station and bought a one-way ticket home. Unfortunately, the school staff made it to the station before the train did. Hilton was bundled into a van and driven back to school, where he was caned in front of everyone. Six strokes left his backside so badly injured, he couldn't sit or lie on his back for several days. The wounds took a month to heal.

When he was finally released from the school, Hilton returned home. Now too old to go back to his previous school, he found work on the fruit and vegetable stall at the local market. He was doing well and staying out of trouble until one day, a friend of his who had previously worked at the stall suggested a way of stealing the takings.

One lunch break, Hilton hid himself in the cellar where his boss stored all the produce. When the manager locked up the building to take his customary hour-long lunch break, Hilton's friend knocked on the door and Hilton let him in. Together, they broke into the office and stole the cash, which amounted to £250 – quite a lot of money in the 1940s.

Hilton thought he had got away with the robbery and carried on working at the greengrocer's, but a few days later he was called into the boss's office to see him flanked by two police officers. Hilton was arrested and taken to the police station for questioning. Apparently, some workers had spotted him coming out of the building just after the robbery.

Hilton pleaded not guilty and was held on remand until the trial. He was sixteen years old now, so faced more than an approved school if convicted. In court, he was forced to change his plea to guilty after he realised the strength of the witnesses' testimony. When the judge asked if anyone wanted to speak on Hilton's behalf, his mother stepped forward again. This time Hilton dared to hope that she would say something positive to prevent him from being incarcerated. He was disappointed again. Instead of trying to help him, his mum told the court he was unmanageable and asked that they place him in an institution. It was the last time he would ever trust her.

Hilton was sentenced to three years in the borstal wing of Wormwood Scrubs in West London. The regime was harsh. The boys, aged sixteen to twenty, had physical exercise routines in the morning, followed by work stitching mail bags until lunchtime. Lunch was a thin soup with a hunk of stale bread that left him still feeling hungry. There was another period of exercise before more mail-bag stitching until dinner time. Fortunately, Hilton made a good friend to help him counter the tedium, an Irish boy named Pat Murphy, and the two stuck together, avoiding the intimidation of the various gangs.

Hilton decided to combat his constant hunger by getting a job in the kitchen, where he could feed off the extra scraps. One day, another boy approached him and asked for a share of the leftovers. Hilton explained that there was barely enough for himself and Pat, but the boy was having none of it. He started to get aggressive and demanded some food. Hilton had learned from his experience in the approved school that it was best to nip intimidating tactics in the bud. He stepped forward and headbutted the bully before downing him with a right hook, then kicking him savagely in the face. The fight was over before it had even begun.

However, the incident led to him and Pat being transferred to another borstal, this time in Rochester, Kent, which had a tougher military-style regime designed to knock the young men into shape. Hilton and Pat were soon forced to face up to the reality of constant hunger again. At mealtimes, they were placed on long tables, each one with a pecking order. The food was delivered to one end, where the table leader took his share before passing it on to the next inmate and so on, until finally it reached the other end where the newcomers, Hilton and Pat, were placed. By the time the food got to them, there was barely more than a few leftovers.

Unafraid, Hilton approached the table leader and pointed out how little food he and his friend were left with, asking if there was a fairer way of sharing it out. The table leader told him unceremoniously where to go and Hilton was left fuming. That evening, he and Pat came up with a plan to show the leader he had picked the wrong people to disrespect. Hilton decided to wait until the boy was in the bathroom brushing his teeth the next morning.

'The bed legs used to unscrew,' he told me. 'I unscrewed this bed leg and wrapped it in a towel, and I said to my mate, "When he comes in, just whistle." I went and sat on the toilet with the door shut. I heard the whistle, opened the door. He was bending over, cleaning his teeth, so I walked up behind him, pulled this bed leg out and beat him over the head with it four or five times as hard as I could, and he fell unconscious, bleeding heavily.'

Hilton quickly washed the bed leg and screwed it back onto the bed before heading to the hall for breakfast, leaving no one the wiser. The table leader was taken to hospital and a few days later, several of the other boys approached Hilton about becoming the new table leader but he refused. He didn't want to be top dog, just to have his fair share of food.

Hilton and Pat soon got themselves jobs as trash collectors. This allowed them access to parts of the prison other inmates never saw. On one of their shifts, they found a yard that contained all kinds of maintenance equipment, including ladders. The yard was only separated by a fence of around six feet. The two inmates suddenly realised they had an easy means of escape: they could scale the fence, then use one of the long ladders to climb the prison wall. The only tricky bit would be getting out of their dormitory at night.

They decided the best way was to tie bed sheets together to make a rope to lower themselves from their dorm-room window. To open the high window, Hilton needed to climb a metal conduit pipe to the top of the wall, then put his foot into an air vent and lean over to pull away the protective metal mesh. He could then smash the window and with the bed sheets tied around his waist, scale down the outside wall.

However, when he climbed the pipe and was trying to pull the metal mesh away, it suddenly gave way and Hilton found himself falling some fifteen feet to the floor below. He lay stunned for a couple of seconds before springing back up and running to the dining area, where he sat down at one of the tables. People were staring at him in shock and horror. Looking down, he saw why. The third and fourth fingers on his left hand had been completely severed, the bones gleaming whitely up at him, and the index finger on his right hand was hanging off. There was blood everywhere.

Hilton was taken to the nearby hospital and had an emergency operation to patch up his wounds. After treatment, he was placed on a stretcher and taken back to the borstal, where he was dumped unceremoniously in a punishment cell and left in complete darkness overnight without medical supervision or pain relief.

'I was there for twenty-four hours,' he told me, 'and during that time I was in absolute agony. I've never been in so much pain in all my life. Blood was seeping through the bandages. I urinated myself. I couldn't do nothing.'

Still no one came to check on him, except for one of his fellow inmates who happened to be passing. Shocked by Hilton's state, he told the other inmates, who later spoke to the prison governor, threatening to riot unless Hilton was taken to hospital. The governor gave in and Hilton finally got the proper medical attention he required. He stayed in hospital for three weeks but the experience alone in the punishment cell stayed with him for the rest of his life.

'I think it was a seismic event in my life,' Hilton told me. 'And I said, I will never show fear and never show that I'm missing my family, or missing whatever. I might be raging inside, I might be frightened inside, but I'd never show it.'

Hilton still had to face his punishment for the escape. Despite his serious injuries, he was put on bread and water rations for several days, which left him constantly hungry, depleted of energy and malnourished. He was also deprived of his exercise privileges, missing out on the Sunday 'route march' where the boys trekked through the local countryside. After finally being allowed back on the walks several months later, he was so thoroughly fed up, he decided to make a getaway at the first opportunity. When he was sure no one was looking, he climbed inside a large bush and hunkered down.

Despite the chaos of shouting and searching that ensued, no one thought to look inside the bush. One officer was standing so close to Hilton's hiding place he heard him say, 'If I catch that little bastard, I will kick his arse all the way back to borstal.'

Soon the coast was clear and Hilton was able to make his escape, finding his way back to London. It turned out that, following his example, Pat had done exactly the same and they stayed in London together at Pat's aunt's place in Bethnal Green. Pat's uncle ran an illegal trade in stolen textiles. The boys began working for him, breaking into warehouses and tailors' shops to steal rolls of fine cloth that could be made into suits. They acquired a van and soon had a regular business breaking into factories and warehouse all around the East End. They earned enough money to have their own tailored suits and to spend their free time partying in the West End.

Unfortunately, one night they were spotted carrying a heavy roll of stolen cloth by two police officers. They dropped the roll and ran, but Hilton was caught after a neighbour spotted him hiding in her garden. He was arrested and sentenced to three more years in borstal.

Hilton was sent back to Rochester, where he faced punishment for his previous escape. Deprived of his mattress, he was forced to sleep on the cold stone floor. He was also forced to live off just bread and water for fifteen days, which left him so malnourished he suffered heart palpitations. He was then transferred to another borstal at Portland which, despite the bleak and windy atmosphere of the peninsula island, suited him much better. The borstal there concentrated heavily on exercise and Hilton was able to play lots of football and practise boxing and swimming. The last twelve months of his sentence were much more enjoyable and he was soon on a train back to London.

He went back to Pat's aunt's flat in Bethnal Green, only to find that Pat had moved to Birmingham for work. Nevertheless, Aunt Vera gave him his old room back and Pat's uncle, Sam, soon had some more work for him. Sam hooked him up with an old professional burglar called Fred, one of the best thieves in London but now in his sixties. His knees were failing so he needed a younger partner.

Under Fred's mentorship, Hilton began to really learn his trade as a thief. Fred taught him how to break locks and other tricks of the trade, and soon they were breaking into four or five upmarket properties a day, clearing them of all their cash and jewellery. Their partnership lasted ten months until, after one hasty escape, Fred's bad knee gave way and he decided to retire. Hilton chose to continue on his own, but soon he had become so well known around the East End that rumours started to circulate that the police were after him. He decided to move out of Bethnal Green to Tottenham in North London.

One day, while having a drink in a pub, Hilton got talking to another thief who offered him work robbing the wages of an engineering firm in North London. The plan was to surprise the car that delivered the wages outside the factory and jump the four minders with pickaxe handles and bottles filled with ammonia, before escaping with several thousand pounds in cash. Hilton was introduced to the other robbers: Bob, an ex-boxer; Gus, a tall man with an intimidating look; and Philip, a smaller man with a gambling addiction. They planned the heist and on the day of the robbery, everything went to plan. Hilton knocked his minder unconscious with one blow of his pickaxe handle and the robbers were soon bundling the money into the back of their getaway car.

Hilton and his colleagues made a grand each from the robbery – not bad money in the 1950s. In fact, the robbery had gone so smoothly the four men were soon planning more heists together. Hilton's gang, or 'firm' as it was called in those days, was born.

In the meantime, Hilton's personal life was developing too. He met and married his first wife in 1956. A year later, their son, Steven, was born. But family life didn't suit him, especially as he was forced to live with his wife's parents. He felt stifled and spent more and more time on the road with the firm, travelling the country to find new targets for their robberies. The money was rolling in constantly and they pulled off a big job in Brighton on the South Coast. Instead of going home afterwards, Hilton sent some money to his wife and stayed on in the coastal resort to party with the rest of the firm, even buying himself a Jaguar sports car to cruise around the town in.

Hilton's friend owned a nightclub in Brighton and one night the firm were enjoying their usual VIP treatment at the club when a bouncer burst in and asked if it was their friend outside. Hilton and the others rushed outside to find their friend, Morris, bleeding badly with a terrible wound to his face. The bouncer told them that a local hardman called Bob Wetherby had attacked Morris, hitting him so hard his eyebrow was hanging off.

Drunk and seeking vengeance, the friends jumped in a car and set off to find Wetherby, all carrying weapons, Hilton with a large blade in hand. They drove to Wetherby's house and piled inside as soon as he opened the door. Enraged and seeking blood, Hilton told me, 'I tried to cut his arm off.' Fortunately for everyone concerned, the men were too inebriated to inflict any lasting damage and were soon piling back in the car to make their escape. Unfortunately for them, the vehicle ran out of petrol and they ended up stranded on a roundabout on the A23. Hilton decided to hail a passing van for a lift, but luck wasn't with him that night as the vehicle behind it was a police car. The car stopped and Hilton tried to brazen it out, telling officers that he and his friends had run out of petrol, asking for a lift to the nearest petrol station. The officers agreed, but little did Hilton and his friends know, a call had gone out looking for five men regarding the assault on Wetherby. As soon as they arrived at the petrol station, several more police cars came speeding up, surrounding them. They were arrested for grievous bodily harm and taken to the station.

Hilton received a five-year sentence for his part in the attack. He served eighteen months in Wandsworth before being transferred to Dartmoor, which had a reputation for being one of the worst prisons in the UK because of its terrible conditions, including dense fog that would enter the building and freeze the prisoners in their cells. But Hilton ended up enjoying his time for one reason: the manual labour – 'I was breaking rocks with an eighteen-pound sledgehammer,' he told me, 'and pleased to be doing so.'

On his release, he went straight back to London, where the rest of the firm were waiting. The first thing he asked his colleagues was if they had a job planned. They told me one was coming up on the Tuesday. Hilton was straight back into the game. He bought a new flat and a car and moved his wife and son in with him, settling down to a life of armed robbery.

Hilton and his firm were good at what they did. Once they had identified a target, they would meticulously plan the robbery, working out an escape route and using two getaway cars. The first car they would use to race away from the scene of the crime before transferring to a second car parked down a quiet back street, which they would drive away sensibly. The cars themselves would be stolen. Hilton would find a quiet commuter car park to steal from, then use a sledgehammer to smash the window of a vehicle. Once inside, he would screw a self-taping screw into the ignition then yank out the entire ignition before inserting a small screwdriver to start the car. He would store the stolen car in a lock-up and change the registration plates by going to a car accessory store and saying he had damaged his number plate. He would then order a new one with a completely different registration number.

Hilton would pull off robberies in the daytime but then be home by four o'clock to pick his son up from school. It was a surreal double existence which he revelled in. 'I lived the life,' he told me. 'I bought a couple of cars. I was booted and suited. My wife had what she wanted. The kid had what he wanted. We used to go out in the West End once a week.'

At this point, the firm were still using pickaxe handles and bottles of ammonia, but in the late fifties, all that changed when they planned to do a job stealing the wages from a building site. Hilton and his colleagues steamed in as usual, taking out the minders and seizing the cash. However, they failed to plan for a dangerous contingency: the builders getting involved. Seeing their wages being stolen, two dozen enraged brickies attacked. Hilton and his gang were now in a fight for their lives. Even with their weapons, they were no match for more than twenty tough men. A fierce fight ensued and for a while, Hilton thought he might not make it out alive. Somehow the firm managed to fight their way to the exit and escape, but they had suffered a severe battering to their bodies and their egos.

The building site fiasco caused Hilton and his firm to rethink. They decided they needed guns to avoid any further confrontations and to get them in and out of places with more speed. Hilton managed to obtain a couple of shotguns and soon they were back in business, taking on bigger jobs. They would hold up a bank every fortnight. Hilton would rush in and wield his shotgun in the air, screaming that he would shoot 'the first fucker' to move. The others would grab the money while Hilton subdued the hostages. If anyone didn't play ball, he would fire a shot into the ceiling, causing white polystyrene to shower down like snow, which always had the intended effect. The one big rule was not to shoot anyone unless it was absolutely necessary and then only in the leg – the guns were merely deterrents and the firm didn't want any murders on their hands.

But sometimes it was a fine line between deterrence and self-protection, as Hilton found out the first time he shot someone during a bank robbery. 'As I come out of the bank, I see a big old boy in a blue suit,' Hilton told me. 'He'd followed us out. Something made me turn around. I just see him about to launch himself onto my mate's back, so I shot him in the leg, and he screamed.' The firm got away.

Hilton had been forced to shoot, but he had been disciplined. Unfortunately, not all of the firm were so calm and calculating when holding a shotgun and this would ultimately be their demise.

They had been doing armed robberies for about a year when Bob the ex-boxer pulled the friends together to tell them of a potential job involving particularly rich pickings. He had followed a security van which delivered money to the head offices of a dairy firm in Mitcham, south-west London. The company was huge and he estimated there could be takings of around £40,000.

The firm went about their usual work of monitoring the target, finding the best way to enter and exit, and the best escape route. Hilton discovered that a school playground bordered the offices and that they could lay low on the roof of the toilet block before hopping over a small fence, straight to where the money was delivered. It looked pretty straightforward. All they needed was to steal three cars for the getaway. Hilton, Bob and Gus decided to steal a car each and Philip was to have them re-plated. Hilton and Bob stole their cars without a hitch, but Gus was tardy and ended up buying a stolen car from another firm whose job had fallen through. This was usually a big no-no, but there was nothing Hilton could do about it. Gus had left it to the night before the job so there was no time to get another car. Reluctantly, Hilton agreed to use the vehicle Gus provided, but it was a decision he would regret for the rest of his life.

The day of the robbery came and Hilton packed his balaclava and gloves into a bag and stowed his automatic .45 pistol in his shoulder holster. He would be carrying the money while Bob and Gus held the place up with a .38 revolver and Second World War Luger pistol. Having left the getaway cars in pre-arranged locations, they drove to the dairy firm headquarters. Then they made their way to the toilet block in the school playground from where they could watch the security van arrive. Like clockwork, the van pulled up and the guards delivered the bags of money to the office. The four men waited impatiently for the van to pull away and were poised to spring into action.

But just then, two of the office workers strode out to have a cigarette just where they were planning on making their entry. The four men looked at each other, questioning whether they should carry on as arranged or cancel the robbery for now. Hilton had a bad feeling about it but the other three were keen to go ahead. Instead of going over the wall, they decided to drive through the main gate, past a security hut manned by an ageing guard.

After running back to their car, they drove through the main gates and past the security guard, who rushed out of his cabin in surprise. They screeched up outside the office and rushed inside, Gus and Bob pulling out their guns and screaming at everyone to get on the floor while Hilton went for the bags of cash. Hilton screamed at one of the office workers, asking where the money was. 'In the back!' she cried, her voice distorted by fear. Hilton thought she had said, 'In the bag' so he rushed over to grab one of the bags, only to find it almost empty. He didn't have time to voice his surprise, however, because just then he heard a shot ring out from behind the office door.

'Gus come running,' Hilton told me, 'shouting, "Everybody out! I've just shot someone!" I thought, I don't believe it. I looked at him and I thought, you fucking idiot. I went out and saw this geezer just lying there, hands in his pockets, a bullet hole here,' – Hilton pointed to a spot just below his right eye – 'blood out the back of his head, dead as a door nail.'

The men rushed outside, where they saw a lorry heading straight towards them. Gus fired another shot which smashed the windscreen, causing the driver to throw himself to the side. They piled into the getaway car and screamed out of the grounds as fast as they could, making their way to the second getaway car and then, at a more leisurely pace, to the third. They made their escape successfully, but all four men were stunned. They had broken their number-one rule: not to kill anyone.

Over the next few days, the robbers got rid of the guns and the getaway cars except, fatally, the vehicle Gus had obtained from another firm. They were too scared to approach the vehicle in case the police had it under surveillance. The friends laid low and didn't see much of each other until Gus called one day and asked to meet with Hilton. When they got together, Gus had bad news – Philip had been arrested in connection with the getaway car. They decided not to panic; they knew Philip would hold out and not give away any information about the robbery or their parts in it.

Both went back to lying low but one night soon after, Hilton was filled with a premonition of danger while lying in bed. Leaping up, he grabbed his car keys and left the house. He soon realised that his premonition had been correct. 'I had two cars,' Hilton told me. 'One was a Zodiac convertible, the other was a 3.8 Jag. I got into the Jaguar. As I got into the Jaguar, all these policemen headed right by me with headlights and dogs, everybody had come out, and one of them banged on the bonnet of the car and said, "Move on, move on." And they all ran to the car I wasn't in. They never knew I had a Jag.'

Thanking his lucky stars, Hilton drove off as he watched the police banging down his front door. Now he was on the run. He hastily arranged to meet Gus and Bob at the pub to tell them what had happened so they could do the same. All three agreed that Philip must have grassed them up and went their separate ways. Hilton drove to King's Cross, where he stayed the night with a friend. He then went to Earl's Court and he rented a one-bedroom flat to lie low in over the next few weeks.

It was while living here during the cold winter of 1962–63 that Hilton had another close scrape with the law. 'I'm walking down the street towards my flat,' he told me, 'and there's a plain-clothed policeman and a uniformed policeman walking towards me. They looked at me, I looked at them. They knew I was John Hilton. I was wearing mittens at the time. I thought, I've got to bluff here.'

Hilton pulled off one of his mittens with his teeth and put his hand inside his jacket as if reaching for a gun. The two policemen suddenly showed less interest in him and pretended not to notice as he sauntered past with his hand still inside his coat.

On another occasion, he was taking the Tube to Baker Street to meet Bob when two policemen boarded the train. Despite it being an empty carriage, they sat opposite Hilton, whose mind was racing and body pumped full of adrenaline. Hilton was armed this time and was reading a newspaper so, from behind the paper, he pulled his gun out and cocked it.

'I thought, what I'm going to do is this,' he told me. 'I'm going to get off at Baker Street. If they get up at Baker Street, I'm putting them both down and I'll fuck off . . . I got up at Baker Street and they both stayed where they was. Those two policemen will never know how lucky they were that day.'

Hilton now found out that Gus had been arrested too, so he decided it was time to try and leave the UK. He contacted an old friend who said he knew a sailor based in Liverpool who could smuggle him out on a ship for just £500. Hilton was delighted and agreed. The plan was that Hilton would call his friend every day to find out if the ship was ready to sail. He did as requested every day, up until Christmas. But on Christmas Eve, assuming there would be no ships sailing over the holidays, he didn't call his friend. He waited to get back

23

in contact after the New Year but he was surprised to find his friend was exasperated with him, asking why he hadn't called on Christmas Eve – he had the sailor with him that day and was ready to take Hilton up to Liverpool for a ship sailing on Christmas morning, bound for New Jersey. Cursing his bad judgement, Hilton went back to lying low. He didn't realise at the time that he had just missed his last chance of freedom.

Now it was only Hilton and Bob who were still at large and soon Bob was feeling the heat in his hideout in Southampton, so he asked to move in with Hilton. Meanwhile, Hilton had secured another place on the sailor's ship. It was his ticket to freedom and the evening before he was due to depart, he and Bob decided to have fish and chips to celebrate. While Bob was out getting the food there was a knock at the door. Thinking it was his friend returning, Hilton answered and was instantly overwhelmed by police officers. He didn't know it at the time, but his brother-in-law had been arrested for driving a stolen car and the police had put so much pressure on him, he had revealed Hilton's whereabouts.

Hilton was taken to the police station and soon joined by Bob, who had also been caught. Hilton was remanded in Brixton Prison where, one day, he was asked to see the doctor. The doctor asked some cursory questions about his health before checking Hilton's weight and height. This was all most unusual and Hilton wondered what was going on until finally the penny dropped.

'Suddenly I thought, they're weighing and measuring me to get hung,' Hilton told me. 'I said, "Dirty bastards, I'm not even convicted yet!"'

It was 1963 and death by hanging was still a possibility for crimes like murder. Suddenly it struck home that Hilton and his three colleagues could all be facing death.

The trial soon came and the days in court passed quickly. It turned out that the getaway car Hilton had worried about had been a large reason for their capture. The other firm that Gus had bought it from were arrested on suspicion of the murder and had quickly given Gus up when faced with the prospect of jail. The police also claimed that Hilton had admitted to the robbery when he was struggling with the cops during his arrest. This kind of evidence was still admissible in court in the sixties and it was enough to convict Hilton, along with the rest of his firm.

When the moment for sentencing came, the four thieves stood side by side in the dock. Gus was sentenced to death by hanging for the murder. Hilton and the other two were sentenced to whole life sentences.

Hilton was transferred to Wandsworth Prison to contemplate his fate. Deemed a high risk of escape, he was forced to wear a bright yellow-striped uniform. He was kept under strict observation, having to sleep in a bare cell with a red light shining on him all night. All he had to look forward to was his appeal, which came six weeks later. The four men appeared at the Royal Courts of Justice in Westminster, where, finally, some good news was delivered. Gus's death sentence was reduced to life in prison. Bob's appeal was also successful and his charge was dropped to one of armed robbery, greatly reducing his sentence. Unfortunately for Hilton, despite not having killed anyone, his appeal was unsuccessful and his life sentence stood.

Hilton was returned to Wandsworth to stew on his fate. He soon had a visit from his wife and son, but that only made matters worse. 'My son stood there against the glass,' he told me, 'and said, "When are you coming home, Dad?" And that slaughtered me. And even today that slaughters me, the way he said it.'

Hilton told his wife not to visit again. The pain of seeing them was too much to cope with on top of having to come to terms with spending the rest of his life in prison. He told her to divorce him if that is what she wanted and was relieved, a few years later, when the divorce papers came through. After that visit, he never saw his wife and son again.

Unable to face a lifetime in prison, Hilton soon began looking for ways to escape. In Wandsworth, he noticed a maintenance yard that could be reached through a barred window. If he could get through the window, he could easily use the equipment in the yard to scale the wall. One of the other prisoners said the storeman was willing to bring in a hydraulic jack that they could use to prise open the bars. For a while it seemed like the escape was on but the storeman got cold feet and the attempt was thwarted.

Hilton was transferred to Winchester Prison, which had a less strict regime than Wandsworth. However, he soon got himself in trouble again when a guard unexpectedly cut short his exercise time. When he asked the guard why he was doing this, the man shouted at him and Hilton flew into a rage, all his pent-up frustration rushing to the surface. He stepped forward and tried to punch the man, but another prisoner stepped in the way and stopped him. He was then taken to the office, where other guards told him he would be sent to the punishment block. Still seething, Hilton picked up a nearby bucket and threw water over one of the guards, then hit him over the shoulder with it. He was bundled to the ground and carried to the punishment block, where he was thrown into a cell. Outside, a group of guards was waiting to beat him up for attacking one of their own. Unfortunately, they didn't realise who they were dealing with.

'You can come in,' Hilton warned them, 'and beat me up. I don't give a fuck, but in the morning, I will gouge the first screw's eye out who comes in my door.'

The guards hesitated, then slammed the door shut and left.

Hilton was punished with fifteen days of bread and water plus confinement to his cell before being transferred to Parkhurst Prison on the Isle of Wight. Parkhurst was another relaxed prison and this time Hilton got himself a job in the laundry. However, this too went wrong when a guard challenged him over a glass jar of coffee he was carrying for his break time. Hilton explained that he had been bringing the jar to work every day for several months and no one had told him he couldn't have it. But the new guard insisted he hand it over. Hilton asked if he could give him the jar but keep the coffee, but again the guard was having none of it. Enraged, Hilton grabbed the man and started hauling him over towards a big tub of acid that was used to clean the clothes.

'He managed to get hold of something and hung on for dear life,' Hilton told me. 'The bell rang and they came down and rescued him, otherwise he'd have been head-first in.'

The guards gave Hilton a good pounding before taking him to a punishment cell. After two weeks of punishment, he was transferred to Dartmoor. While there, Hilton began to hear rumours of new high-security wings being built around the UK to house high-risk prisoners like himself. Realising he was in a race against the clock to escape before the new wings were built, he hastily concocted a plan. He got a friend to fashion him some metal bars that could be fitted together to make a hook. With this and a rope made out of torn bedsheets, he intended to scale down from his cell window. He was just waiting for some hacksaw blades to be smuggled in to cut through the bars when he received the news he had been dreading: he was being transferred to one of the new high-security wings in Durham, in the north-east of England.

E Wing in Durham was worse than Hilton had expected. The guards were intimidating and did everything they could to wind him up, hoping he would give them an excuse to punish or beat him. His cell door was heavily reinforced and set with alarms. The cons were locked in their cells twenty-three hours a day and talking with neighbours wasn't allowed. In his introductory speech, the governor warned Hilton that unruly prisoners had a habit of falling down stairs and walking into doors but even this was no warning of what was about to come.

One evening, Hilton was looking out of his cell window when he saw a van pull up and a group of soldiers jump out, carrying rifles with fixed bayonets. He and the other prisoners watched astonished as the soldiers loaded their weapons and proceeded to patrol the area. In the morning, the scene was even more bizarre. The soldiers had built a sandbag wall in the exercise yard behind which they had stationed a heavy machine gun. As the prisoners walked around the exercise yard, the soldiers trained the machine gun on them as if itching to shoot.

Hilton even had an escort of four soldiers with fixed bayonets when he visited the prison dentist. When the dentist saw Hilton's guards, his hands were shaking so badly they were in no fit state for dental work.

After a few months of this brutal regime, rumours began circulating that a new governor was going to make it even more harsh by increasing the prisoners' workloads and reducing their privileges. The twenty Category A prisoners now making up E Wing decided enough was enough: it was time to make a stand.

They chose an evening when a football match was on. Hilton asked a guard if the radio in the guards' office could be tuned into the match. The guard agreed and went into the office to do so. When he returned, Hilton and a colleague were waiting, hidden in a cell doorway. They jumped out on him and ripped his key from its chain, then all twenty prisoners stormed into the guards' offices. After barricading themselves in, they ransacked everything, finding their prison records and taking great delight in tearing them to shreds. Eventually the wing governor came down and the rioters presented him with a list of their demands. He agreed that if they came out, their demands would be looked into. They conceded and emerged two at a time, with Hilton in the first pair, half expecting a beating from the enraged guards. But the beating never happened and the prisoners were even treated to a shower and a slap-up meal.

The rioters were all charged with mutiny and sentenced to forty-two days in solitary confinement, but their protest had its desired effect, highlighting the harshness and brutality of the regime. E Wing was closed down shortly afterwards in 1971. After four weeks of punishment, Hilton was informed that he was being transferred again, this time back to Parkhurst, which now had its own high-security wing.

But Parkhurst wasn't the relaxed prison Hilton remembered. The high-security wing was staffed with sadistic guards who were constantly looking for any excuse to inflict violence or punishment on the inmates. It was a running joke at the prison that there were two shifts of guards – the nicking shift, who punished inmates at the drop of a hat, and the kicking shift, who beat them up.

Hilton spent two years there before growing tension among the inmates finally exploded. It happened when the whole wing was told they would be moving to a landing that had even worse cells, which were damp and freezing. They all got together and decided to barricade themselves in, much as Hilton and the crew had done at Durham.

The protest was planned for recreation time. As soon as all the prisoners were out on the landing, they began ripping up any furniture they could find and throwing it down the stairs to form a barricade. They managed to take two of the guards captive and put them in an empty cell, where they were left unharmed. After an hour, a wave of guards attacked the barricade and fought their way through. The violence was fierce. One guard had his throat cut with a knife. Another hulking bully of a guard was struck over the head with a snooker ball and had to be dragged away by his colleagues. Eventually, the guards pushed the prisoners back along the landing until around twenty-five of them were trapped in a room. The guards besieged the room and called out prisoners by name, ordering them to come out.

When it was Hilton's turn, he emerged into a corridor that looked like a war zone, with wreckage everywhere, bloodstains and even a bloodied handprint that slid down the wall. As he reached the bottom of the stairs, an even nastier surprise was awaiting him.

'I got to the end,' Hilton told me, 'and then I saw them. I thought, fuck me – a gauntlet of fifty screws! They had black leather gloves and truncheons. I hesitated then. I thought, whatever you do, don't lose your footing. So I just put my head down. I plunged through and I was getting bang, crash walloped, thumped . . . I got through to the end and there was an assistant governor from another prison with a big stick in his hand. As I came through, he beat me right across the kidneys and that was absolute agony.'

Hilton vomited with the pain but forced himself back to his feet and hurried on to the punishment cell, where he lay on the floor for several hours, unable to move. He received five months in solitary confinement for his part in the infamous

Parkhurst riot of 1969, but as with the Durham riot, it high-lighted the brutal prison regime which was soon exposed in the press, leading to a damning inquiry.*

Hilton was transferred to Hull Prison which, thankfully, was much more relaxed. He spent four years there before being taken off the Category A list. Compared to Parkhurst, Hull was a revelation. 'Every weekend we used to drop acid,' Hilton told me. 'The whole prison was on acid.'

After the delights of Hull, he was then transported back to his old haunt, Lewes, in Sussex. He was finally given a release date from his life sentence and was transferred to Coldingley Prison in Surrey to serve his last six months. In 1977, he was released from Coldingley and sent to a pre-release hostel in Maidstone, Kent, where he would be allowed out during the day to work and reintegrate into society.

Hilton found work on a night shift in an engineering firm in Stroud, but he wasn't particularly interested in reintegrating into society. On the first weekend of his release in January 1978, he contacted an old friend to see if there was any work to be had. His friend told him about a job stealing the week's profits from a clothes shop in Hackney. By the end of the month, Hilton and his friend had pulled off the job. Hilton had bagged £3,000 for himself. It was almost like the life sentence had never happened.

Soon, there was more and bigger work on offer. One day Hilton got a call from a fellow armed robber he had met in Coldingley called Alan Roberts. He met Roberts in a pub and listened to his plan to rob a load of diamonds from a jewellery

---

* https://hansard.parliament.uk/%E2%80%8CCommons/1969-03-20/debates/576b1d2a-8e57-4782-b93a-853a023d1b59/ParkhurstPrison(In-quiry)

store. Roberts estimated the value of the diamonds at £400,000, which was music to Hilton's ears. They went about planning, which meant following the man who carried the diamonds from his shop in Hatton Garden to a house in Golders Green. When they managed to track the man to his ultimate destination, they set about planning the heist. Hilton would hide under a parked lorry with his shotgun while Roberts was to lurk in the shadows, armed with a cosh. When the man went past, Roberts would spring out and attack him with the truncheon while Hilton emerged from under the lorry to threaten him with the shotgun. Then they would seize the black bag carrying the diamonds and make their getaway. It seemed simple and foolproof except for one small detail that bothered Hilton – the size of Roberts' cosh. 'He had a little truncheon about that big,' Hilton told me, indicating about two feet. 'It wouldn't hurt a fly. I said, "What's that? My fucking dick's bigger than that!"'

Despite the inadequate size of Roberts' truncheon, the job would have to go ahead, but it would come back to bite them. When they accosted the man with the bag, he put up a fight and used his briefcase to fend off Roberts' attack. This forced Hilton to shoot, missing the man and hitting Roberts in the thigh. He then shot the jeweller in the back as he tried to run away, before grabbing the bag and bundling it, along with Roberts, into the getaway car.

Hilton drove back to his flat in North London, with Roberts bleeding heavily in the back of the car. He parked outside and helped his friend across the road and into the block of flats. Hilton's flat was on the top floor, but the lift wasn't working so he now had to carry Roberts all the way up the stairs, leaving a trail of blood behind them. Once inside the flat, Hilton laid Roberts on the floor in front of the fire. Blood was still pumping from the massive wound in Roberts' thigh so Hilton called a doctor he knew. There was no answer. Then he tried a nurse he knew. Again, no answer.

'Now I'm on the horns of a dilemma,' Hilton told me. 'As far as I'm concerned, I've got a dead man lying there. He's on bail. If I take him to hospital, what's going to happen? They may link him to me. He would certainly have gone to prison for thirty-odd years and so if the position had been reversed, I'd have expected him to have done what I done. I've done the best I could, I'm sorry.'

Hilton made Roberts as comfortable as he could and started thinking about how to clean up the tell-tale trail of blood leading from the car all the way to his front door. Just then the doorbell rang. Hilton drew his revolver and went to answer it, ready to shoot on sight if it was a policeman. Fortunately, it was just the next-door neighbour checking if everything was all right. Hilton spun a story about getting into a fight in the pub and said he was just about to clean the blood up. This placated the neighbour, who went back to his flat.

When Hilton went back inside, Roberts looked terrible. He asked Hilton to remove his shoes, which Hilton did. Once the shoes were off, Roberts made a gurgling sound and died. Hilton wrapped his body in a duvet and dragged it down the stairs to his car. Just as he was about to lift the body into the boot, he saw a woman across the road watching him. 'I thought, whatever you do, don't come over,' Hilton told me, 'because you'll fucking join him.'

Fortunately for the woman, she walked on. Hilton got the body into the boot and drove the car to a garage he used for stowing stolen vehicles. Once the car was safely stashed in the garage, he got a taxi home and set about the momentous task of cleaning up all the blood. 'I was wiping up blood for days after,' he said, 'lumps of blood here and fucking everywhere. I never stopped for about three or four days cleaning up blood. I felt like Jack the fucking Ripper.'

After a long night of cleaning, Hilton went back into his flat and poured himself a large drink. He had only been free for twenty-eight days and already he had two murders on his hands.

The next day he woke up early to set about getting rid of the body. He knew the police would be looking for the getaway car so he went to a friend's firm and hired a car and a van for two days. The car was to scout for a good place to bury the body and the van to transport it there once found. He headed towards the Kent countryside and pulled off the motorway at the Dartford Tunnel, where he quickly found a suitable spot up a country lane at the top of a railway embankment, under an electricity pylon.

Hilton drove back to his flat and waited nervously for night to fall. At eleven thirty, he left the flat and took the van to his garage. There, he transferred the body into the van and drove it to the burial spot. He hauled Roberts' body up the embankment and set about the long and tiring process of digging a grave. 'First, I took all the turf up,' Hilton told me, 'put it to one side, then I started digging a proper grave, six-foot long, about three-feet wide, and I dug and I dug and I dug. The rain was pouring down. I felt like Burke and Hare. I dug and dug until I got down to about that level,' he said, indicating neck height.

Hilton pushed Roberts' body into the grave then began the equally long process of filling it back in. By the time he had finished, it was nearly dawn. He scrambled back down the slope to his van and drove home.

Now, there was still the problem of the getaway car. Hilton decided to take it to his friend who owned a scrap metal yard, where it could be crushed. Thankfully, there was a slot available the next day. Without sleep and running on adrenaline, Hilton drove the car to the scrap metal yard and watched with relief as it was hoisted up to be crushed. But he hadn't banked on one last hitch: he didn't know he was supposed to empty the petrol tank. When the car was crushed, it burst into flames. Soon, the yard was inundated with firefighters and police officers, alongside dozens of other spectators who had all come to watch the spectacle. Hilton couldn't have made more of a scene if he'd set off fireworks.

Incredibly, however, the car was crushed without further ado and sent off to Belgium that afternoon. Somehow, Hilton had got away with the whole thing without being caught. 'How I never got nicked, I will never know,' he told me. Yet even this didn't deter him from committing more robberies. He earned £60,000 from the diamonds and used this to take a few months off and lie low, but after that he was back in the game. At the same time, he met a new girlfriend and after a few months of dating, they got married and moved in together, along with her two children.

One day, Hilton spotted a van that collected money from an office block in Stratford, East London. He realised that in order to wait around on the busy street for the van to arrive without attracting attention, he would need some form of cover. He eventually settled on disguising himself as a window cleaner. The day before the robbery, he stole a window cleaning van and the next day parked it on the street outside the office block. He then took a ladder across the road and started cleaning the windows of the building next to the door where the money would emerge.

When the security van arrived at three o'clock as usual, four big men escorted the cash out with the driver. But this time, instead of waiting on the steps of the building as they had done every other time Hilton had observed them, the four men formed a protective barrier from the steps all the way to the back of the van. This meant Hilton didn't have the easy access to the money he had expected. Still, he wasn't going to let a little detail like this prevent him from getting his hands on the cash.

Hilton waited while the guard went into the building and returned, carrying a large black bag of money, then he pulled a revolver out of the bucket where he had stashed it and shouted, 'Hey!' As everyone turned towards him, Hilton shot the nearest minder in the leg, crushing him against the side of the van with the force of the blow. The man crumpled and screamed in agony as blood fountained from his thigh. Hilton pointed the gun at the guard, who instantly threw the bag of money to the ground in front of him. After grabbing the bag, Hilton ran across the road, jumped in his van and raced to a nearby back street. He left the van on the side of the road, then tore off his window cleaning clothes and walked away through a maze of winding pedestrian streets to the nearest Tube station, where he got a train home. Another successful job, and this one had bagged him another £27,000.

Hilton's new wife had always wanted to own a clothes shop and so with his illicit funds, he decided to help her set it up. It would give him a useful cover to launder some of his proceeds as well as providing something to focus on other than armed robberies. Hilton was surprised to find himself happy and content living as a family man for the first time in his life. He even stopped committing robberies for a while. But it wouldn't last long. The clothes shop did well until the financial slump of 1979. Customers stopped spending and the business suffered. Unwilling to accept a drop in lifestyle, Hilton decided to go back into action. He pulled off some robberies on his own before finding a new partner called Don Barrett, who he had got to know in Hull Prison. But right from the beginning, things didn't go well with Barrett. All their jobs seemed to go wrong in some way or another and they weren't making much money.

Hilton decided to ditch Barrett and go back to working on his own. He was lying in bed one night when a sudden premonition of danger swept over him, as it had several times in the past. But this time he decided to ignore the feeling and went to sleep. The next morning, he was in the kitchen preparing breakfast when there was a knock on the front door. When he looked through the windows, he saw armed police waiting in the road outside. He rushed through the back door and into the back garden, aiming to jump over the fence and escape but before he could get far, an armed policeman jumped over the fence from the neighbour's garden and caught him.

Hilton couldn't work out how he had been arrested or for which crime. He soon found out when he was taken to the police station and identified as his partner in crime by Don Barrett. Hilton had long suspected there was something iffy about Barrett. Now he knew – the man was a grass.

Hilton was sent to Brixton Prison to await trial for six armed robberies. He knew what the outcome would be. As someone let out after a life sentence, his licence would be revoked and he would be re-imprisoned for life. When his trial came round at the Old Bailey in 1981, he was proved right. He was sentenced to fourteen years in prison but soon after found out that his licence had been revoked and he was due to serve life.

Hilton was back on the Category A list. He spent ten months in Wandsworth before being transferred to Long Lartin in Evesham. Hilton spent four years there, managing to survive without too much trouble due to his reputation and his connections. During this time, his marriage fell apart and he learned that his sentence would total eighteen years, meaning he wouldn't be released until he was sixty-eight years old. He began seriously considering escape, but first, he would have to wait until he was downgraded from Category A status.

His chance came when he was transferred to his old favourite: Lewes Prison. He had served eight years now and was fifty-seven years old, but his spirit remained unquenched and he still yearned to escape. Hilton got a job in the kitchen and could see an easy means of escape early in the morning, when he was allowed out into the yard to access the vegetable store. All he would need was a few friends to throw a ladder over the wall at an appointed time and he could be free. He organised this with some friends from the outside, but as the day of the escape approached, he found himself randomly seized and placed in a punishment cell. He soon found out that another inmate had grassed him up. Fortunately, he was able to talk himself out of the situation, saying it was just another prisoner trying to get him in trouble as revenge. The governor believed him and he was allowed back into the normal prison, where escape was still possible.

While in Lewes, Hilton met the infamous gangster, Reggie Kray, a man he didn't like at all. 'He was disgusting,' Hilton told me. 'He loved the young kids.' Apparently Reggie used to sit on the stairs watching the inmates of the number one landing, where the younger men were housed. He had a favourite who he bought presents for – first, a jumper and then a gold chain. Soon, according to Hilton, the young man was to be found inside Reggie's cell being sexually abused.

'He once came into my cell,' Hilton told me. 'I didn't want to speak to him if I could help it. He came in and said, "I thought I'd come and introduce myself." I said, "I know who you are." "How are you?" he says. I shook his hand, and you know how you read about people saying I wanted to wash my hands afterwards? Well, that's how I felt. I wanted to wash my hand afterwards because he was a vile man. He had nothing about him whatsoever – a treacherous, vile man.'

Hilton was offered a transfer to Kingston Prison, which he accepted when he found out that the security there was laxer than Lewes. He secured himself a job in the kitchen at Kingston, which he soon found offered a similar means of escape. The kitchen back door was left open in the mornings to allow access to the vegetable store. Just across the yard was a wall with no barbed wire that could easily be scaled by a ladder. Hilton contacted the same friends who had agreed to break him out before and a time and date were fixed.

The morning of the escape, Hilton waited in the kitchen until the clock struck the appointed hour, then walked out into the yard, past the vegetable store, taking three glass jars from a bin that he had stored the night before. He threw the jars over the wall until one of them made a smashing sound on the other side. Immediately, a ladder poked over the top of the wall, followed by a head with a balaclava on it. Another ladder was slid down into the yard and he was able to scale the wall. At the top he pulled up the ladder and clambered down to freedom. His friends showed him the way to where their car was parked and then he was gone. 'As I went by, there was two or three screws waiting to come on duty,' he told me, 'and I laughed. I thought, you wait till you get in there.'

Hilton holed up in a hotel in King's Cross until he found a new flat in Walworth, South London. He was almost sixty but had no intention of going straight. In fact, he had a plan to do as many robberies as he could in three months, then use the money to escape the country. His first job was with a man his rescuers had introduced him to. With his new partner, Hilton decided to target his old haunt, Brighton, where he knew of a jewellery shop that was an easy mark.

The plan was for Hilton to hold up the shop with his revolver while his accomplice smashed the window with a sledgehammer and grabbed as much jewellery as he could in ninety seconds, before they both fled. The robbery went like clockwork and the two made their getaway in the car. They dropped the vehicle off by some gardens and Hilton's partner went into the cubicle of a public toilet to remove the jewellery from the bag, while Hilton waited outside. Just then, two police officers came by and descended into the toilets.

'Now I went into overdrive,' Hilton told me. 'The gun come out under my coat. The safety catch went off. I thought, if they come out with him, I'll shoot both of them in the legs, drag the first person I could lay my hands on out of their car and fuck off. I knew Brighton like the back of my hand, I'd get away all right.'

Luckily for the policemen, they emerged without Hilton's accomplice. It turned out he had heard them coming and pulled his trousers down. When they peered under the cubicle door they had just seen someone using the toilet and moved on. Hilton and his partner left the toilet and enjoyed a leisurely meal in a seaside restaurant before catching the train back to London, where they shared out the spoils, totalling £8,000 each.

Hilton's next plan was to rob a jewellery shop in Burlington Gardens in Mayfair. The shop contained what he estimated to be £400,000-worth of jewellery, a good start for his fund to escape the country. He could rob the shop and make his getaway on foot down a nearby arcade. He had a plan; now all he needed was a partner. His last partner from the Brighton job wasn't trustworthy as he had tried to hide some of the jewellery from Hilton when they were dividing the spoils. The trouble was, no one else would work with Hilton because he had so much heat on him. After much deliberation, his mind settled on one name: Rab Christie, a fellow prisoner he had befriended in Long Lartin. He tracked Christie down and found him in a pub about to celebrate his birthday.

Hilton explained his situation but Christie wanted nothing to do with the robbery. But Hilton was insistent and forced Christie to get in his car and visit the shop in Burlington Gardens. Still, Christie didn't want to do the job, but Hilton was becoming desperate. He pulled Christie into a nearby phone box and pulled a gun on him, telling him he'd shoot him unless he helped. Christie reluctantly agreed and Hilton took him back to his flat that night, knowing he had to keep him in sight so he couldn't slip away.

The next morning, he took Christie, virtually at gunpoint, to the shop. They burst in and Hilton held up the staff while Christie seized all the jewellery he could, before they both fled down the nearby arcade. But here things started to go wrong. Hilton suddenly heard shots being fired from behind and turned to see two men sprinting after him. He fired and they ducked out of the way, but still resumed coming after him. Hilton fired again and began to run. He turned again and fired a shot into one of the men's legs, dropping him to the floor, but now the arcade was filling with people who had come out to see the commotion and the crowd was making it impossible to escape.

Suddenly, several off-duty policemen jumped on Hilton and he was quickly overpowered. He was bundled into a police car and taken to a station. Stunned, he couldn't believe his bad luck. How had such an apparently easy escape route turned into such a nightmare? Only later did he find out the truth about how bad his luck had been that day. 'What I didn't know was the Home Secretary was round the corner in some building,' Hilton told me, 'and there was three rings of his bodyguards, and I ran, I think, into the third ring. You couldn't make it up.'

Hilton was taken to Wandsworth but, incredibly, the prison refused to house him. He was just too much trouble, according to the governor. Instead, he was taken to Wormwood Scrubs, the prison where he first went to borstal as a sixteen-year-old boy. Now he was a sixty-year-old man. As a Category A high-risk inmate, he was soon transferred to one of the high-security dispersal prisons, this time Parkhurst, one of his old haunts where he had taken part in the bloody riot.

In the September of 1991, Hilton found himself back in the dock at the Old Bailey to face trial alongside Rab Christie for the Burlington Gardens robbery. Hilton pleaded guilty but Christie pleaded duress, meaning he had essentially been forced into doing it. However, to win a duress case he would have to prove that his life was in danger and thus that Hilton was capable of murder. Hilton felt sorry for the way he had treated his old friend and since he was now resigned to dying in prison anyway, he decided to own up to the murder of the diamond jeweller and his old partner, Alan Roberts, in order to help Christie win his case.

Unfortunately for Christie, the jury wasn't convinced and found him guilty of armed robbery. Then came Hilton's turn. The judge sentenced him to two life sentences with a recommendation that he never be released. It hit Hilton hard but he wasn't particularly surprised and had already made peace with the fact that he would spend the rest of his life behind bars. He was sent to Whitemoor, a high-security prison in Cambridgeshire, where he spent the next sixteen years trying to make the most of the remainder of his life: 'I spent my time drinking and smoking dope,' he told me, 'cooking, reading and going down the gym.'

Hilton was prepared to live out the rest of his life this way, but one day he received a letter from the Minister of Justice with some unexpected good news. Due to his age, his confession to the two murders and his good behaviour during his 16 years in Whitemoor, one of his life sentences was being quashed. He would now only have to spend twenty-five years in prison, which meant he had around six years left to serve.

Hilton was in his eighties when finally released. Now in his mid-nineties, he is still going strong. He looks twenty years younger than his age and still has a sharp mind and an incredibly detailed memory. Talking to him, you can see the incredible vitality, sharp wits and cool demeanour that made him such a formidable armed robber.

Apart from his sprightliness, what is most striking about Hilton is his lack of regret or remorse, despite spending forty-five years in prison and being directly involved in the murders of three people. Since his release he has written a book about his life called *Armed and Dangerous: London Gangster's Path to Multiple Murders and 45 Years in Prison*. In it, he makes a remarkable admission about the mindset of an armed robber:

Most people wonder and question what gives a normal human being the urge to take what belongs to someone else. What drives someone to live a life where they hold a gun to someone's face, or beat them with a cosh? Then you are asking the wrong question entirely. You are making the assumption that robbers have the capacity to have empathy, have remorse or care about anyone's individual feelings. We don't care, we have no regard for anyone, we are not normal people. We live on the outskirts of society, doing what we want, when we want, and take whatever we like. We don't show remorse for the death of anyone; it is part and parcel of the job. Things go wrong and lives are lost. We don't feel bad for taking anyone's money, we don't have bouts of regret or shame. We just don't give a fuck. No conscience, and certainly no regrets. This may be hard for people to understand, but I believe telling the real truth of the mindset of a robber is far better than pretending we have a conscience.

2

Michael Thompson

'You couldn't build an effective business structure with a bunch of psychopaths'

The man is sitting on a bench, enjoying the sun on his face, when the attack comes.

He hears something move behind him, but he barely has time to curse his stupidity for letting someone get the better of him before the blow lands. It hits him hard in the back of the head, knocking him forward off the bench. Everything goes black and he wonders for an instant if he is unconscious, or even dead. But he can still hear the sounds of his attacker moving behind him. He realises dimly that the blow has blinded him, but he has little time for further thought.

He feels a hand grab his long hair roughly. He knows that the other hand will be carrying a weapon. With his vision gone, his other senses have become hyper-aware now he's fighting for his life. From the feel and sound of the man's motions, he is able to raise a hand just in time to block the blow that was aimed at his neck. The strike is deflected upwards and his body flinches in pain as he feels the makeshift knife cut deep into his ear, slicing it in half.

He feels the attacker moving to strike again. With his preternatural awareness he can predict the blow's trajectory through

45

the movements of the man's body. This time, he senses, the man is aiming deeper. He manages to block the blow again and it cuts into the back of his throat, missing the anterior artery by millimetres.

The next strike comes even deeper. The attacker, he senses, is trying to cut the artery and his windpipe with one deadly blow. But suddenly his vision returns and now he is able not only to deflect the blow, but to grapple the weapon – a modified box cutter – from his opponent's grip.

He takes the weapon and flips his attacker into the prone position, where he is at his mercy. For a split second, his hands go instinctively to the other man's throat. The element of fire – one of his most destructive fighting styles – courses through his veins. He knows he could snap the man's neck with a mere twist of his hands. Every cell in his body is urging him to do so and finish his attacker off. Instead, he leans back, takes several deep breaths, places the weapon underneath his body and waits for the guards to arrive.

The inmate has taken a vow of non-violence and that must take precedence over his killer instincts. Twenty years ago, his attacker would be dead. Today, he is a lucky man.

Of all the people I have interviewed, Michael Thompson has served the most time in prison, totalling forty-five years behind bars. Raised with Native American traditions, he was convicted of two murders in Orange County, California, in 1973 and received a sentence of seven years to life. Once inside, he was targeted by the Black Panthers prison gang for defeating their leader in a knife fight. Thereafter, he had to fight for his life numerous times, fending off a constant stream of knife-wielding opponents, while at the same time dodging bullets from the guards who had orders to shoot to kill prisoners engaged in knife fights. Bulking up his muscles to absorb bullets bought Thompson extra seconds to fight.

His fighting prowess drew the attention of the Aryan Brotherhood prison gang (America's oldest white supremacist prison gang and crime syndicate), which Thompson joined, eventually becoming one of its most influential leaders by serving on the gang's California council. But when the gang's methods of revenge began to contradict his personal code of ethics and his spirituality, he turned his back on them, swearing an oath of non-violence. Thompson spent another thirty-five years incarcerated with his life under constant threat from the Aryan Brotherhood, other gangs and the prison guards themselves. He has survived numerous assassination attempts, been shot twenty-two times and knifed more times than he can remember, before finally achieving his release in 2019.

Michael Thompson's life story is so extreme, it is sometimes stranger than fiction. He has lived through enough violence and trauma to fill several lifetimes, but throughout his struggles he unflinchingly embodied the ideals and ethics of a warrior code and a spiritual path which not only kept him alive but maintained his humanity through some of the worst conditions imaginable.

Thompson's mother, Jackie, called him the 'Dirt Baby' because she was picking cotton in the fields outside Bakersfield, California, when he was born on 2 October 1951. Jackie had been raped when she was thirteen and was left pregnant. She ran away from home to prevent the child being taken away from her and provided for herself and the baby, doing whatever work she could pick up. She met Thompson's father and the two settled down, having six more children together, of whom Michael was one.

The Thompsons were poor and there was not enough money to feed all the little mouths. Jackie was forced to send

Michael to live with his eldest sister, Pat, who was already grown up with a family of her own. Pat lived on the Big Pine Native American reservation at the foot of California's Sierra Nevada range of mountains. It was a place of poverty and deprivation, and Pat's circumstances were no different. Pat, her husband and two children lived in a small trailer. Their lack of means meant that Thompson was again surplus to requirements. Pat made him sleep underneath the trailer and refused to feed him. He was continually hungry and malnourished and only survived by scrounging or stealing food and catching the occasional rabbit.

'The reservation was abject poverty,' Thompson told me. 'You had tar paper shacks and little twelve-foot travel trailers, and starvation and alcoholism and everything else that goes along with abject poverty.'

With Thompson's fair skin and hair, he didn't fit in on the reservation. He was bullied or ignored by the other children and periodically beaten by the men. One time, a group of the reservation men caught Thompson on their way back from the liquor store. They punched him repeatedly around the head and face. One of the men pulled down Thompson's shorts and drew a knife, saying he was going to cut the boy's penis off so he couldn't 'create any more half breeds' with the native women. Fortunately for Thompson, the man had to release him to draw his knife and the skinny boy was able to run away.

Thompson got his revenge on the men by sawing through a bridge they used to cross the river on the way back from town. He watched from the bushes as the weakened bridge collapsed under their weight, plunging them into the freezing water.

A confrontation led to Thompson's eventual ejection from the reservation. An older boy lay in wait for him and jumped out on him as he was walking along a path. In the ensuing scuffle, Thompson threw the boy over his shoulder, injuring his back badly enough that Thompson was forced to leave the reservation. For a while, he went back to his mother's house, but she was with a new man who took a dislike to him. One day, when he was eleven years old, two police officers turned up at his house to tell him his mother had declared him 'incorrigible' and they were going to take him to Juvenile Hall in Orange County. He was placed in a cell and later told that his mother wouldn't be coming to pick him up – she had left the state.

Thompson was put into a children's home in the countryside. Most of the children at Joplin's Boys Ranch were there for behavioural issues and the place was run along strict lines by a bunch of men who were mostly former marines. Under this disciplined regime, Thompson thrived. For the first time in his life, he was fed adequately. The adults were strict but fair and gave him an education in how to be a man for the world he would inhabit. The work was hard, but he soon found he enjoyed difficult physical labour and it was through this that he found his foster father.

Jack Martin, or 'He who Walks on Top of the Wind', was a half-Irish, half-Native American who owned a nearby horse ranch. Martin was watching the kids at the orphanage one day, looking for an eager worker to help him out, when he spotted Thompson. Noting how hard the boy worked, he told the head of the children's home that he would like to foster him.

Ranch life suited Thompson and he soon settled down to the satisfying outdoor regime. He was to help Walks on Top of the Wind look after his ranch of Arabian horses and Black Angus and Hereford cattle. Thompson learned how to groom, ride, breed and teach the horses. He also learned skills that would keep him alive in prison for over four decades.

One hot day, Walks on Top of the Wind and thirteen-year-old Thompson were heading back for lunch after building a bull pen. Noticing how hot Thompson looked, Walks on Top told him to lie down on the cold concrete floor of the porch. Thompson complied hesitantly and as he lay there, his whole body began to shake uncontrollably. After the abusive traumas of the reservation, Thompson thought Walks on Top was about to give him a beating. Shocked by the boy's reaction, Walks on Top asked why he was shaking. When Thompson explained, Walks on Top spat out a large gob of tobacco juice and said, 'Well, boy, we are going to make sure no one can ever hurt you again.'

Walks on Top was an army veteran who had been a close-combat instructor. He had studied all the Eastern martial arts and was also proficient in Native American fighting styles. Under his tutelage, Thompson learned how to fight one-on-one or against multiple opponents, how to fight with a knife and how to make his own weapon. He also learned how to make his own bow and arrows and how to hunt bears with them in the mountains. At the same time, he was growing quickly. He was soon six-foot-four and nearly three hundred pounds. With his size, strength and fighting skills, he was now a formidable opponent.

What helped hone his fighting was his time at the rodeo. With his horse-riding skills, he would travel and compete at the rodeo, where he would often win. This would attract the ire of the older cowboys who, after a few drinks, would come seeking revenge. 'At night we all camped out in the olive groves around the rodeo,' Thompson told me. 'I don't drink, but they got liquored up and then they'd come looking for me because they wanted to best me where they couldn't best me in the rodeo ring. It allowed me to hone my skills with multiple attackers and to use the techniques that my elder taught me.'

As well as a close-combat instructor, Walks on Top was a Native American 'man of spirit' or medicine man. When he hit puberty, Thompson was initiated into his local tribe in a coming-of-age ceremony that involved four days of fasting followed by a secret ritual. At the end of this, Thompson was given his Native American name, 'Two Eagles'.

But not everything in life went so smoothly. At school, he was still unable to read or write due to his dyslexia. He eventually managed to graduate from high school solely on the strength of his athletic prowess and his ability at woodwork, but was still illiterate. After he left, he travelled around California doing odd bits of construction and scrap work between periods of helping out on the ranch and excursions to hunt bears in the mountains. He tried to join the military, but suffered a severe form of colour blindness that ruled him out of every branch of the armed forces.

Thompson was hunting bears in the mountains of California's Cleveland National Forest when he got caught up in the trouble that would eventually land him in jail. Surprised by an early snowstorm and caught out with only light summer clothing, he was forced to trek down the mountain in three feet of snow. Suffering severely from pneumonia, he found a tavern in the middle of nowhere, where one of the waitresses – Berdel – offered to put him up while he recovered. Berdel told Thompson that her parents had taken over custody of her son and that she could get him back if she were married. To help out, Thompson agreed to wed the waitress.

A cousin of Berdel's told Thompson about a plot by two local drug dealers, who were out on bail, to kidnap the children of a cartel boss named Solis and use the ransom money to escape to Canada. Alarmed by the threat to the children, Thompson decided to call Solis and tell him about the danger. Solis reacted by killing the two men and burying their bodies on Berdel's property.

Unfortunately for Thompson, when the cartel boss and his henchman were arrested for the double murder, they tried to pin the blame on him. 'He said that the phone call I gave him about his kids going to be kidnapped was just a plot on my part to steal away with the wife of one of the victims,' Thompson told me.

In return for implicating Thompson, Solis had bargained himself preferential treatment, but Thompson now faced charges of first-degree murder in a double homicide case. Still, the case against him had so many holes in it, a decent lawyer should have been able to beat it. That was where the next problem came in.

'I was in the process of adopting two little children,' Thompson told me, 'and I'd hired this attorney for that purpose. He was a family law attorney and I didn't know the difference. He was an attorney so I went ahead and I hired him for this murder trial, and he knew nothing about it, of course. The money he was being given was lucrative so he didn't tell me that he had no experience in a criminal case. This was his first criminal case so he really had nothing to advise me on, and he didn't make objections that he was supposed to. I had a prosecutor, then I had two co-defendants who had three attorneys that they had hired that were opposing me, so I was going up against four attorneys.'

With these odds against him, the result looked less appealing and indeed it proved to be so. It took a year-long trial before the jury came to a decision. When the trial did finally end, Thompson was found guilty of first-degree murder alongside his two co-defendants and sentenced to seven years to life behind bars. It was 1975. He was just twenty-three years old. Little did he know, but he would not ride another horse or hunt bears in the mountains for another forty-five years.

Thompson began his stint in jail at the reception centre at the California Institution for Men (CIM) in Chino. Despite the enormity of his sentence, he soon fitted in and got himself a job in the kitchen, spending the rest of his time exercising or working on his appeal.

At Chino there was a hall with a stage where the prisoners would watch guests give talks. Occasionally it would be used as a boxing spectacle where a certain big inmate would challenge anyone to come up and fight him, then give them a good drubbing.

'He was more about shaming people by beating them,' Thompson told me. 'He was a bully.'

One day, spotting the six-foot-four Thompson walk into the room, the man challenged him to come up and fight. At first, Thompson demurred but the other man insisted until it became impossible to back down.

Rather than wait to be hit, he stepped straight in with two jabs and an overhand right, knocking the man to the floor. The big man got up and came at Thompson with a wild haymaker. Thompson put him down again. This time the man was raging, shouting, 'Motherfucker! I'm gonna whup your ass!' But it didn't help. Thompson laid him out again and this time he didn't get up.

Thompson's time at Chino was relatively comfortable, but it didn't last. After eight months he was transferred to the Deuel Vocational Institution (DVI) at Tracy, where he was allocated a job as porter for the chaplain of the Protestant chapel. The chaplain took a shine to Thompson and when he realised the big man couldn't read, he offered to teach him. His dyslexia made it hard but the chaplain's patience and kindness helped him to pick up the basics, which he supplemented later at Folsom with a handy trick: 'The Black Panthers and the BGF [Black Guerrilla Family] used to read Mao's *Little Red Book* on the tier,' Thompson told me. 'That was part of their discipline. And so I got a hold of a copy and I would follow along.'

There was a small grassy space between the Protestant and Catholic churches and the chaplain allowed Thompson to use this area to practise his spirituality. However, the Catholic priest was less understanding and took exception to what he saw as Thompson's devil worship. The priest complained to some of his congregation, who were from the Hispanic Nuestra Familia (NF) gang which ran the prison, and soon Thompson had a target on his back.

The attack came one day when Thompson was in the outside space between the chapels. He knew something odd was happening when he saw the side door of the Catholic chapel being opened. Nobody ever entered the garden from that door so his survival senses were immediately on alert. He dropped his religious regalia and moved towards the door, where seven Mexican men emerged in a wedge formation, each with a homemade knife taped to their hands.

Moving quickly, he attacked the man at the point of the wedge, striking him in the chin with the heel of his hand and knocking him to the ground, unconscious. The rest of the men stumbled over the prone figure of their leader and were thrown into disarray. Quickly taking stock, Thompson used a Native fighting technique he had learned from Walks on Top, which allowed him to channel the spirit of an animal to aid him in combat. Seeing that he had to work quickly with the utmost ruthlessness, he decided to channel the spirit of the grizzly bear. He crashed into his attackers, using the full weight of his body and all his strength to put them out of action in a kind of fluid trance, where he allowed the spirit of the animal to control his actions. When he was done, seven men lay on the ground, five of them unconscious, the other two screaming in pain with broken bones protruding from their arms.

Thompson had made short order of seven knife-wielding attackers, but as he told me with characteristic modesty, this accomplishment was perhaps not quite so impressive as it sounds: 'They weren't warriors,' he said. 'They weren't fighters. They'd probably never been in a fight in their life.'

The NF had sent what they called 'expendables', non-gang members whose lives could be sacrificed. As Thompson took stock of his handiwork, a guard who had been watching the fight stepped into the garden and congratulated him on teaching the NF a lesson. He told him the NF leaders who had sanctioned the hit were in the prison yard and at Thompson's request, he unlocked the door to the main yard, adding that there was a box of baseball bats in the yard shack.

In the yard, he met two bikers who were on their way to take on the same NF leaders for threatening their friend. Thompson led the men to the shack and, armed with baseball bats, they tore into the NF, some of whom produced knives. Thompson managed to down two of the leaders' guards with a kick, then floored one of the leaders with a thrust of the bat to his solar plexus and an elbow to the nose. He turned and crashed the bat into the next man's leg, shattering his knee, before the guards finally reacted and began spraying the ground with bullets. Thompson rolled away from the gunfire but came up in front of a group of guards who were all pointing their weapons at his chest. He was handcuffed and removed from the yard while staff rushed in to treat the wounded.

Thompson spent the next two weeks in the hole for the attack, a surprisingly short amount of time, and on release no charges were filed against him. Back on the mainline, however, he was prey for the NF's revenge, which was bound to be more professional next time. It came quickly.

The morning after his transfer to a new cell on the third tier of the mainline, Thompson was up bright and early. He heard the sound of the cell doors being opened and immediately spotted a group of four inmates running up the stairs from the bottom tier. Knowing they were coming for him, he acted quickly. After waiting for them to pass below him on the second tier, he jumped over the guardrail and came up the stairs behind them.

He caught the two rear men by surprise as they stood at his cell door, acting as guards for the two other men who had entered to do the hit. In quick succession, he grabbed the two men and threw them over the tier railing. He then moved into the cell where the two assassins still had their backs to him. He hit the first man over the shoulder with his forearm, flooring him instantly. The second man just had time to turn around in the cramped cell and thrust his knife towards Thompson's heart. It was a good blow and Thompson understood instantly that it would do him serious harm. The only way to counter this was to use his hands to take the force of the strike. He put his hand in the way of the knife and it plunged through his palm and out the other side. He wrapped his fingers round the knife and ripped it from the attacker's hands before chopping his throat with his other hand and following through with a knee to the groin. Job done, he calmly walked down the tier with the knife still stuck in his hand and presented himself to Medical.

After this victory, he knew that all hell would break loose in the NF-run prison with white inmates being targeted. He persuaded the other whites to take the advantage and act first. They agreed and attacked six of the NF associates' cells with Molotov cocktails. He then arranged for a gun and ammunition to be smuggled in, with the plan of shooting six NF members in each of Tracy's four units. Unfortunately, word got out about the gun and Thompson was caught, put in heavy chains and transported immediately to Folsom State Prison, where security was tighter.

At Folsom, he walked into an establishment where gang warfare was already in full swing. Several gangs were competing to control the prison's resources of drugs, prostitution and money lending. The Aryan Brotherhood (AB) and Mexican Mafia (Eme) were in charge of the mainline in an uneasy truce, while the Black Panthers and Black Guerilla Family (BGF) were trying to establish a foothold. The AB were smuggling in heroin, marijuana, methamphetamine and alcohol with the help of some guards, while the Eme were bringing in black tar heroin and the Hell's Angels meth. Thompson was a recruitment target for these gangs because of the rumours of his strength and fighting prowess which had preceded him. The first to try to recruit him was the leader of the Black Panthers, Hugo 'Yogi' Pinell, who had been transferred to Folsom after taking part in a takeover of the hole at San Quentin. Pinell and his companions had taken several guards hostage and slit their throats alongside those of several white inmates.

Pinell approached Thompson on the yard and introduced himself as the commander-in-chief of the Black Panthers. He asked Thompson to join them and gave him a recruitment speech about the benefits of communism and the struggle against the imperialism of the United States. Most of Pinell's discourse went over his head, but Thompson knew one thing: he was a patriot and he had heard no less a man than the actor John Wayne speak up about the dangers of communism. Thompson liked Pinell but told him he didn't want to join his organisation. Pinell's reaction was immediate and decisive: 'He said, "Young Mike, if you're not with us then you're against us,"' Thompson told me. '"So what you need to do is, you need to go in and make yourself a piece and I'll meet you out here in the morning."'

Thompson and Pinell may have been housed in the hole at Folsom but that didn't stop gang violence from occurring regularly. The inmates made their own shanks or had them smuggled in and would regularly engage in knife fights when they got onto the yard. These would be hurried affairs which would have to be conducted before the guards on the tower started shooting. Sometimes the prisoners would blow fake whistles to attract the guards to a different location and buy themselves extra time. Other times they would fight in a relative blind spot beneath the guards' tower or they would just carry on fighting, doing their best to dodge the bullets as well as their opponents' knives.

Back in his cell that evening, Thompson faced a problem: he had no knife for the next morning's fight. Fortunately, one of the inmates near him fashioned a 'kite' – a way of passing messages and small items by tying them to pieces of string and passing them from cell to cell – with a metal pen clip attached to the end. The metal of the clip was harder than the sheet steel that the cell bars were set in, so Thompson was able to use the pen clip to etch the shape of a blade into the sheet steel, then gradually cut it out. It took him six hours to cut the blade from the sheet steel and the rest of the night to sharpen it against the cement floor of his cell.

Finally, Thompson needed to 'keister' the weapon in order to smuggle it onto the yard. This meant sequestering it inside his rectum. Fortunately, the other inmate had sent him some plastic sheeting for that purpose. He wrapped the blade in plastic and smothered it with soap for easier insertion and withdrawal.

When the next day finally dawned and the prisoners were allowed onto the yard, Thompson, who was new to keistering items, had problems getting the knife out of his rectum. He tried squatting against the wall but nothing was moving. Finally, he managed to get it out by lying on his back and massaging his lower abdomen while contracting his muscles to force it out. He was just in time as Pinell was let out of his cell. The two men squared up and Pinell began the fight with a quick thrust at Thompson's chest, which Thompson parried.

Both were skilled knife fighters and both were agile men, with speed and precision. 'We both understood that we needed to move,' Thompson told me. 'We knew that instinctively because we had three gunners on the rail, so we began our knife fight and we began our dance.'

Pinell kept slashing at Thompson's face but each time he did so, Thompson would slash a nick on Pinell's hand or wrist. The steadily mounting flow of blood caused Pinell's grip on his knife to loosen and this affected his rhythm and confidence. When the first round of bullets hit the ground around them, Thompson noticed Pinell glance towards the gun tower. Quick as a flash he stepped in and slashed a shallow wound across Pinell's chest. Thompson saw the fear flash in Pinell's eyes, then the other man sidestepped onto a low wall and began to run.

Thompson chased his opponent until two Black Panthers blocked his progress. One tried to plunge a knife into Thompson's chest but he blocked the thrust and slashed the man's abdomen so deeply that he collapsed to the floor, trying desperately to hold his intestines in. The next man attempted to headbutt Thompson. His blow was met by Thompson's knife, which thrust into his forehead, slicing the top of his head open. At that moment Thompson was knocked to the floor by a blow from behind. He just had time to realise that he had been shot before he lost consciousness.

When he woke in his cell, he couldn't move most of his body. The 223-calibre round fired by the guard's M14 rifle had lodged in his spine. The doctor had elected to leave the bullet in there and it would stay in Thompson's body for the next thirty years. In the meantime, he could only lie in a pool of his own blood and do his best to eat the food that was slid under his door. This he managed by rolling over until his face was lying in the food. He then did his best to hoover up what he could before rolling back over with food stuck all around his face – 'The cockroaches would come up out of the sewer,' he told me, 'and of course I couldn't do anything to stop them, so I could feel them, the large antennae crawling up my leg and onto my body. I think it's a natural response, you kind of blow air to see if you can discourage them, and they weren't having it. They wanted the food on my face, so ultimately, I named them and invited them to the party.'

It took ten days before some limited movement returned to Thompson's body. He could barely manage a shuffle, but when the guards asked if he wanted to go to the exercise yard, he answered 'yes'. It was a bad move. Out in the yard, several Black Panthers were waiting for him. Four of the men immediately jumped on Thompson, who was unable to respond. They slammed him to the ground and began stabbing him in the chest.

'The interesting thing about that,' he told me, 'is that I knew they weren't going to kill me. First, they were hitting me high, but I could actually hear and feel the knives go through my body and chink the asphalt underneath me, but they were extremely fearful, probably because there were three gunners on the rail.'

Almost as soon as the attack began, it was over. Shots were fired and the black prisoners retreated. The guards tried to carry Thompson off the yard on a stretcher but he refused, insisting on shuffling off the same way he had come in.

The next time he was allowed on the yard, he was healed enough to defend himself properly. This time he was approached by a muscly white man with a bristly moustache, who introduced himself as T.D. Bingham – the most influential member of the Aryan Brotherhood at that time. He told Thompson that he had called a truce with the Black Panthers and invited him to join his gang. Bingham's recruitment spiel was different to Pinell's. Rather than politics, it concentrated on power. Bingham explained that the AB, or 'the Brand' as it was also known, controlled most of the resources in Folsom, so being a member would allow him greater access to the commodities that made prison life easier. Thompson was somewhat surprised to hear that racism wasn't a huge part of the Aryan Brotherhood's mission. Their task was practical and focused on maintaining power and control. Furthermore, Bingham himself had a Star of David tattooed on his upper arm. He told Thompson that while he wasn't religious, his mother was Jewish and he was proud of his heritage. Thompson took an immediate liking to Bingham, nevertheless giving the same answer as he had Pinell before.

Although Bingham had negotiated a truce, it was an uneasy one and individual members of the Black Panthers and BGF were allowed to challenge Thompson to head-to-head fights with the sanction of all the gangs. This meant that for the next four months Thompson was in a string of more than a dozen knife fights with various members of the black gangs looking for revenge after their leader's humiliation. These events became regular entertainment for the guards, who would take bets on the outcome. The fights would be situations of double jeopardy where Thompson would have to dodge the thrusts of his opponents as well as bullets from the guards – 'I can't remember an altercation ever being less than eight shots fired,' Thompson told me. 'Sometimes many, many more.'

To dodge the bullets and continue the knife fight, he developed a fighting style similar to a kind of dance, where he would be continually on the move, ducking, spinning and rolling to make himself the hardest possible target for the guards' bullets. That didn't stop him being shot several times. He also received multiple shrapnel wounds from where the bullets kicked up asphalt, particles of which are lodged in his body till this day.

'It knocks you down,' he told me about the feeling of being shot. 'It knocks the wind out of you. It drops you like a sack of potatoes. If you stay conscious, you realise you've been shot. There's not much pain.' He contrasted this with the way it feels to be stabbed: 'If it's a weapon that's been finely crafted then it's razor-sharp – you know what it feels like to cut yourself with a razor blade? So, intensify that a hundred-fold, that's what it feels like. If it's a rougher weapon, it's more ragged, it's not as well manufactured, and that can be painful because it's like being stabbed with a sharp stick. You feel it going in and you feel it coming out.'

After several months of fighting off numerous attackers, Thompson was approached by the AB again. This time it was by a group of five Native Americans who were all members of the Brand. The gang members were all old 'rez dogs' like Thompson and could sympathise with his harsh upbringing. They emphasised that they lived better in prison than they ever had on the outside, thanks to the gang's power and control of resources. This resonated with Thompson and after some consideration, he decided to join them.

Given the name of the gang and its reputation, it might surprise many people to find that half of the Aryan Brotherhood membership in Folsom at that time was Native American and that one of its leaders proudly wore a Star of David tattoo. But, as Thompson emphasised to me, back in the seventies, racism wasn't particularly high on the gang's agenda there. Instead, it was all about control of the prison resources of drugs, male prostitutes, food, alcohol and loan sharking. Whichever gang controlled those resources ensured the best quality of life for its members. There were no Nazis in the early AB there, as Thompson remembers it. Indeed, part of the AB's formation was in response to trouble that the neo-Nazis caused.

As a new Brand member Thompson was afforded some protection, but if he thought it would mean an end to violence, he was wrong. Gang fights were a common occurrence in Folsom. There were eight Aryan Brotherhood members, including Thompson, in the hole at Folsom and they would typically square up to at least twenty attackers from the combined Black Panthers and Black Guerrilla Family (BGF) gangs, as well as some members of the Texas Syndicate, a Mexican gang from Texas. These fights would all take place in the yard under the watchful stare of the guards so everyone risked being shot, as well as stabbed by an opponent.

Thompson received some of his twenty-two bullet wounds during these fights. One was during one of his toughest fights ever against an opponent called Roland, a former professional boxer. Roland was so tough that no matter where or how hard Thompson hit him, it had no effect. Eventually, Thompson resorted to kicking the big man in the groin, which finally did the job. But in a case of instant karma, Thompson was immediately shot in the leg he had kicked him with.

On another occasion, Thompson was hit in the side of the head with a stinger round, with messy consequences. 'It peeled my scalp,' he told me. 'It literally lifted my whole scalp up, hair and all. I remember thinking to myself immediately that somebody had "Sundayed" me, punched me from the side – that's how hard it hit me, because it actually buckled my knees.' With typical endurance, he pushed his scalp back down and carried on fighting.

Undoubtedly a tough man to deal with, Thompson's martial arts training made him incredibly nimble. Added to this, he could bench press over five hundred pounds and break bones with one hand. He was so strong, in fact, that his most used fighting style was one which he used to limit damage. As well as being able to channel the spirits of animals while fighting, he had learned a Native American fighting style that utilised the powers of the four elements – earth to stay grounded and strong, water to be fluid and mobile, air to be nimble and fast-moving, and fire to be explosively destructive.

Combined with his skill and strength, Thompson embodied a warrior code of ethics. He would only ever fight head-to-head, man-to-man, and would never attack someone from behind. If his opponent didn't have a knife, he would give him one of his own and only used force as far as was necessary. There were numerous occasions when someone tried to kill him, but once his opponent had been disarmed, Thompson would let the man live. He was often criticised by his AB brethren for allowing enemies to live to fight another day, but he found that men he had let live never came back to attack him again. The truth behind his code of ethics is one which many might find surprising, or even hard to believe:

'The fact of the matter is I deplore violence,' he told me. 'I always have. The problem with it is that I'm very good at it and in a controlled environment like prison, that's an asset, and it's why I'm alive today.'

As a new Brand member, one of his first problems was a sudden lack of weapons to fight other gangs. Folsom had recently introduced metal detectors, which meant that weapons could no longer be manufactured in cells then keistered and taken out to the yard. There were dozens of knives already buried in various parts of the prison, but these were dealt with by bringing in the National Guard with mine-sweeping technology. The gangs were suddenly reduced to using sharpened bones from the kitchen. But Thompson thought he had a way to beat the metal detectors: he surmised that a folding stainless-steel knife wrapped in electrical tape would get past the machines. All he needed now was a way to test his theory.

To do so, he used a resource which had come to him via a fellow inmate, one of the most famous prisoners in US history – Charles Manson. Manson still had a gang of loyal female followers from his time before incarceration. The AB offered him protection in exchange for the use of these women to smuggle in drugs and other items. Thompson tolerated Manson for his usefulness to the Brand but he had, and still has, a low opinion of the cult leader. Manson was a 'punk', who, according to Thompson, could often be seen in the showers having sex with two men at a time. But worse, Manson was a paedophile who had his women followers bring their children for visits so that he could molest them in the visiting room. Manson was too valuable to the Brand to get rid of, but Thompson was able to fix it so that these visits were stopped.

Thompson decided to get Manson's female followers to try smuggling in a knife using the new system he had devised.

It worked perfectly. This gave the Aryan Brotherhood a huge tactical advantage the next time a fight broke out. The odds were firmly in the Black Panthers and BGF's favour in their next fight, with seven AB members against over thirty of their enemies. The Brand had two large buck knives against the sharpened bones of their opponents. The Panthers and BGF charged the AB, confident in overwhelming them, but at the last minute, Thompson and an AB colleague – Wendel Norris – spun around and launched into the opposition with their superior knives. The fight was over almost as soon as it started with not a shot fired by the guards. The Panthers and BGF retreated, leaving a bloodbath across the yard where they had been repeatedly slashed and stabbed. Thompson and Norris used the blood covering them to lubricate their weapons and re-keister them.

Although the guards could find no evidence of the weapons that had made such a terrible mess of the black gangs, they suspected Thompson of being behind it. They immediately transferred him and T.D. Bingham to San Quentin State Prison.

Thompson was placed straight into the hole in San Quentin, where several other Brand members were housed. He was immediately caught up in gang politics and thrust right into the middle of a violent situation. On his first night at San Quentin, he received a kite message from one of the members of the Mexican Mafia, Moe Ferrell, which said Ferrell was going to kill a native island prisoner called 'Hawaiian John', who was an AB associate. Apparently, Hawaiian John had insulted Mexicans' courage in battle so Ferrell said he was going to kill him in the morning. Thompson replied that Ferrell was not to kill Hawaiian John, that he was an associate of the Brand and that this could disrupt the delicate truce that the two gangs had established. He told Ferrell that he would deal

66

with Hawaiian John himself the next day, but in no way to touch him himself.

The next day, Hawaiian John was stabbed eighteen times by Ferrell and a colleague despite Thompson's injunction. Thompson was still on lockdown, but a few days later, when he made it out to the yard, Ferrell had anticipated Thompson's anger and moved to attack him and Bingham quickly. Ferrell and a colleague ran at Thompson, attempting to do an American football-style double hit, with one tackling him around the legs and the other hitting his torso. Unfortunately, the lower tackler lost his balance and stumbled into Thompson's boot as it kicked him squarely in the forehead, knocking him out of action. Ferrell's tackle was better, but without the lower tackle to knock Thompson off balance, it was ineffective. Thompson simply grabbed Ferrell's body and slammed him into the floor. Thompson kneeled over the prone man, intending to bust up the Mexican's face, but he hadn't contended with the guard in the tower behind him.

'Fred, who was the gunner, was an ex-Vietnam vet,' Thompson told me. 'He was hell on wheels. I've never seen anybody handle a shotgun that well. While he was firing, he was reloading and he hit both T.D. and I five times each. The thing that stopped us was that that damn shot is so hot and it's burning you so each time you get shot and you've got all that lead in you and it's on fire and it's burning you. And the only reason it didn't hit our heart or our lungs was because T.D. and I were both lifting iron at the time so we had a lot of muscle over our backs and that's the only thing that stopped that.'

At San Quentin, Thompson was still a target for the black gangs and one day when he was being escorted along the tier in handcuffs, he saw a BGF member called Ricky squeezing his body through a hole he had cut in his cell bars. Ricky was wielding a twelve-inch 'bone-crusher' knife which he evidently intended to use on Thompson. Seeing the weapon, Thompson's two guards legged it off the tier, leaving Thompson handcuffed and unprotected. Luckily, he had planned for just this kind of scenario. He rushed to another AB member's cell, where various weapons and handcuff keys were stashed. After getting his handcuffs unlocked, he grabbed a knife before rushing back outside.

Back on the tier, Thompson was shocked to see his assailant still dangling from the hole in the bars. It turned out the man hadn't cut out enough bars and his body had become stuck. Thompson sauntered up to the man, but instead of killing him, as most other prisoners would have done, he pushed him back into his cell and took the knife. It was an example of his warrior code put into practice.

After the Hawaiian John affair, Thompson and Bingham settled down to try to restructure the AB presence at San Quentin. The Brand at San Quentin was run by two men in a homosexual relationship who openly flaunted the 'rules' of such relationships in prison at the time by kissing and fondling each other in public. This was having a demoralising effect on other gang members and was ammunition for the other gangs. On top of that, most of the Brand members at San Quentin were drug addicts so all the money the gang was making was disappearing on chemicals. Thompson, who had never used drugs or drunk alcohol, wanted to restructure the gang more along the lines of a criminal organisation like the Italian Mafia. 'I introduced the idea of a business infrastructure,' he told me, 'utilising our revenues towards expanding the infrastructure of the brand, more like a business, using those revenues to purchase properties – for instance, on the street – to develop businesses out there so that when members of the Brand were paroled, for instance, they had a job; use those revenues to start purchasing real estate, to buy houses, vehicles and so on.'

No growth was possible, however, until the structure of the gang was overhauled and a more hierarchical system installed. At the moment it was one member, one vote. With Thompson's guidance it was arranged that the system would be changed to a leadership structure with a three-person commission at the top, which governed the Brand across the whole of the country. This was eventually accomplished and he, T.D. Bingham and 'Blinky' Griffin were nominated to the commission. With the new structure in place, Thompson was able to start pushing his reforms through and the two previous leaders were sidelined.

One of his new rules was that anyone who wanted to be a Brand member could no longer be an addict. This naturally made him some enemies – those who weren't keen on giving up their lifestyles. One of these, a Brand member called Butch, planned on stabbing Thompson from behind, but the attack didn't go quite to plan. 'He had his arms stuck inside the bars and he was attempting to talk to an individual inside the cell,' Thompson told me, 'but something just didn't seem right to me so I caught it out of my peripheral vision that he had a knife in his hand. So his intent was to stab me as I walked by him. I locked his arm into the bars, took the knife away from him and I put him down. And then, putting him down, he begged for his life and it was a choice on my part. So what I did was I choked up on the knife and I tattooed a series of wounds around his heart to remind him that he had been given his life.'

Another innovation he introduced to the Brand was counter-intelligence. The guards had several moles supplying information about gang activity so he started feeding suspected moles misinformation to confuse the guards and to establish who exactly was feeding them the intelligence. However, his reforms were interrupted, perhaps intentionally, when the authorities suddenly transferred him out of San Quentin. Thompson spent the next two years in several other prisons, but mostly at Palm Hall, which was the name of the hole at Chino.

It was at Palm Hall where he first got stirrings of unease about the methods the Brand was using. It started when an AB affiliate, T-Bone Gibson, insulted Mexicans in front of some Eme members. The Eme head at Palm Hall, Benjamin 'Topo' Peters, informed the AB that he was going to kill T-Bone. Worried that this might spark a gang war between the AB and the Eme, one of the Brand leaders, Blinky Griffin, told Topo he would do the killing for him. A few days later, Griffin and another AB member, Junior Snyder, invited T-Bone to a game of cards in the yard. Snyder came up behind T-Bone while he was playing and stabbed him in the back, then Griffin cut his throat from the front.

The hit went against everything Thompson stood for in his warrior code. In his eyes it was unnecessary because it really only required a straight-up fight to teach T-Bone a lesson. It was also sneaky, involving deception and quite literally stabbing someone in the back.

Another incident that played on Thompson's mind was the murder of Steve 'Loser' Clark. Clark was due for parole soon but he liked the lifestyle in prison so much, he didn't want to get out. In a desperate attempt to create a beef so that he would lose his parole, he called another AB member, Clifford 'Smitty' Smith, a punk in front of his daughter during visitation. But Clark had bitten off more than he could chew with Smith. Instead of a straight-up fight, Smith had other ideas. He came up behind Clark right in front of Thompson's cell and hacked at his neck with a knife so viciously, he almost decapitated him. Thompson tried to shout out to Smith to stop but it was no use.

The brutal killing gave Thompson pause to think about his association with the Brand. It wasn't just the savagery and sneakiness of the previous attack that bothered him, it was the dawning realisation that you couldn't build an effective business structure with a bunch of psychopaths. Unfortunately, he was stuck with them for an increasingly long amount of time. By defending himself against assaults by two AB members bent on killing him for his no-drugs policy, and a third assault for which he was wrongly charged, Thompson received three concurrent seven-year sentences added to his life sentence. While appearing in court for these cases, he got himself in even more trouble. He was being housed in the San Bernardino county jail when he heard three men bragging and telling in detail the account of how they had gang-raped and repeatedly sodomised a twelve-year-old girl.

Something had to be done about these men. The deputy sheriff was the cousin of one of the AB members so Thompson called him over and persuaded him to let him out of his holding cell when these men were walking past. The deputy sheriff agreed and Thompson waited for the men to come past. He had handcuffs on that were chained to a chain on his waist, but he had managed to keister a knife, which he slid out and hid beneath his armpit. When the men came past, he pivoted and with all his weight, thrust the knife into the first man. He then lifted him up, slid him off the knife and did the same manoeuvre into the second and the third. His attack was so vicious and quick that the three men had no idea what had hit them.

A medivac helicopter was called and Thompson was sprawled out on the floor in his chains. When the helicopter arrived, the pilot drop-kicked him in the back of the head with his steel-capped boots. The force of the blow drove the bone in Thompson's nose into his left eye, blinding him and fracturing his skull. Despite the severity of his wounds, he was put back in his cell and transferred back to Palm Hall without any medical attention. His optic nerve had been so badly damaged it took three years for his sight to return in the affected eye. One fortunate result, however, was that he wasn't charged for the assaults. The case was widely publicised in the newspapers and public opinion was overwhelmingly in his favour, so the District Attorney must have decided it was a battle not worth fighting.

Despite his horrendous injuries, Thompson was straight back out on the yard at Palm Hall the next day, playing handball with the rest of his colleagues. But his relationship with the Brand had become increasingly uneasy. The final straw came with the AB's killing of Steve Barnes.

Barnes had been a new AB member when Griffin and Snyder had murdered T-Bone. The nature of the killing hadn't sat well with Barnes and he decided to testify against Griffin and Snyder. With Barnes in protective custody, the Brand couldn't exact their revenge on him so someone came up with the idea of killing Barnes's wife and daughter. Thompson was horrified at the idea, but even more so that most of the Brand members were in favour of the plan.

Thompson managed to argue his colleagues out of killing Barnes's wife and daughter, but then someone proposed killing his parents instead. Again, Thompson protested. It was finally decided to kill just Barnes's father. A vote was taken and Thompson's was the sole dissenting voice. The assassination plans were drawn up. Thompson, meanwhile, began some deep soul-searching about his future with the Brand. He held on for a while, attempting to distract the Brand members from the murder with other plans, like a mass escape attempt. However, he was ultimately unsuccessful and when the news came through in 1983 that Steve Barnes's father had been murdered by Brand member, Curtis Price, Thompson knew he couldn't be a part of it any longer. He told the authorities he wanted to step away from the Aryan Brotherhood.

'Anybody that will take it upon themselves to murder, assassinate innocent people, is not somebody that I want around my family, my loved ones,' he told me. 'And I certainly don't want to see them able to integrate themselves into the social fabric of our society. So I was of the opinion, and I hold to that opinion, that just as I'd taken a responsibility for building the infrastructure of the Brand, I had a responsibility to bring it down.'

It was 1983. Thompson was to face another thirty-five years behind bars that would arguably be tougher than the ten he had already served. He received no parole or benefits for his offer to help the authorities, nor did he want any. His motives were solely to tell the truth and to testify against crimes that offended his personal ethical code. He testified in the case against Curtis Price.

Because he did so, he was subjected to several assassination attempts, the last of which occurred in 2015, described at the beginning of this chapter. It wasn't just criminal gangs he had to protect himself from either, but the authorities themselves too. In the nineties, Thompson was transferred to Corcoran, a newly built maximum-security prison where there was a special protection wing for under-threat prisoners. He shared this wing with inmates like the man convicted of Robert Kennedy's murder, Sirhan Sirhan, Charles Manson and another subject of this book, Joey Torres, a co-founder of the 18th Street Gang.

Corcoran was a ruthless regime where, according to prisoners, the guards formed their own gang called the 'Sharks' and brutalised the prisoners remorselessly. Under the command of Corcoran's warden, George Smith, prisoners claimed the guards were allowed to get away with this behaviour to the extent where they would hold regular 'Gladiator Days', where two inmates were pitted against each other in deadly cage fights. They said prisoners who refused to engage in these fights could be shot to death.

The guards' savagery reached an apogee with the murder of Preston Tate. Tate was a black inmate who had had an altercation with a guard, during which he had spat in the officer's face. The next day, the guard set it up so that Tate was left alone in the yard with two of his enemies. When the men started fighting, the officer who Tate had spat on opened fire, shooting him dead.

By this point Thompson had taken a vow of non-violence and was working as a clerk for a lieutenant at Corcoran. It was his job to write up the reports of incidents such as these, so naturally he was handed the file about Tate being shot. The only problem was, Tate hadn't been shot yet. Thompson had been given the file two hours before the shooting even occurred. Despite how hard he must have known this would make his life, he decided to report what he knew about the planning of Tate's murder and to testify against the guards involved.

This of course led to even more cold-blooded treatment at the hands of the guards and many beatings. In fact, the closest Thompson says he has ever come to death was at the hands of the Corcoran guards. 'These guards had just been indicted,' he told me, 'so they came in and they chained me up and I thought I was going out to court when I wasn't. Once they got me chained up, they took me into a room and beat me pretty severely, to the point where I actually thought I was going to die. I think the only thing that saved my life, I was choking on my own blood and I brought up the blood and I spat it at them, and I made the ridiculous comment, "That's all you got?" And for some reason that stopped them.'

Despite all the travails he had to suffer for speaking up against injustice, he managed to educate himself during his remaining years in prison. He gained a Master's degree in Business Studies and a doctorate in Biology. He also trained to become a counsellor and listened to people suffering from a wide range of problems, from addiction to sexual offences. In 2014, while still in prison, he started his own organisation, 'Live Learn and Prosper', which was designed to help prisoners overcome the vicious cycle of crime, imprisonment and re-imprisonment, and to help them rebuild their lives and careers after parole. He also married the woman who is still his wife today, Ariel Tomioka, who he met in 2005 when she was assigned to interview him as part of a RICO (Racketeer Influenced and Corrupt Organizations Act) prosecution against the Aryan Brotherhood.

Thompson was finally released in 2019 after the introduction of new legislation covering youth offenders and elderly offenders which facilitated his parole. It was his nineteenth parole board. At each previous board, he had refused to admit his guilt for the murders he didn't commit. It took him forty-five years to get out, but even when he did, the DA's office did its best to re-imprison him. When I last spoke to Thompson in January 2025, he was undergoing a court battle in which he faced what he said were trumped-up charges of money laundering through his Live Learn and Prosper organisation. To stop him from speaking out about this miscarriage of justice, he had a banning order placed on him which gagged him and prevented him from accessing the internet.

In October 2023, Thompson released *Warhorse Book 1*, co-authored by his partner, Ariel Tomioka, which documents his life story. The standard of writing is so high, you would never imagine that he was once unable to read, a situation aggravated by dyslexia. The descriptions of his rustic upbringing and the challenges of working on a ranch are on a par with the stories of Ernest Hemingway or Jack London. Thompson credits Ariel for the exceptional prose.

Now in his seventies, Thompson may be free from prison, but his life is still limited by the restrictions placed upon him. Apart from having the authority's boot on his neck, he still lives under threat of death from the organisations he betrayed. Yet he refuses to live under police protection. He lives five hundred miles away from his wife in order to protect her safety and otherwise gets on with his life, fighting his legal battles, training and hunting and fishing in his wilderness home.

Despite the many restrictions placed on him, not to mention the forty-five years of incarceration and brutality he was forced to undergo for a crime he didn't commit, Thompson is still grateful for his life and the people he loves. Much of this positivity comes from his native spirituality. It is this, above all else, that he says enabled him to survive all the brutality he has witnessed, with his humanity still intact. Speaking to him today, you would never guess that this humble, gently spoken, scrupulously polite individual could ever have participated in the things he was involved in. It is testimony to the strength of his faith that it has brought him to where he is today, with an appreciation of life, a wise head and a loving heart, undiminished by the traumas he has undergone.

As Thompson told me: 'My goal in life right now is to be as fully human as I can possibly be, to be the best human being I can possibly be, and understanding what that means, what I believe and why I believe it. To me, that's important.'

3

Dellmus Colvin

'I have the power of life and death'

It is 10 p.m. and the man is just bedding down for the night in the sleeping compartment of his truck.

He has been driving for eleven hours straight on his route from Michigan to Idaho and is dog-tired. Just as his eyes close, they snap open again. There's a knock on the window. Swearing to himself, he sits up and opens the passenger door a few inches to see what's going on. Beneath the harsh lights of the Nebraska truck stop, he sees a woman dressed in gaudy clothes and make-up: a sex worker. He tells her where to go in the harshest terms possible, ensuring she gets the message, then slams the door and clambers back into bed, swearing profusely about hookers who ignore the etiquette of truck stops: if a driver has all his lights off, he's not looking for business.

Ten minutes pass and he's just drifting off into a pleasant sleep when his head snaps up again. Another knock. Seething with rage, he gets up again and opens the door: it's the same woman.

This time there's no cussing or shouting. 'Wait there,' he says calmly. He closes the door and pulls on his shirt, pants and boots, then climbs out of the passenger side door.

As soon as his feet hit the tarmac, his hands go to the woman's throat. She has no time to move or scream, and by the time his hands are around her neck she no longer has a chance. He's a big, three hundred-pound African-American man. The contest couldn't be more unequal.

He drags the woman all the way to the back of his fifty-three-foot trailer, strangling her as he goes. When he gets to the back of the truck, he finishes the job, throttling her until the life has left her body. He opens one half of the trailer door and throws her body inside, then, climbing in after her, he methodically strips off her clothing, leaving her naked. He closes the door and walks back to the cabin of his truck, climbs back in, gets undressed and clambers back into bed.

Within seconds his eyes are closed and a few minutes later he is snoozing. He doesn't lose sleep over the prostitutes he kills. This woman isn't the first and she won't be the last.

She is just one of fifty-two.

Dellmus Colvin is not your average Hollywood depiction of a serial killer. Growing up in rural Ohio, he had a perfectly normal and healthy life. When you speak to him, as I did over the phone from an Ohio prison, he comes across as a normal, bright, easy-going and friendly guy. You might even describe him as 'bubbly'. But his personality masks a history of darkness. Convicted of seven murders and sentenced to two life sentences without possibility of parole, Colvin has privately admitted to fifty-two murders committed between 1983 and 2005, the year he was finally caught. He shows not a shred of repentance or remorse for the dozens of mostly female sex workers he claims to have killed and in his disarmingly cheerful way, says he would happily do so again.

I spoke to Colvin on a phone call from his prison in Lebanon, Ohio, with criminal profiler, Phil Chalmers, mediating the call. Of all the criminals I have interviewed, Colvin is the biggest enigma of them all. How do we get to the bottom of a man who seems so transparently human on one level, but who is also capable of the most inhuman acts?

Born in 1959, Colvin grew up on a farm and as a child, he would get up at 5.30 a.m. to feed the cows before heading off to school. He had a Rottweiler called Max, who he raised from a puppy and trained to be a guard dog. When Colvin's nephews came over to play in the back yard, Max would diligently watch over the children, not allowing anyone to enter the yard. Colvin loved the dog and had no inclination to harm or torture it, unlike many psychopaths and serial killers in the popular conception. But then Colvin doesn't live up to any of the stereotypes of a serial killer. The only harm Colvin said he ever did to animals was when he would go out hunting small game such as ducks and quails, pheasants and rabbits, which the family would eat. But this was no different to any other boy living in rural America.

At school, Colvin was a model pupil, never getting into any trouble and showing no signs of aggressive behaviour. He channelled any violent tendencies he might have into sports such as wrestling and football. There were only two signs of anything amiss in his childhood. The first was bullying at school. He would sometimes be chased home after school by bigger boys and occasionally be beaten up by them. The second was his stepmother. When Colvin was fourteen years old, his father moved in with his new partner, bringing Colvin and his siblings with him. His father and stepmum soon began having children of their own and Colvin felt that his stepmom treated her own children differently to her stepkids. This led to his first thoughts of murder: 'I hated that woman.' He tells me about the first time he felt like killing her: 'I couldn't find a way to dispose of her body. I was trying to enlist my brother to help . . . I had it all planned out too. I had a gun, a shotgun, a twelve-gauge single shot from Woolworths.'

When Colvin left school, he signed up for the army, where he served three years as a heavy forklift driver. At £312 a month, the pay was bad even for the 1970s, and Colvin couldn't wait to get out. After leaving the army, he worked as a taxi driver in Atlantic City, New Jersey. It was in New Jersey in 1983 that Colvin claims he committed his first murder. He told me that the killing was not pre-planned or even considered, but simply a reaction to being disrespected by a female hitchhiker he had picked up.

'One day I did it,' Colvin told me. 'The very first time I did it was in New Jersey. I picked up a hitchhiker. She got to giving me some lip about she wanted to go on this end of the Black Horse Pike [a highway]. I told her I wasn't going on this end of the Black Horse Pike. I strangled that bitch and left her body in Pomona, New Jersey.'

Colvin also explained how the ease of this first murder was one of his primary motivations for committing more: 'I said, "Man, any day they're gonna knock on my door,"' he told me. 'But they never came. So I said, "Oh shit, I actually did it and got away with it. It's too fucking easy." I couldn't believe it.'

Now that Colvin had committed his first murder, the others seemed to come easily. However, he insists that, unlike many serial killers, he never went looking for victims. Instead, his crimes were reactive and motivated by anger whenever he felt someone – nearly always a woman, and usually a prostitute – had disrespected him.

One of his typical truck-stop murders was the one described at the beginning of this chapter. Colvin recounted it to me in a chilling matter-of-fact way: 'I was getting ready for bed. I took my clothes off and laid down. There was a knock on my door. It was a goddam truck-stop prostitute. I been as rude as I can. I've run her away. She leaves. But this son of a bitch comes back ten minutes later, knocks on my door again. Now I'm pissed, in full rage mode. I tell her, "Wait a minute." I get dressed. I put my shorts, my boots and my shirt on, and I get out on the passenger side of the truck. As soon as I hit the pavement, I get to wringing that little fucking neck [laughs]. I drag her to the rear of the trailer – fifty-three foot long – and all the time I'm still wringing that damn neck. I get back to the end of the trailer. I finish the job, open up one door, slip her in head-first, strip her off, asshole naked. She ended up in Nebraska and her clothes ended up in Idaho.'

This was a typical murder for Colvin. It was unpremeditated, opportunistic and motivated by rage. He told me of another murder that was also caused by anger, except this one had a premeditated element because it took him two and a half years to get his revenge. The original incident happened in Tulsa, Oklahoma. A truck-stop sex worker was having an argument with another truck driver. She turned and threw a rock at the driver but it missed and hit Colvin's truck, smashing the mirror. Replacing the mirror would cost $1,500, which he would have to pay out of his own pocket, so Colvin was naturally angry. He didn't have the opportunity to kill the woman then and there, but he remembered her face and he recognised her at the same truck stop two and a half years later.

'She didn't recognise it was me,' Colvin told me. 'I called over to her and while I reminded her about it, it was too late. That's when I had her by her throat [laughs]. She had just climbed off the truck of another truck driver. My truck was three trucks away so I dragged her by her hair underneath the trailers of the other three trucks.'

Another murder occurred when Colvin pulled into a truck stop to get a Wendy's, his preferred takeaway meal. A woman – presumably a sex worker, but it's not clear – asked to use his mobile phone. When he refused, the woman replied, 'You don't have to be a bitch about it,' which was one of the last things she ever said. As Colvin put it, 'That was curtains for her right then and there.'

The vast majority of his victims were women, but he claims that two of his fifty-two murders were men. Colvin told me that if a man disrespected him, he was more likely to threaten him or beat him up. But he recounted one of the situations when a man went too far and his killer instincts took over: 'He butted into a conversation I was having with another trucker,' Colvin told me. 'I was trying to sell him a mic and he said some really horrible things. He called me the N word . . . I don't use that word, I don't play that game. That's how he ended up in the fucking bushes.'

Colvin said he averaged one to two murders a year, sometimes killing three people in a 'good year'. He said he never came close to being caught at any time until he was finally arrested in 2005. However, he did have some narrow escapes by sheer accident. On two occasions he was stopped by police while he had a corpse in his truck. On one of these occasions he was stopped for a speeding violation just outside of Columbus, Ohio. According to Colvin, the state trooper stepped onto the step of his truck and looked at the sleeper compartment, which was curtained off, concealing a body that was 'as dead as a fucking door-nail'. The state trooper called, 'Anybody back there?'

Colvin knew he had to think quickly so he said, 'Get the fuck off my truck! Are you going to give me this speeding ticket or not?' It was a ploy to anger the law enforcement officer into giving him the speeding ticket and forgetting about the sleeping compartment. And it worked. The man couldn't give Colvin the ticket fast enough and the corpse remained undiscovered.

The ease with which he was getting away with these crimes made Colvin become almost blasé about carrying corpses around in his truck. On one occasion, he said he carried a body around for months and even parked his truck outside a court where he faced burglary charges, with the decomposing corpse still in the back.

He told me that he thinks one of the reasons he got away with so many murders so easily is because the police don't work sex-worker murder cases as hard as other killings. Added to this was the peripatetic nature of the job, which meant he was constantly on the move and could dump the bodies in a different state to the one where he had committed the murder and leave the victims' clothes in a third state. Also, due to the nature of his victims' work, they were hard to trace, often being homeless and with no fixed source of income, meaning they could go months without anyone noticing they were missing.

On one occasion, Colvin said he met another trucker who was also a murderer. Colvin got to know the man by chatting with him on his CB radio, but they hadn't met in person until one day when they both happened to be at the same truck stop in Davenport, Iowa. Colvin went over to the driver's truck for a chat and what he saw made even the hairs on his neck stand up. In the man's truck there were straps, posts and a cage door across the sleeper compartment, with a lock on the outside. Colvin immediately knew what this man did and he could tell the man knew that he knew. Eventually, Colvin broke the ice by bringing up their shared interest and the man pointed him to a website he might enjoy. After several more minutes of conversation, the man asked Colvin if he could get him a woman. When Colvin asked how long he wanted the woman for, the man answered chillingly, 'I want somebody that won't be missed.'

Colvin sold the driver a sex worker called Catalina for $500 and said he never saw her again. Catalina had been missing for six months before anyone even noticed. Even more chillingly, according to Colvin, her murderer is still at large.

Colvin says he has met several serial killers among the truck-driver community and that he thinks there is something about the profession which either attracts them, or breeds them. Perhaps, as in Colvin's case, it's the ease with which they can get away with their crimes. Perhaps it's the long hours spent alone with nothing but their dark thoughts that drives them to such acts. Whatever the case, he suggests it would be a rich vein to explore if murder investigators were to look into the world of truckers.

Colvin is clear that the motivation for his crimes was anger. He insists he never went looking for victims but only ever reacted to being disrespected. But it is clear that there is also a misogynistic element to his crimes. He constantly refers to the women he murdered as 'bitches' and 'hoes'. In one telling answer, he insisted that his victims were not women at all, instead they were 'crackitutes', dehumanised creatures whose life is worth little or nothing. The fact that he refuses to acknowledge the humanity of his victims is highly revealing.

Colvin also admits that he obtained satisfaction and pleasure from killing these women. Otherwise, as he pointed out, why would he have killed so many? In one chilling answer, he expanded on the feeling he got when he was taking a life. 'It felt good,' he told me. 'It felt good to let her know right there and then that I have the power of life and death. Like one, she said, "Oh God!" and I said, "He can't help you." [Laughs].

It's a hell of a feeling. Some people go their whole life not knowing that feeling. I do. I have the power of life and death, and I always choose death.'

When I asked Colvin if he had any sympathy for his victims to the point where he ever considered sparing their lives, he answered, 'No. The reason why is 'cause I didn't know them from a can of beans. I can't be sympathetic to someone I don't know because I care nothing about them.'

Strangulation was his preferred method of killing because it was 'clean' and 'fun', and was another reason his crimes were so hard to detect. 'First of all, it's personal,' Colvin told me. 'Shooting and killing, that's too messy. There's blood every goddamn where. Strangulation is clean. If they find the body while still mummified, cause of death will be undetermined. They have no way of knowing. Because the ones they found of mine, I told them I strangled them.'

Although he had never timed it, it took a long time to kill victims using the strangulation method. The victim would lose consciousness at first, but it would take a long amount of time to finish them off. 'One time I got a cramp in my hand,' he told me, 'so I had to switch hands. When that happens I usually lay my forearm on the Adam's apple and just lean down. I'm three hundred pounds.' He also told me that his victims rarely struggled while they were dying, which was another benefit of strangulation because it, 'takes the fight out of you'. The same was true of speaking or calling out for help. Colvin made choking noises as he described a typical murder: 'All you hear is [choking noises]. What you saying bitch? [more choking noises] Speak up, I can't hear you.'

Another problem could be interruptions. Colvin described one occasion when he received a phone call halfway through a murder. He took the call with one hand while continuing to strangle his victim with the other. The call was from his mum, checking to see why he was so late coming home. He patiently explained that he was just outside Chattanooga, Tennessee, and that he would be home at five in the morning, while with the other hand he was throttling the life out of a young woman.

When Colvin completed a kill, he had the same problem as all murderers – how to dispose of the body. His preferred method was to strip the body naked and dispose of the corpse and its clothes in two different states, a process that led to him eventually being dubbed the 'Interstate Strangler'. Although he stripped the corpses naked, he said there was never any necrophilia involved in his murders. As a precaution he would also cover the head with a plastic bag and duct tape it around the neck. This was in case the victim wasn't actually dead because, he said, 'The last thing you want is someone popping up while you're going down the interstate about seventy or eighty miles per hour.' As his killing spree progressed, he began to learn tricks of the trade such as storing the corpse in a foetal position – this made the body easier to carry once rigour mortis set in.

Colvin would dump the bodies in the woods, making the effort to carry them deep out into the trees, but he didn't bother burying them. Most of his victims have never been found, despite a serial killing spree that lasted twenty-two years and spanned several states. What makes this even more surprising is that during this time, he was arrested and imprisoned several times on charges unrelated to these murders. In 1989, he was charged with a slew of crimes including attempted murder, felonious assault and illegal possession of weapons. He was convicted and sentenced to fifteen years in prison. On release in 1996, he continued his murder spree as if nothing had happened. Incredibly, during the whole process of his arrest and incarceration, no link was found between him and any of the murders he had committed.

Although his run continued for over two decades, it wasn't to last forever. He was finally arrested in 2005 and charged with the murders of Melissa Weber and Jackie Simpson. His capture came through an act of sloppiness that saw him work together with an accomplice, a practice that he had always avoided up until that point. Like many of Colvin's actions, this mistake came from an impulsive act of anger. He discovered that a cousin of his had taken a local prostitute he was dating, Melissa Weber, to Colvin's house and had sex with her there. On learning this, Colvin was so enraged that he decided to kill them both. He told his cousin to bring Weber to a nearby motel, where he planned to strangle her and shoot his cousin.

As instructed, his cousin brought Weber to the motel. Colvin strangled her in front of his relative. However, the second part of Colvin's plan didn't work out: he found that he couldn't murder his cousin because of the man's three children. Colvin knew the three boys well and had watched them grow up from babies. They would often stay around his house and that same day, one of them had been at his house polishing the chrome on his truck. Instead of killing his cousin, Colvin instructed him to dispose of Weber's body. This was his major mistake: his cousin wasn't as thorough as he might have been and the corpse was discovered. DNA evidence linked the corpse to Colvin's cousin and he was arrested and taken into custody. It didn't take much questioning by the police before he gave up Colvin's name and he too found himself in custody, answering questions.

From Colvin's DNA they were able to link him to another murder, that of Jackie Simpson. Simpson was another sex worker who Colvin had had intercourse with in a hotel room, before smothering her to death with a pillow. He hadn't originally planned on killing Simpson but he said her moaning was aggravating him because she wouldn't stop talking about her mother and 'creepy' uncle. 'I don't care nothing about that,' Colvin said. 'I just got tired of her whining.' Colvin kept Simpson's corpse in his truck for several months and it was her body that was in the trailer when he parked it outside the court to face burglary charges. Simpson's body was found in 2003 and DNA testing linked it to Colvin. Now linked to two murders, he was in a lot of trouble. 'I was charged with two counts of aggravated murder,' Colvin told me, 'for the killing of Jackie Simpson and Melissa Weber, which was a capital offence. I was on my way to death row.'

He soon realised that his only way to avoid the death sentence was to arrange a plea deal so he agreed to plead guilty to the murders of Jackie Simpson and Melissa Weber and also to help solve five other cold cases by admitting to the murders. 'I struck a deal to take the death penalty off the table,' Colvin told me. 'I tried to get thirty-five years but they wasn't going for that. And I tried to close some cases for them. At first they didn't believe me, but I gave them two and led them to the bodies and I got sentenced to two consecutive life sentences.'

Colvin admitted to the murders of Valerie Jones, Jaquelynn Thomas, Dorothea Wetzel and Lily Summers, all of whom he had murdered within the last five years. According to his testimony, he lured Valerie Jones into the cab of his truck in January 2000, strangling her to death then dumping her body in Lake Erie in Ottawa County, Ohio. In September of the same year, he said he murdered Jaquelynn Thomas after luring her into his truck cab and raping her. He dumped her body near a roadside in Monroe County, Ohio. In the same year he killed Dorothea Wetzel, dumping her corpse by the banks of the Maumee River in southern Toledo. Colvin murdered Lily Summers in 2002 and dumped her body in an empty tractor trailer. During this period of confession, he said he had police officers coming to him from all over the country looking to solve cold case murders. But, unlike many convicted murderers looking to make their life easier, he refused to admit to any killings that weren't his own. He also kept the cases to Ohio, where he had the protection of the deal that would save him from death row.

However, one out-of-state murder was added to his list of convictions in 2010, when he was linked to the murder of Donna Lee White in 1987 in Atlantic City, New Jersey. Colvin had been a suspect in the original case but had not been convicted and her death was ruled as an overdose. However, the case was re-opened following Colvin's 2006 conviction. He pleaded guilty to the murder, which had happened when he was working as a taxi driver in New Jersey. White was a prostitute who Colvin said he had brought back to his apartment for sex. Afterwards, she had overdosed on drugs. Rather than helping her, Colvin suffocated White with a plastic bag before dumping her body on the outskirts of the city. 'I put the bag over her head and laid her down on the bed, and I sat there and watched football,' he told me.

In 2006, he was sentenced to two life sentences without the chance of parole. His reaction, according to him, was one of pure relief that he was off death row. 'Death row, that's a cruel and unusual punishment,' he told me. 'If you're gonna kill me, get it over with. Don't drag it out for twenty, thirty years.'

Colvin was incarcerated in Lebanon Correctional Institution in Ohio, a Level III medium-security prison. He kept his head down and tried to keep out of trouble as much as possible.

But he also had his limits, and he wouldn't allow anyone to treat him like a punk. When he was first moved to the prison there were no dividers in the showers. One day he was taking a shower next to another inmate and had just turned to leave when the other man said, 'You got soap all in the crack of your ass.' Colvin didn't respond but he instantly knew two things – the other inmate was checking out his ass, and the man thought he was soft.

Colvin quickly went back to his cell, where he dried himself off and got dressed. He came back to the shower fully dressed while the man was still naked. Colvin knew that he would have the advantage over a naked man on the wet floor, and so he did. He beat the man badly and tried to kill him, but was unable to do so before the alarm was raised. As punishment, he got six months in the hole and was charged with assault – inconsequential to him as he was never getting out of prison anyway.

On another two occasions he choked inmates who he felt had disrespected him. One of them had made a sexual pass at him. He received sixteen hours extra duty in the kitchen.

One of the biggest irritations of Colvin's time in prison was the constant barrage of media attention. He was approached by almost every television network looking to do interviews with him, but he wasn't interested in gaining fame from his crimes and so he turned them all down. One offer came from NBC, who wanted to make a documentary involving Colvin. He said he wasn't interested unless he was compensated financially. This was a no-go due to laws preventing criminals from profiting from the publicity of their crimes, so the dialogue ended there. Some time later, however, Colvin was interrupted one day by a guard, telling him he had to accompany him to the conference room. The guard handcuffed Colvin and took him to the room, where he sat him down and handcuffed him to the table.

Soon after, a man walked in accompanied by another man holding a camera and microphone. The first man was John Douglas, a former criminal profiler from the FBI's Elite Serial Crime Unit, whose 2012 book, *Mindhunter*, had inspired a popular drama series of the same name on Netflix. Douglas sat down opposite Colvin and said he was there to interview him for the documentary. Colvin responded, 'No conversation without compensation,' which Douglas didn't react well to. He told Colvin that he didn't pay the likes of people like him. Colvin responded by beckoning Douglas closer with one hand. The man obliged and Colvin said in a soft voice, 'Get your punk ass on this table and suck my dick.' Douglas's face dropped and Colvin could tell the man was unused to being spoken to like this. Unfazed, Colvin went on to explain how lucky Douglas was that he was handcuffed to the table, otherwise he'd feel more than harsh words. The celebrity profiler left without his interview and with a bruised ego to boot.

The only person Colvin ended up speaking to was Phil Chalmers, another criminal profiler. Chalmers hosted a podcast called 'Where the Bodies are Buried', where he interviewed murderers and serial killers. He wrote to Colvin in 2020 requesting an interview and received the usual response. But there was something about Chalmers that made Colvin have second thoughts: 'We got off to a bad start,' Colvin told me, 'because I read his letter and wrote him back something jazzy, and he took it on the chin. He came to see me and I said, this guy got a lot of spunk.'

Colvin ended up agreeing to an interview for Chalmers' podcast and the results were explosive – Colvin revealed the full extent of his killing, saying he had murdered fifty-two victims. He also revealed the details of another murder, even giving the exact location where the body was buried. Colvin described to Chalmers how in 2004 or 2005 he had stopped at a Flying J Travel Center off the Interstate 80 highway, just outside of LaSalle, Illinois, when a woman knocked on his truck door. The woman was a sex worker with her hair combed over one eye to mask a black eye. He shouted at her, 'Beat it! Get the fuck out of here!'

The woman left and Colvin went into the shop to buy a couple of log books. He then returned to his truck when the woman knocked on it again. This time he let her into the cab, where he strangled her to death. He put the body in the sleeper compartment and drove to a nearby abandoned truck wash. 'The road is deserted,' Colvin said. 'No one comes down there, it's dark and it's scary. I pulled all the way in the back. The weeds are so high, and I just remember picking [the body] up on my shoulder and into the woods I go.' He dragged the body some thirty or forty feet into the woods and left it there, making it, as he told Chalmers, 'one of the easiest of his bodies to find'.

His admission led to a search by Illinois police using cadaver dogs. The search turned up two bones which might have been of human origin, but later testing identified them as belonging to an animal.

Colvin and Chalmers' interview aired in 2020, which was a notable year for Colvin for another reason. He caught a severe case of Covid-19 and nearly died. 'The worst part ever was when I came back from the hospital,' he told me. 'They stuck me in a hospital cell in the hole and that did more damage than good 'cause you need oxygen, you need to be cool. And this was during August when it was the worst weather ever. It was bad. I could have died here faster than I could in the hospital after they'd already treated me for the Covid.'

Colvin survived, however, and is now sixty-four years old. He is treated as a Level II prisoner within the Level III Lebanon prison. He says he has made his peace with never being let out and that the prison lifestyle doesn't faze him. On the contrary, he says that thirty years of working as a trucker has prepared him for the isolation and boredom of prison life.

His routine starts at 5.30 a.m. when he wakes up in his single cell. At 6.30, he leaves and goes to get his injection for diabetes. He then has breakfast and heads off to work in the mail room, where he makes mail tags along with two other prisoners. At 10 a.m. he comes back to the block for count, where he reads some news and sports. At 11.30, he heads back to work until 2.15 p.m. He then comes back to the block and has a shower. For the rest of the day, he watches sports or movies on his tablet, or he might play a game or two of chess before getting his head down at some time between 7 to 9 p.m. He seldom socialises, saying he deters most people who try to approach him.

'There's over two hundred people in this block,' he told me. 'I'm in range 3. Range 3 is all single-room cells and there's twenty-two cells on Range 3. Out of twenty-two cells I talk to about four people. On Range 2, I talk to one person. On Range 1, I talk to one person. People outside of the block, I talk to no one. I'm not a very sociable person, and it's not good to be sociable, especially in here.' The rest of the inmates he describes as 'assholes', who he 'wouldn't piss on if they were on fire'.

With all this time on his hands you might think that he has spent many hours reliving, analysing and trying to come to terms with the crimes he has committed. On the contrary, Colvin says he hardly ever reflects on the murders and doesn't even think of himself in those terms. When I asked him if he saw himself as a serial killer, his answer was revealing. 'I don't

93

give it a second thought,' he told me. 'When people ask me what I'm in here for, I say, "Mind your own fucking business." I don't even think of it like that. The media sees it like that but I never give it a second thought.'

He said he never suffers from nightmares and sleeps 'damn well'. For twenty years he has been having the same dream – that he's driving a truck with no brakes, heading for an intersection, but he always wakes up before the truck hits the junction. Not an unusual dream for a trucker and not one that seems to show any hint of remorse for his murders, even on a subconscious level.

Unsurprisingly for someone who reflects so little on his crimes, Colvin has no repentance for what he has done. When I asked him if he was remorseful, he answered, 'No, I am not. Remorse is for suckers on television shows. None whatsoever.' In fact, he went further. When I asked if he would kill again, he answered immediately, 'Hell, yes! If someone pissed me off, hell, yes! I know I would.'

A clue to how Colvin can be so unemotionally involved in his crimes comes from the way he speaks about his victims, constantly dehumanising them. He referred to them as 'worthless' and went on to explain, 'They didn't give a shit. All they cared about is smoking crack cocaine and they'd fuck and suck and steal and rob or do anything they can just to get it. That was their main focus in life – to get high. And they don't care what they got to do, who they got to fuck, suck or whatever as long as they get it.'

Colvin doesn't extend this feeling to all women. This is illustrated by the way he speaks about his fiancée, the woman he was engaged to when arrested in 2005. He said that love was a 'beautiful thing' and that he had experienced it at least twice in his life. He also said that his fiancée, Robin, was the love of his life. Robin never knew about Colvin's crimes and when he was arrested, he says it hit her hard. With a typical lack of empathy, however, he followed this up by saying it had pissed him off that after five years of looking after her, he had never received a phone call or letter from her following his arrest.

How can someone who says love is a beautiful thing, and talks about a woman being the love of his life, bring himself to murder fifty-two women? Anger is the reason Colvin gives, but clearly there is a deeper misogyny, hatred and rage that led to countless murders. The one hint at the reason behind the anger came when he told Phil Chalmers, 'I took a lot of shit. I took a lot of crap from a lot of different goddam people. I was never the one to go looking for trouble but I've always been prepared for it. There's a difference, the military taught me that. But when it builds up, now it got to the point where I quit taking shit. I just quit.'

It seems that Colvin was particularly affected by the bullying he experienced at school, where he would often be beaten up by the bigger kids. Perhaps he felt he was something of a walkover, who was treated badly by the people he came into contact with throughout his life, until one day he just snapped. Combine this with the hatred he had for his stepmother and we can see the misogynistic element which focused his rage on women – women he could dehumanise, thus keeping any sense of remorse or guilt out of the equation.

The sixty-four-year-old serial killer says he has come to terms with spending the rest of his life in prison. In fact, his positive mental attitude to his situation is almost astounding. 'It is what it is,' he told me. 'I lived a good life, I got caught. I'm guilty. Hell, I'm the only guilty guy here. I put it like this – all this is extra. I should be sitting on death row right now, and any minute someone gonna stick a needle in my black ass . . . Instead, I've got a single cell with a colour TV, some chicken breasts up here, some Jack mackerel, some crackers and hot sauce, a few chips and an apple pie . . . I ain't mad at the world, I don't go round frowning and shit.'

This positive attitude is the flip side of the darker aspect of his nature – his callous attitude to his victims. And this points to a deeper underlying problem in the US and society at large – the phenomenon of 'the less dead'. There is an underclass of people such as sex workers, addicts and the homeless, a population that lives on the fringes of polite society and who are ignored, devalued and often not missed if they disappear. It has spawned something of an epidemic of serial killers in the US, as Phil Chalmers explained to me after my conversation with Colvin.

'There are many serial killers like Dellmus,' Chalmers told me. 'Fifty to a hundred serial killers in the US at any given time. A lot of these guys are driving around the country just like him. They're targeting "less dead" victims who are drug addicts, prostitutes and sex workers. There's thousands of women being murdered.'

We know from Colvin's testimony that he was aware of several other truck drivers who were serial killers, at least one of whom is still at large. Continuing to catch serial killers like Dellmus Colvin is ongoing, of course, but won't tackle the root of the problem. We need to stop devaluing people like drug addicts and sex workers and prevent them from being pushed beyond the bounds of normal society. Studies have shown that ending the war on drugs and legalising prostitution would go a long way towards doing this and would make life far safer for the kind of people who are the prime targets of an ever-growing band of callous murderers like Colvin.

DELLMUS COLVIN

As for Colvin himself, he is someone who fascinates us, yet makes us deeply uncomfortable. He certainly presented these two sides to me. It can't be overstated how the facts of his crimes jibe with his personable, affable, polite and friendly manner. He is the kind of person you would describe as a 'nice guy' after an everyday conversation with him. Neither is it easy to write him off as a psychopath who is incapable of normal human emotions. He talks about being in love and a certain amount of human warmth is evident in the way he responds to questions and engages in conversation. He is generous and good to his friends. In short, he is about as far away from the 'typical' serial killer of the popular imagination as it's possible to conceive.

Colvin's case defies any easy and artificial boundaries we try to draw around it and, as such, I find it hard to draw any simple or clear-cut conclusions about him. Except for one: a serial killer can be the most 'normal' person you ever meet.

The Hollywood, Hannibal Lecter-style serial killer is a myth in many circumstances, so we shouldn't be fooled into thinking it's only the weird guy down the street who never comes out of his house, and has a pale complexion and some serious social problems, that we need to be careful about.

Don't get into uncomfortable situations with strangers because they seem 'nice' or 'normal'. As so many found with Dellmus Colvin, you might be getting into a situation you never come out of.

4

Wild Bill

'I'm going to show them the best damn criminal there is'

As the twin-engine turbo prop touched down at Albrook Airport, just outside of Panama City, the fugitive looked out the window to see something that made him question whether he was really awake or dreaming.

He had suspected media attention, but the sea of people, the hordes of cameras, the journalists and reporters from seemingly every country in the world – it couldn't all be for him, surely?

The plane rolled to a stop on the runway and the SWAT team soldiers around him pulled their masks down and made themselves look professional again. Just a few minutes ago they had been laughing and joking with him, feeding him fried chicken and getting souvenir photographs with the famous serial killer hitman.

He was led down the aeroplane steps in chains and handcuffs and across the tarmac to the waiting cameras. On a makeshift stage he was sat next to Omar Pinzon, Director General of the Panamanian Police. Dozens of cameras focused on him as the head of police stood up and delivered a long victory speech in Spanish, detailing how they had managed to catch Panama's most wanted criminal, the American 'Wild Bill'.

However, the speech didn't last too long before it was interrupted. Pinzon was just thanking the Panamanian forces for their great work in Wild Bill's capture when a pair of manacled hands rose into the air. A sea of heads turned his way. The criminal, the monster, wanted to speak!

A hush descended as the man spoke in halting, American-accented Spanish. 'Hey, wait . . .' he said. Silence reverberated around the airfield. 'The Panamanians didn't capture me. The Panamanians let me get away. It was the Nicaraguans that captured me.'

The silence extended for several moments, then the voice of a female reporter shouted out a question, 'Hey, Bill, what would you like to say to all the Panamanians?'

He smiled in response. 'I'd like to say thanks for the free private jet ride, and for the long vacation I'm about to take. I hope there's a jacuzzi.'

This statement was met with more stunned silence. Then someone began to laugh. More people joined in and suddenly everyone was laughing. More questions were fired at him and he tried to answer them as best he could in his broken Spanish.

Next to him, the upstaged Director General of Police was fuming. Pinzon started screaming at the guards to take the prisoner away. As he was led off, Wild Bill couldn't help smiling to himself. It looked like he'd made himself another high-profile enemy, but it had been worth it.

William Holbert, otherwise known as 'Wild Bill', was a professional hitman from the US who plied his trade in Panama from 2006 to 2010. His multiple homicides made him the most wanted criminal in Central America until he was finally captured while on the run in Nicaragua. Sentenced to forty-seven years in prison for five homicides, he spent several years in the maximum-security section of one of Central America's most dangerous prisons.

During his time in jail, Holbert experienced a religious conversion and eschewed all further criminality. After angering the Panamanian authorities for an exposé of their human rights abuses, he was placed in an even worse prison where troublesome inmates are left to rot and often die, and where human rights are non-existent. He is now the pastor of this prison, which he calls 'hell', where he helps to get the young inmates out of their gang lifestyles. I spoke to Holbert on my true crime podcast in June 2024.

As a professional hitman and multiple murderer, you would expect Holbert to have had a traumatic childhood. Not so. According to him, his upbringing in rural North Carolina couldn't have been much better. 'I had a really good mother and father,' Holbert told me. 'We lived together in a house. We were religious and not more religious than anybody else or not less than anybody else. We went to church on Sundays, prayed before meals. Five evenings out of seven everybody ate together around a big table and in a semiformal way . . . typical American family . . . I couldn't imagine anybody having a better childhood than I did.'

The young Holbert wasn't particularly violent either, or any more so than a typical red-blooded boy from North Carolina. He played American football and got into the occasional fist fight, but that was about it. As a country boy living in the rural south, he had an incredible amount of independence from a young age. From the age of eleven he could drive a tractor and shoot a gun, and he would often escape into the wilderness to hunt game with his rifle.

If there was one factor Holbert pinpoints as leading to his career as a criminal, he thinks it came when he was around sixteen years old. 'I got a driver's licence, I became free and opened up to many things, probably too quickly – sex with girls, booze, partying. I went from one day being totally repressed to the next day being totally free, and that's probably a bad thing.'

Once he had gained this freedom, Holbert threw himself into partying and with it came violence. He found himself getting into a lot of bar fights. Soon, he discovered he was pretty good at fighting and would often pick fights with the biggest, fiercest-looking men he could find. He also found himself getting into low-level illegal activity. He started selling stolen heavy machinery and when he was eighteen, he set up an illegal business selling cigarettes to other states. In his early twenties he got married and had children after completing two years at a local agricultural college.

Despite dabbling in illegal money-making schemes, Holbert's real ambition was to be a politician. When he was twenty-three years old he formed his own political party with a staunch anti-illegal immigration stance, which he describes as being more like an armed militia consisting of five hundred members. He even had his eye on running for state senator the following year.

Life was looking pretty rosy for Holbert and his future was full of promise, but everything went wrong in 2004 when his marriage ended in divorce. During the court proceedings, Holbert was sentenced to two weeks in prison for contempt of court for insulting the judge. With that on his record, his immediate political ambitions took a nosedive, a disappointment which caused him to make a radical decision that would change his life forever.

'I should have done the time,' he told me. 'My God, if I could go back in time and just do the time and continue on the same path I was on, I would have been okay. But I didn't and I told my lawyer . . . I said, "If they want to see a criminal, I'm going to show them the best damn criminal there is." That's what I said. I'll never forget saying that, and that's what I did. From that point I took a complete right-angle turn, or maybe a one hundred and eighty-degree turn, and became the best damn criminal that anybody had ever seen in that part of the world.'

Holbert started working as a debt collector, a job which, at one point, nearly cost him his life. He had caught a man who owed a debt and was beating him with a piece of rubber hose filled with lead when the man reached down to his ankle and pulled out a small semi-automatic pistol. The man fired five shots before Holbert managed to wrestle the gun from him.

'I looked down and there's blood everywhere,' Holbert told me, 'and I said to my partner, "He shot himself," because I didn't feel anything. And he had actually shot me. He shot my ankle and he shot literally my ass, like literally right next to my asshole . . .'

Because of the nature of his activities, Holbert couldn't go to a regular doctor. Instead, he was forced to use a crooked veterinary surgeon. The vet dug the bullet out of his ankle and put pins into the bone using nothing more technical than a cordless electric drill. He also told Holbert that one of the bullets had lodged in his spine and would have to be left there because removing it could risk permanent spinal injuries. He told him to go home and rest in bed for four weeks. The next morning, Holbert woke up with no feeling in his legs. He called the vet, who told him all he could do was continue to rest and pray that he recovered. Holbert did just that and was fortunate to be up and about again within a few weeks.

Holbert's time as a criminal in the US came to an end after he fraudulently sold a house that didn't belong to him and was featured on the crime TV show *America's Most Wanted* in 2010. After several close escapes, he fled the country and travelled to Costa Rica with several hundred thousand dollars in cash. Still just twenty-five years old, he was looking to build an illegal criminal empire outside the US. He left Costa Rica and moved to Panama when a friend of his, who was a fisherman, invited him down to fish for cocaine. 'When the drug boats go north from Colombia they have to run from the cops,' Holbert told me, 'and so they throw all the drugs overboard, and those drugs kind of just go like a shotgun, they go everywhere, and they're wrapped in these twenty-five-kilogram condoms . . . and they throw them in the water and sometimes you can pick them up. And in Costa Rica white was $7,000 a kilo, so just do the math – twenty-five times seven thousand – that's a lot of money.'

While staying in Panama, Holbert got speaking to a man who operated a human trafficking operation, smuggling Asian immigrants into the US via the Panama Canal, through the Caribbean to Jamaica, then on to the east coast of America. As a proficient sailor with a coastguard's licence, Holbert landed himself a well-paid job ferrying these illegal immigrants on part of their journey to the States. Holbert's leg of the journey was between Panama and Jamaica and he would skipper a large open boat that could carry sixty-five to eighty passengers at a time. He would make a little over a thousand dollars per journey and would make the trip two or three times a week.

Holbert enjoyed the work but he saw some bad things, which mostly involved the mistreatment of the passengers who, despite having paid around $10,000 to be smuggled into the US, were often treated like cattle. The worst incident he saw was when he was transferring the passengers from his boat to the Jamaican ship. The sea was rough so the two boats had to be loosely moored to each other to prevent them capsizing. However, this meant that the two boats would periodically bang together quite violently, making the crossing between them hazardous. Holbert had got around two-thirds of his passengers safely across when it came the turn of an attractive young Chinese woman. The woman was standing on the railing of the boat about to jump across when a wave crashed through the gap and she slipped and fell. At the same time the two boats crashed together, snapping her leg so badly that the femur was sticking out above her knee.

'I don't know what to do,' Holbert told me, 'because I'm a day and a half away from help and I can't take her back with me because she'll die on the way, she'll bleed out because you can't have a bone sticking out of your skin for a day and a half. And I thought, the Jamaicans, I don't know what they'll do with her, and then I saw them shoot her in the head and throw her overboard. And I thought to myself, it's both a terrible thing and a kindness that they did to her because they can't take her to a hospital because we're in the middle of a criminal activity. They could have just thrown her overboard without shooting her, I guess. That sounds very callous on my part, and it is, but it is a kindness that they at least shot her first.'

The man who ran the trafficking operation was part of a criminal cartel operating in Central America, made up of twelve loosely affiliated, high-level criminals, including drug traffickers, money launderers and dirty lawyers. Holbert was doing a good job as a boat captain and getting along well with everyone until one day he was attacked by a man who happened to be an associate of the cartel. In defending himself from his attacker, Holbert accidentally killed the man. The crime was investigated by the authorities and Holbert was cleared of homicide, having been found to be acting in self-defence. Still, this wouldn't wash with the cartel bosses, so he ended up going on the run for the best part of a year before the cartel caught up with him. When they did, Holbert owed them several large favours, which they cashed in by forcing him to become a hitman.

Holbert had been involved in his fair share of violence as a bar brawler and a debt collector but he had never premeditatedly killed anyone before. Still, he had little choice now and so, as with everything he did, he set about doing it in the most thorough and professional way possible. He soon realised he excelled at it and so, on the side of his cartel work, he started operating as a freelance bounty hunter and hitman, hunting down fugitives for clients and liquidating their wealth. Some of these people were paedophiles on the run from the US authorities, others were former Mafia associates who had ratted on their colleagues. At first, Holbert would charge $20,000–$30,000 for a killing, but as he got more of a reputation his prices went up. By the end he wouldn't accept a job for less than $250,000.

Although killing people became his job, Holbert insists he never took pleasure in his work. Instead, he would require weeks to get over a killing, time which he spent partying as hard as possible to try and take his mind off what he had done. 'I hated it when I had a contract,' he told me. 'It stressed me out, the thought of killing someone. It wasn't something that was pleasant to me at all, it was very, very unpleasant.'

A typical job would last a month, most of which would be spent researching the target. This was in the age before smartphones, plus Holbert lived off-grid in the jungle, so most of his tracking would have to be done the old-fashioned way. Once he had finally hunted down his target, he would go about the job as efficiently and painlessly as possible. He preferred to inflict as little suffering as possible too, so he would typically come up behind his target and shoot them in the head from behind, killing them instantly. He is aware that this might sound cowardly, but his intent, he says, was not to inflict a period of suffering and terror where the person knew they were about to die.

After a hit Holbert would require a month of hard partying to escape the reality of what he had done. He wasn't happy and his only consolation was that he thought he himself wouldn't be around for long. 'My thought process was that I'll never get out of this,' he told me. 'Somebody will kill me. There's no retirement for professional killers. The retirement is when they put a bullet in the back of your head – that's what I assumed would happen to me.'

Holbert spent a year as the cartel's underling, carrying out contract killings whenever they required it and supplementing the money with freelance work of his own. But his fortunes changed when, after one hit, he chanced upon a safe that had $650,000 in it. With his newfound wealth, he went to some of the cartel higher-ups and told them he wanted to become one of them. Several of them weren't too keen on this proposition but when they voiced their doubts, Holbert suggested that he might start killing them one by one, at which point they changed their minds and welcomed him to the club.

With his position secure, Holbert now began making serious money. He bought a large property in a secluded cove in Bocas del Toro, a peninsula off the southern tip of Colón Island, on Panama's Caribbean coast. The property was over two hundred acres, with a six thousand square foot main building. It was completely off-grid and powered by a large generator. On the land, Holbert kept cattle and grew plantains and cacao for chocolate. He had two hundred-feet-tall ancient mango trees near his house, which were homes to two war-ring families of howler monkeys who would wake him up at sunrise each morning with their loud screams. He also had a sailing yacht and several speedboats moored to his dock, which he would take into the tranquil waters of the bay. Holbert liked his toys and it was one these which would earn him the moniker 'Wild Bill'.

Another resident on the island owed Holbert several thousand dollars which he couldn't afford to pay back. Holbert visited his house and in lieu of cash, decided to take a bro-ken-down old Cessna seaplane, which he thought would look good moored to his dock. The plane was in several pieces so Holbert returned with an army of local helpers, who put it back together. They then towed it by boat back to his property.

Holbert had a friend who was former aeroplane mechanic in the navy and he offered to fix the engine for a small fee. Holbert agreed and within three weeks, he had a perfectly running sea plane. The only problem now was that he couldn't fly it. He was waiting for someone to come down to teach him when he hosted a party for about eighty people at his house. During the party the navy mechanic kept winding him up about the fact that he had let the seaplane sit on his dock for three weeks without even taking it out for a spin. By the end of the night and several strong drinks later, Holbert had had enough. He marched out to the dock and did something that definitely merits the name 'wild'.

'There were two mangrove islands about two miles out from where the dock was,' Holbert told me. 'My plan in my drunken mind was to fly out, bank left around the islands, come back and settle it easy into the water, just to prove that I can fly. I'd never flown an airplane before but I'm Wild Bill, and where there's a Bill, there's a way. So, I put the flaps down, maximum throttle, up in the air, drop the flaps, gained about two hundred feet of altitude, bank left around the mangrove island, everything's going really good. Now I look back, everybody's on the dock watching me, ready to watch me kill myself – there's eighty people out there watching . . . I've got about a mile's worth of approach, maybe a little bit more, so I dropped the flaps, pull the throttle back down to about 25 per cent, let the plane settle into the water. But something bad happened. I didn't realise how much drag was going to be on those pontoons when they hit the water. I didn't really even think about it, but there's a lot of drag. The water grabs the pontoons pretty hard, and you're not going that fast, like forty-five knots, it's not really moving that quickly, but when those pontoons hit, the plane almost nosed over in the water, and I pulled back on the stick really hard. It was a really, really ugly landing but at the end I saved it.'

As Holbert strode unsteadily back down the dock to the crowd's roaring cheers, someone shouted out, 'That's our Wild Bill!', and the name stuck.

Another of his pride and joys was the bar that Holbert built on his property called the Jolly Roger Social Club. Sharing the island with around forty other eccentric expatriates, he liked to entertain these people with lavish parties at his house, so building his own bar seemed the next logical step. The Jolly Roger Social Club was finished in 2008 and was built on stilts over the water so that boats could float straight up to it and moor alongside, which was good as it was only accessible by water. Holbert and his guests would party for up to three days straight, where cocaine was served alongside alcohol and cut into lines on the bar. At the end of the third day, as the sun was rising, Holbert would don a Viking helmet, stand on a milk crate and deliver the 'Words of Wisdom' which he had prepared beforehand, then everyone would go home unsteadily in their boats.

But the good times couldn't last forever and they ended abruptly in 2010 when one of Holbert's contacts inside Panama's version of the FBI warned that the police were going to call him in for questioning. Holbert decided to get out of the country for a while and fled to Costa Rica, where he stayed in an isolated cabin on the flank of an active volcano. He had been staying at the cabin for six weeks when he turned on the news to see his own face staring back at him and the headline that Panamanian police were on the hunt for Wild Bill, the most wanted hitman in Central America, a fugitive responsible for hundreds of deaths.

The heat came even closer to home when he was sat in the local internet café, where he would check his emails daily. He was sitting in the corner one day when an American man entered and sat next to him. His suspicions were raised immediately – everything about the man, from his haircut to his clothes to the way he walked, screamed 'cop'. The man asked him several questions as if starting a polite conversation, but Holbert was having none of it. When the man asked where he came from, Holbert responded, 'My mother's womb!' He then went to the toilet and escaped out of the second-storey window. On the ground, he doubled round to see the man exit the café angrily and jump into a Chevrolet Caprice, a car that was practically unknown in Costa Rica. Holbert had no doubts any longer – the authorities were zeroing in on him.

'I crammed my girlfriend in the car,' he told me, 'a bag that had about $32,000 in it, a 38-calibre pistol and two changes of clothes, and left everything else. I thought to myself, if I can get to Bluefields in Nicaragua, where I have some friends who are embedded in the Nicaraguan military, I'll be okay, if I can just get there.'

Holbert set off with his girlfriend and his few meagre possessions in the Nissan Pathfinder he had recently purchased and headed for the border with Nicaragua, using dirt backroads that turned the three-hour journey into a gruelling eight-hour marathon. At the border town of Sarapiqui, he arranged for boat transportation up the river to the Nicaraguan town of Bluefields. There, he had friends among the Nicaraguan paramilitaries whom he used to smuggle arms to. These paramilitaries could hide him, but first he and his girlfriend had two days of boat travel to negotiate through a country full of police checkpoints.

They found a boat captain who agreed to take them upriver and set off at 5 a.m. the next day. By the afternoon they had reached the border, where they holed up overnight in a small cabin. The next morning, they set off, but, strangely, the captain of the boat insisted they must stop near a small checkpoint on the way. Holbert protested but the captain insisted that it was unavoidable. Holbert found out later that the boat captain's wife had informed him that his passenger was most probably the Wild Bill that everyone was searching for and he had called the police, who had told him to bring Holbert to the nearest checkpoint.

When they arrived at the rickety old shack that passed for a checkpoint, the two policemen insisted that Holbert must accompany them back downriver to check his passport. Holbert pretended to comply and asked if he could go and explain the situation to his girlfriend, who was still sitting in the boat. The police agreed and when Holbert got to the boat he simply jumped in, turned the ignition on and raced off in the stolen vessel. But he didn't get far before he noticed another craft coming up behind him. He heard shots ring out and quickly realised the boat was firing on him. Holbert slowed down and allowed the boat to come alongside. It was occupied by a Nicaraguan army captain and two soldiers. They arrested him and took him to the nearest checkpoint. However, by some miracle, the captain didn't seem to know who he was, instead assuming he was a drug trafficker. Holbert was down but not out. He still had one weapon left in his armoury – cash.

'I said, "I'm not a drug trafficker,"' Holbert told me, '"You didn't find any drugs and I'm being honest, I'm not a drug trafficker." And he said, "Well, how can you account for the $32,000?" And I said, "I can't account for $32,000. I can account that I have $16,000 and that you have $16,000." And he blinked and he said, "We've made a terrible mistake, we've arrested an innocent man." And he ordered everybody out of the room.'

Holbert counted out the money then and there on the table and he was free to go. The Nicaraguans even gave him his pistol back. But his luck was due to take another turn. Little did he know but the Costa Rican police and military had been patrolling the river with helicopters, looking for signs of him. While he was waiting to leave the Nicaraguan checkpoint, one of these helicopters flew over and a policeman announced through a bullhorn that the Nicaraguans were holding Holbert, the most wanted man in Panama and the most dangerous killer in all of Central America. Before he had time to react, Holbert felt a rifle butt crunch into the back of his head and he lost consciousness.

He woke up on the floor of a cell next to his girlfriend. Soon, they were moved out and put on a boat. They were told they would be taken to the Nicaraguan capital, Managua, for interrogation. The journey took three days by boat and military truck with nothing to eat the whole time. But the journey itself would be nothing compared to the ordeal he would face in Managua.

In the capital, Holbert and his girlfriend were first questioned by American Embassy staff, who at last gave them some food. After the Embassy staff left, it was the Nicaraguans' turn. The lead interrogator questioned Holbert for about an hour in fluent English before asking him to sign some papers. What he didn't realise was that Holbert could read Spanish. As he scanned the document, he could see that he would be admitting to four homicides committed in Nicaragua between 1999 and 2010. He refused to sign and the tone of the interrogation swiftly changed. The guard raised his baton to hit Holbert but the American hitman was faster. Despite weighing nearly three hundred pounds and being chained by the ankles, he managed to close the distance between himself and the guard and crash him to the ground with a shoulder barge. The interrogator began screaming for help and the room quickly filled with guards, who beat Holbert thoroughly around the body with their batons.

He would be interrogated a further four times and each session would begin and end with a beating, each one done with an expert thoroughness. 'They began to beat my ribcage and ample belly with these bats that have foam wrapped around them,' Holbert told me, 'and it doesn't hurt at first, it really doesn't, but after they do it for about an hour, it starts to hurt pretty damn bad, and you bruise and shit, but then they put a shirt on you and take you out for photographs and they're like, "We interrogated him. Here's a photo of him, he's not been beat up."'

Holbert faced a tough future in Nicaragua, which is why he jumped at the chance of extradition back to Panama when the head of the Panamanian FBI, Omar Pinzon, came to visit him. Pinzon promised that there would be no more beatings in Panama and that his girlfriend would be safe there. The papers he asked Holbert to sign contained no hidden admissions of guilt, they were merely an agreement to return to Panama to face trial. Holbert accepted and before too long, he and his girlfriend were on a plane. It was there that he got the first hint of just how much publicity his case had attracted when the eight fully armed SWAT team soldiers who had been assigned to guard him took off their face masks, untied his chains and asked him to sign autographed pictures with them.

When the plane touched down in Panama City in 2010, the media circus was like that for a rock star or famous actor. As mentioned at the start of this chapter, Holbert attracted even more attention to himself by upstaging Pinzon at the press conference at the airport. After this little stunt, the media attention would only continue despite his capture, with items about him on the news every day for the best part of a year.

After the press conference Holbert was whisked away to a holding cell to await questioning. The interrogation techniques in Panama were indeed much more civilised than in Nicaragua; however, the aim seemed to be the same – to get him to sign up to a whole lot of crimes he hadn't committed. The lead district attorney, Angel Calderon, tried to get him to sign a seventeen-page document in Spanish legalese that Holbert couldn't understand. He refused to sign. They also wanted him to give up the names of all his associates. This he wasn't about to do because he knew how easy it was to have someone killed in a Panamanian prison.

In fact, what Holbert wanted to do was the opposite: he needed to admit to everything they knew about which he had actually done, say it was all his fault, and get a copy of his signed confession out to his former associates as quickly as possible to prevent himself from being murdered. This he was able to do with the help of a half-Panamanian, half-American lawyer whose number someone had passed him. The lawyer helped get the government and the press off his back. He pleaded guilty to two initial homicides with which he was charged and a copy of this plea was swiftly passed to his former crime associates in the cartel.

His new lawyer also advised him that his best bet would be to admit to every crime that he had ever committed in Panama, leaving nothing that could come back to haunt him later. This was because the Panamanian legal system had a maximum single sentence of thirty-five years. In admitting to everything and squeezing it into one case, Holbert could avoid multiple sentences that could last beyond thirty-five years. The thirty-five-year sentence could also be appealed, hopefully getting it dropped to twenty-five years for cooperating with the authorities. Holbert confessed to five homicides and would ultimately be sentenced to forty-seven years behind bars. But this didn't happen until 2017, seven years after he was first arrested.

Meanwhile, he was coming to terms with life in Panama's prison system. There were some odd things to get used to, such as the way the Panamanian guards would have sex with the female prisoners every night as a matter of routine. He also noticed how the Panamanian prisons were run almost exclusively by the prisoners themselves. There was no violence in the prisons, no beatings or even stabbings, because of the simple fact that everyone had guns. All conflicts were settled with shootings and, indeed, the Panamanians seemed to eschew, even fear, physical violence. Even stranger, although the prisons were run by gangs, these gangs were not run along racial lines. And in fact, he told me he never saw a single case of racism during his time in the Panamanian prison system.

Holbert was soon to find out even more about Panamanian prison life as he was scheduled to be transferred from his holding prison to Panama's most notorious jail – La Joya. On the day of his transfer, he learned that he would be taken to the infamous Cell Block 7, the supermax section of La Joya, where the most dangerous criminals in the country were kept under strict supervision. He knew he would be in for a rough ride and on the way there, he tried to prepare himself mentally for the challenges to come. But no preparations could prepare him for the reality of what he would experience when he arrived at Cell Block 7.

He told me: 'They march me down, turn me loose in this place, and there's just one cop guarding and one cop in the guard tower and that's it. And the cop guarding takes my chains off and my cell is the one in the middle. There's only six cells and my cell's number 3. So I walked down to number 3 and I put my stuff in the cell and I noticed the cell doors were just open, and this guy, this tall white-headed man, comes down and with a British accent says to me, "Hey, Bill, welcome to hell!" and he throws something at me and I catch it out of the air, and it was an ice-cold can of Heineken beer, and I'm like, "What the fuck?!"'

Instead of the hell Holbert had expected, Cell Block 7 was a rather pleasant place to live. He had his own cell, and inmates were allowed out from 6 a.m. to 5 p.m. The five other cells were inhabited by ten high-risk prisoners – a mixture of gang leaders, drug barons and murderers. They shared a communal kitchen with well-stocked provisions and a refrigerator full of cold beers. The man who had initially tossed the can of Heineken to Holbert was an English gangster called Leo Morgan, who came from Birmingham and would go on to become one of Holbert's best friends. Morgan helped introduce Holbert to the prison's vagaries and routines and a guard supplied him with a mobile phone with which to contact his friends and family. The other prisoners were friendly and helpful and no one ever fought. In fact, the inmates were so scared of Holbert's reputation, they had nominated him to be the only one of them who received a cell to himself.

If he thought he had landed on his feet, Holbert had no idea what was coming, especially when two attractive female guards arrived one day. 'There were two women who were police sergeants,' he told me, 'who would come down and fuck us for money. And so I was sitting at this little desk that they had there and my friend Leo Morgan's sitting beside me, and he's like, "Oh shit, Bill!" And I said, "What?" And he's like, "You want to get laid?" And I'm like, "What are you talking about?" And so these two girls come in and I'm like, "What?" And he's like, "Yeah, they'll fuck you for a hundred bucks." And I'm like, "No man, I'm not paying for sex." And so the girls come down, and he spoke perfect Spanish. So they ask me, and Leo says, "He's a weird guy, he won't pay for sex." And the one girl says, "I don't care, I want to fuck Wild Bill." And so they took me into my cell and I ended up fucking both of them there in prison, if that tells you anything about how we lived there.'

But things weren't going quite so smoothly on the outside. One day, the mother of Holbert's lawyer – also a lawyer and the head of the family law firm – came to visit. She asked him to sign a document handing over all his possessions in Panama as payment for the firm's services. He refused to do so until they had secured his girlfriend's release from prison (she was later released with no charges). From that day on, the attitude of his lawyers changed towards him and, rather than being helpful, they actively tried to hinder him in any way possible, telling the press, falsely, that he hadn't paid for their services.

The problem with the lawyers would resurface soon when things went bad inside Cell Block 7. A new warden was appointed who had different ideas about how the maximum-security wing should be run. He wanted the cushy lifestyles to be over and the prisoners placed on full lockdown. He also wanted to bring in more dangerous prisoners. To this end, the cell block started to fill up with gangsters and hitmen who had committed multiple murders for their respective gangs. Even worse, the warden moved in the most dangerous members from rival gangs, immediately setting up an atmosphere of tension and impending violence.

When Holbert complained about the new system on the phone to his lawyer, their reaction was bizarre. They whispered down the line in a weirdly insistent voice that Holbert should kill the new warden. Holbert realised they were trying to set him up for another murder that would see him put away for even longer than the sentence he was already facing. When he put the phone down, he decided never to deal with this dangerous person again.

In the midst of the newly escalating tensions in Cell Block 7, something happened which changed Holbert's life forever. The La Joya prison chaplain, who Holbert affectionately knew as 'Chaplain Bob', regularly visited Cell Block 7. Chaplain Bob had a happy disposition and a wonderful singing voice, which he would use to boom out hymns whenever he was on the wing. One day when Chaplain Bob was chatting with Holbert and Leo Morgan, it came out that Holbert had been brought up in the Southern Baptist church. Chaplain Bob immediately burst into song, singing in English hymns which only a Southern

Baptist would usually know. Holbert found himself joining in while he was transported back to a time in his childhood when he was still innocent and guilt-free. He began to belt out the hymns and for fifteen minutes the two sang while the rest of the prisoners stared, mesmerised. It was a deeply spiritual experience for Holbert and that night he began to hear the tiny voice of his conscience speaking to him again. He started to take stock of the things he had done and took the first steps in a long process of spiritual rebirth.

Holbert had to survive eight more months of the new regime before he was transferred out when his case file moved to another part of the country. The timing couldn't have been more fortunate. Just after he was transferred, the escalating tensions finally exploded into violence: 'Three days after I got transferred out of there,' he told me, 'there was a shootout inside which killed three men.'

In late 2010, Holbert was transferred to the David Public Prison in a rural location in the Chiriquí province of northern Panama. The long and boring bus journey was made notable by the guards stopping to bring some prostitutes on board for their own amusement. When the two working girls discovered that one of the prisoners was the famous Wild Bill, they insisted on offering him their services, which they did on the moving bus while he was still chained and handcuffed, with the guards looking on.

This journey was a taste of things to come. David Public Prison was a laid-back institution where the inmates ruled and anything could be had for a price. When he was introduced to the warden at David, the first thing the Panamanian asked was if Holbert was a businessman. He responded that he most certainly was and from that moment on, the two had an understanding which allowed Holbert to rise quickly within the

118

hierarchy of the prison: 'I began building a relationship there in prison with the authorities,' he told me, 'one of corruption, and I literally took over that prison completely, as the inmates elected me as their representative of the government.'

One of the first things he managed to do was end the gang violence that periodically racked the prison. He called a meeting between the rival gang leaders and proposed a truce that would assign certain territories to each gang, within which they could sell their drugs freely. Without the constant shootings and police lockdowns, he argued, everyone would make a lot more money.

The scheme was incredibly successful and no one else was murdered the whole time that he was the prisoners' representative. It also meant a lot more freedom and privileges for Holbert. 'I had lots of sexual relationships with the girls who worked in the office,' he told me. 'I got conjugal visits every week. It wasn't like being in prison at all. I had the key to my cell, literally. I left my cell at five in the morning and I came back about midnight after drinking booze with the guards at night.'

But just as with his comfortable time at La Joya, the good times were soon destined to end. The authorities built a new prison called the Chiriquí Public Prison and all the inmates were moved. Things went on as comfortably as ever in the new institution for a while until the fateful day that Holbert agreed to do an interview with the British tabloid newspaper, the *Daily Mirror*. The interview was supposed to be about the human rights abuses in Panamanian prisons and Holbert claims his name was supposed to have been kept anonymous. However, when the piece came out, it focused solely on Holbert himself and how he lived like a king inside Panama's justice system.

The authorities were furious. They transferred him back to La Joya and its infamous Sector C, a section where all human rights were ignored or discarded when the prison authorities wanted rid of them. There was no food provided in Sector C, or rather, there was food, but it was so bad, it was completely inedible. On the two occasions when Holbert attempted to eat the prison food he broke his tooth and was violently ill. There was no toilet paper provided, no bedding and no healthcare. Everything came at a price. Inmates had to look after themselves and those with no money were forced to join gangs or do without. When he was initially transferred to Sector C, Holbert didn't eat for three weeks. Mortality rates were unusually high.

According to Holbert, there were three ways the Panamanian authorities finished you off in Sector C. One was through natural causes – lack of food, nutrients and ill health. The second was by purposefully celling you with a psychopathic murderer (which they attempted with Holbert), and the third was by driving you to suicide by the sheer unpleasantness of the life there. 'The death rate here is about three per cent per year,' Holbert told me, 'Three per cent per year, so the longer you stay here, the higher your chances of dying in here are. If you can figure that the average stint in Sector C is about three years, you have a ten per cent chance of being killed, or killing yourself, or dying of natural causes. That's insane, that's a one-in-ten chance of not making it back out.'

Needless to say, none of these tactics worked on Holbert, who managed to thrive even in 'hell'. His spiritual progress continued and by now he had given up all illegal activities and was trying to live a pure life. His chance for the next stage in his spiritual journey came when Sector C's chaplain proved himself unworthy of the job. The young man who had taken on the role was trying his best, but he was more often than not drunk or high on cocaine. The end of the road came when another prisoner kicked him in anger. The young chaplain came running to Holbert, asking for a knife to kill the man who had attacked him. Holbert calmly pointed out that he was the pastor of the prison chapel and couldn't do such things, but the chaplain was too enraged to listen. He told Holbert he could be the preacher instead and raced out of his cell, hell-bent on revenge.

When the next service came around there was no one else but Holbert to take it, so he became the prison's de facto chaplain. At first he was terrible at the job, but with practice, grew into the role. This is the job he still does on Sector C. It has brought him some privileges – for example, he is the only inmate who is free to leave his cell all day, but the privileges are outweighed by the massive responsibilities that he has taken on as part of the role.

One of these is trying to get his fellow inmates out of gangs. In this he has been quite successful, having got fourteen people out in the same year I spoke to him, with a total of around sixty since he began his ministry. Another, and perhaps more dangerous, responsibility is acting as an official mediator between the various gangs in his prison. 'When the gangs fight, I have to go and be their mediator,' he told me, 'which is a very dangerous and delicate thing, I assure you, because you can't show any favouritism. But I'm the perfect person to do it because I'm a foreigner and the Panamanians all respect me. The Panamanians hate Americans, but they love me because I became fairly famous. And I'm not affiliated with any gangs so I can go into any cell block without getting killed. Being a slight celebrity, people are always willing and ready to receive Wild Bill.'

Apart from this important work, Holbert also finds time to fight for his own freedom and to campaign against the human rights abuses in the Panamanian prison system. He hosts a regular podcast called *Life Inside Hell*, which documents the day-to-day life inside Sector C. He has also written a book about his story called *Long Live the King Wild Bill: The Hero is a Villain* and he hopes to write several more. More than anything else, Holbert spends his time trying to help others. It is a conscious decision to make amends for the sins of his past and to find spiritual redemption. Not that he has much time to ponder such things – he is too busy trying to make things better.

'Even though,' he told me, 'I am totally repentant for the things that I've done, I don't wallow in remorse. Ain't nothing I can do about that. The Bill that did those things fifteen years ago isn't alive anymore. The new Bill is here, and nobody – not you, not anybody else listening – is the same person they were fifteen years ago. So, I can't go around punishing myself for shit that I did when I was stupid and young, even though it was terrible. I've got to do something about it now. I've got to do something better now, and so that's what I'm doing.'

Despite having committed some of the most horrific crimes in this book, Wild Bill has actively tried to do good, including putting his life on the line to mediate gang disputes. Beyond his tough-guy persona, I suspect there exists a part of Bill that is trying to balance his karma for the lives he has taken.

5

Two Tonys

'I know you want me dead. But guess what, I'm coming for you guys!'

It was late when they got back to the house so he should have sensed something strange was going on when nobody was home.

But he was still preoccupied with the events of earlier. He had gone over to his best friend Sal's house, but had been met at the door by Sal, who had a gun to his head.

It was members of the Aryan Brotherhood, the white supremacist prison gang that ruled and terrorised the Arizona prison that he had spent time in. He had killed one of their highest-ranking members and now they were after revenge.

He'd barely got away with his life. Reacting quickly, he'd shot the guy behind Sal in the shoulder, then engaged in a running shootout with the other gang members as he retreated down the street to his car, where his daughter was waiting.

Sprinting down the road, he'd screamed at his daughter to get ready to drive, then taken one last pot shot and jumped in the passenger seat. As the car had screeched away, a bullet blew the back window out and they had both flattened themselves against the dashboard.

His daughter was terrified and had almost crashed the

car several times but somehow they made their way back to Phoenix, Arizona, and his mother's house. But it was late and no one was home. He barely had time to register this when suddenly the lights went out. When he peered outside the window, he saw that the streetlights had also gone dark. Suddenly cars screamed up outside and men wearing SWAT team outfits jumped out and pointed their weapons at the house.

Ducking down, he screamed at his daughter to get on the floor of the house. He heard a helicopter overhead and then a familiar voice coming over a megaphone, the homicide detective who for years had been trying to put him behind bars. Next, another familiar voice came over the megaphone: his ex-wife was begging him not to let their daughter get hurt. He knew the game was finally up, but he also knew that going back to prison was a death sentence. With the murder of a top-ranking member of the Aryan Brotherhood on his hands, he would survive maybe five minutes behind bars – he had to think quickly.

Inching the front door open, he shouted to the cops that he would come out peacefully on one condition – that TV news crews would be filming his arrest live. The detective on the bull horn confirmed that the cameras were already present. That was good, but he needed confirmation. He shouted out that he wanted the electricity back on so that he could check the news. The detective agreed and within minutes the lights in the house were back on. He turned on the TV and saw the surreal sight of the house he was in being filmed from outside, with crowds of armed police and news crews standing by.

Satisfied, he turned to his teenage daughter and said his goodbyes. He told her that no matter what happened, he had always loved her and always would. Then he picked up an old cowboy hat that he saw lying around and placed it on his head – might as well go out looking cool.

When he stepped outside the house with his hands up, a dozen gun barrels and almost as many cameras were pointing at him. The detective told him to approach the vehicles slowly. As he passed the waiting cameras, he turned and spoke straight down the lens, 'Hey, Aryan Brotherhood, I know you want me dead. But guess what, I'm coming for you guys!'

With that, he was forced to his knees and cuffed. It was over. He knew he was going to jail for a long time but with those words, he might just have saved his own life. By announcing his beef with the Aryan Brotherhood live on the news, the Arizona prison system would have to ensure he was locked down in a secure cell or else his death would be on their hands.

As the cops swarmed around, he allowed himself only a moment of satisfaction. He might have bought himself some time for now, but how many years could he evade one of the country's most powerful prison gangs in their own back yard? He sighed as he tried to come to terms with the inevitable – the rest of his life was going to be a long, hard struggle to stay alive.

Two Tonys was my first-ever sitdown with a murderer. Although not someone I interviewed on my podcast, I probably spent more time listening to his stories than several of my guests combined. I met Two Tonys when I was in prison in Arizona. I had moved to the US from England in 1991 and got into ecstasy importation. After my criminal enterprise was noticed by the authorities, I was arrested and sentenced to nine and a half years – all documented in my *English Shaun* trilogy of books.

My story intersected with Two Tonys' in Tucson Prison, where he was serving 141 years for multiple homicides, having left the corpses of rivals from Arizona to Alaska. I was walking down the corridor one day, on my way to a visit from my parents, when I was attacked from behind by a burly prisoner. When an inmate is the target of an unprovoked attack they face a stark choice: take the blows and be forever labelled a punk who can be used and abused for favours and services of all kinds, including sexual; or fight back and risk time in a punishment cell with loss of all privileges, plus the chance of added time on your sentence. Not wanting to be labelled a punk, I turned and threw some punches at the hulking thug, but it was like hitting a big bag of cement. Unperturbed, he knocked me down, injured.

When I told my cellmate about the attack, he suggested I meet Two Tonys, an old school Bonanno crime family associate who had gained a lot of respect in the prison and could offer me protection. In order to effect the meet-up, my cellmate arranged a game of chess. After hearing about Two Tonys' crimes, I was nervous. He arrived looking like Uncle Junior out of *The Sopranos*. Over chess, he was judging me: I was a 'fish', a new prisoner. Even though I beat him at chess, he took a liking to me. The game had been a test of my character and by being honest and straightforward, I had passed.

I had started writing a prison blog called *Jon's Jail Journal* and, knowing that I was a writer, Two Tonys asked if I would write his life story. I agreed and from then on, I visited his cell almost daily, scribbling down his words in my nearly indecipherable scrawl as he took me on his life's journey. I would then smuggle the manuscript out to save it from being discovered and used against him in murder trials, for which there is no statute of limitations. It turned out that we shared a love of books. We gave each other recommendations and began exchanging books too.

With the many hours we spent together, our partnership

blossomed into friendship and he even told me that he looked on me as the son he never had. Two Tonys' respect among the other inmates kept me safe from any further attacks. Our friendship could have saved me from getting killed or seriously injured when an Aryan Brotherhood shot-caller put a hit out on me for blogging about something he had taken exception to: how to make a syringe from items sold at the inmate store. For a few days, Two Tonys ensured that I was protected, even personally intervening to stop a man who was approaching my cell with a shank (a homemade knife) before calling in a personal favour to get the hit quashed.

Two Tonys would spend the rest of his life in jail, but my release came in December 2007 after serving almost six years. When the time came to say goodbye to Two Tonys, I felt incredibly sad. I knew this man was a hardened killer who had done some unspeakable things, but he was also an honest and caring man who loved his daughter with all his heart and who had saved several people's lives in prison, including my own. Most of all, he was my friend and a kind of mentor, who had taught me several life lessons I would never forget.

When we said goodbye at the chain-link fence I knew I would never see Two Tonys again. We both had tears in our eyes but I consoled myself with the thought that I would make sure his incredible story would be shared with the world, which I achieved in 2010 with the publication of his book, *The Mafia Philosopher: Two Tonys*.

Born in 1941, Two Tonys grew up in the shadow of the Chrysler factory in Detroit, Michigan, where his father worked. It was a working-class neighbourhood and he, his mother and father and two older sisters lived on the ground floor of a shared house with another family living upstairs. Violence became commonplace to him from a young age. He was a paperboy selling the *Detroit Free Press* in the evenings, which exposed him to a lot of bar fights, especially among the servicemen who had just returned from the Second World War. Other violence was closer to home. His mother used to take him to the basement and whip him with an ironing cord. His dad's preferred weapon was his belt. One time, Two Tonys' mother pressed the points of a two-pronged turkey fork against his neck and threatened to kill him. Two Tonys put his propensity for violence down to these early traumas.

Perhaps because of the abuse at home, Two Tonys looked elsewhere for role models and found them among the hoodlums and tough guys who hung out on the streets around his house. He got his first chance to emulate them when one of them contracted Two Tonys and his friends to smash up a barber shop that was undercutting the prices of all the other barbers in the area. Two Tonys and his friends took a bunch of rocks and smashed the shop's windows and mirrors. They were rewarded handsomely with a trip to the bowling alley.

Two Tonys got in more serious trouble when he turned sixteen. He was at a drive-in movie show with some friends when he saw some other kids he knew in a fight. Two Tonys and his friends dived in to help and when he was attacked by a bigger guy, Two Tonys drew the knife he carried tucked under his belt and stabbed the man twice in the stomach.

Two Tonys got away, but his friend was arrested and he was later told to go to the police station. He went down with his oldest sister's husband, a Detroit cop. The policeman told the cops and a judge he knew that Two Tonys was going to join the navy. The judge agreed to let Two Tonys off if he went ahead and joined the services.

So, at seventeen years old, Two Tonys found himself in the navy. He wasn't a model serviceman, often getting into bar fights on shore leave. When stationed at Okinawa in Japan, he stole a navy car and drove it, drunk, to a brothel. He crashed, rolling the car end over end and sending his drunken accomplice to hospital. In the Philippines, he absconded with a sex worker and spent almost a week ashore before finally returning to his ship when he ran out of money. He was court martialled again but didn't learn his lesson. He continued to steal and fight and fall asleep on watch. Despite his antics, he survived his five-year stint in the navy and somehow received an honourable discharge. It was 1958. He was just twenty-one years old and looking for trouble.

He soon found it.

Two Tonys' connection to the Mob began in 1962 when he befriended another young man called Teddy Licavoli. Teddy's father, Peter Licavoli, was a Mob boss who had been indicted seven times for murder but had beaten the rap every time. Two Tonys enjoyed the prestige of hanging out with a mobster's son, getting served for free in restaurants and bars, and was soon doing odd jobs for the Licavolis – simple stuff like driving their kids to music lessons.

At this time Two Tonys' best friend, Sal, suggested they take a road trip to live in LA. Two Tonys agreed but an engine breakdown meant they cut short their trip to stay at the Licavolis' ranch in Tucson, Arizona. Two Tonys fell in love with Arizona and started working for Teddy's older brother, Mike Licavoli, doing construction work on the ranch and shaking down tenants of their local motel who were behind on their payments. Unfortunately, Two Tonys got on the wrong side of Peter Licavoli when Teddy's partying lifestyle gave him cold feet about his impending marriage. Peter blamed Two Tonys for Teddy's behaviour and banned him from seeing his son if he valued his health.

Two Tonys got a job working behind the bar at a smart club back in Detroit before moving back to Tucson, Arizona, and hooking back up with Sal. Through Sal he was introduced to a crime family far more powerful than the Licavolis – the Bonannos, one of the big five crime families of New York. At the time, the Bonannos were still run by their legendary founder, Joe Bonanno Sr, one of the inspirations for *The Godfather* movie. Sal was fronting a jukebox vending company for the Bonannos in Tucson and doing odd jobs for a Bonanno lieutenant called Charlie 'Batts' Battaglia.

One day, Sal told Two Tonys that Batts had a job for him moving some dynamite. Two Tonys picked up the dynamite and some detonation caps and drove them in a truck to the drop-off point. A few days later, the dynamite was used to bomb a local restaurant. Two Tonys had passed an initial test with Batts and was now hired for more work, mostly busting heads and collecting debts. He soon graduated to helping Batts dispose of the various bodies he had whacked, a job that would teach him a lot of useful lessons for the times to come.

Two Tonys impressed Batts and was introduced to the Godfather's son, Joe Bonanno Jr. They hit it off straight away and started hanging out together. Soon, Two Tonys had moved into Joe Jr's house and was acting as a friend who also kept an eye out for Joe Jr's safety. Through Joe Jr, Two Tonys met an accountant called Walter, who splashed a lot of cash around. Always on the lookout for a scam, Two Tonys decided to relieve Walter of some of his money by offering him a slice of a shady deal, whereby Walter would front up $30,000 and receive $10,000 interest. With Walter's money, Two Tonys started living the high life. He moved into a plush apartment on Tucson's upmarket Miracle Mile and threw parties attended by rich guests.

TWO TONYS

At one of these parties, Two Tonys met Katy, a florist from Arizona. They hit it off instantly and were soon in a steady relationship. Things were looking good for Two Tonys, but took a turn for the worse when it transpired that Walter, the man he had conned $30,000 from, belonged to the Bonanno crime family. Two Tonys was called to a meeting with Batts and Bill Bonanno, one of the high-ups in the organisation, and told in no uncertain terms that he had to pay the money back or forfeit his life. He tried to talk his way out of it, saying Walter was lying, but instantly found himself lying on the carpet. One of Bill's goons, a big guy named Hank, had laid him out with a punch. Sal, who was also at the meeting, tried to intervene on Two Tonys' behalf and promptly found himself on the carpet with two front teeth missing. Bill Bonanno told Two Tonys to kneel. He held a gun to the bridge of his nose and asked him one last time where the money was.

Fearing that he was about to be whacked, Two Tonys was forced to admit that he had the money. When Bill demanded it back, he was also forced to confess that he had spent most of it. The rest, he said, was in a bank account that he couldn't access until Monday morning. Bill agreed to wait until then to receive the remainder of the money, which allowed Two Tonys to get out of there with his life, for now.

Monday morning came and Batts was on the phone, demanding the money. Two Tonys hung up and then changed his phone number. Not long after, he moved to a house out in the desert and gathered a crew of tough guys around him, including a six-foot-four hulking monster called Blake. If Batts came round asking for the money, Two Tonys was going to defend himself.

With his crew for protection, Two Tonys continued to live the high life and did his best to avoid the Bonannos. This went horribly wrong one day when he was in the grocery store and ran into Bill Bonanno alongside the Godfather himself, Joe Bonanno Sr.

Bill spotted Two Tonys straight away and took him to one side for a chat. Two Tonys knew they wouldn't whack him in the supermarket but he also knew he was in serious trouble so it was a relief when Bill told him he would let him off the hook if Two Tonys would do him a favour. The Bonanno family in New York had undergone a split and people were beginning to get whacked. Bill was worried that the violence would follow him and Joe Sr out to Tucson. He wanted Two Tonys and his crew to keep their eyes open for any shady characters moving into town and asking questions. In return, Two Tonys was off the hook.

Not long after, Katy told Two Tonys she was pregnant. Delighted, he asked her to marry him and decided to go straight. He borrowed $10,000 as a down payment and got a mortgage on a club called the Cabaret Lounge in Katy's name. By doing everything in his wife's name he knew he could keep the Bonannos from sniffing around, trying to get a slice of the pie.

With his name cleared with the Bonannos, Bill was soon asking Two Tonys to do jobs for him. One was to plant two bombs to smash up some properties and send a message to certain people. Two Tonys agreed and placed the bombs where Bill had asked, one outside a residential house and the other at a beauty salon. On 18 September 1968, Two Tonys planted the sticks of TNT as requested and lit the fuses with a cigar. The next day he read in the newspapers that the residential property he had bombed belonged to Arizona Supreme Court Justice Evo DeConcini, who had once worked with the Bonannos, but had drifted away from the crime family.

Despite the bombings, Two Tonys was still trying to go straight. He decided to get a job selling real estate and was doing well until his name was mentioned in the press as a suspect connected with the bombings. He was promptly fired. Undeterred, he used his real estate knowledge to set up his own scheme selling land just outside Las Vegas. With the money he made, he bought a house in Scottsdale, Arizona, for his new family. Katy had given birth to a baby daughter.

But just as things were going so well, Two Tonys' dark side caught up with him again and his life imploded. Two Tonys and Katy were out having a drink with Sal and Blake and their partners when Blake's girlfriend came out of the bathroom saying two guys had pinched her ass. Two Tonys, Sal and Blake attacked the men and beat them up so badly, they were left with a $3,000 dental bill. Katy had long been having doubts about Two Tonys' lifestyle, especially with a newborn daughter. Seeing him engaged in such an intense act of violence, she freaked out completely and said she wanted an end to their relationship.

With Katy and his daughter gone, Two Tonys' life went into a tailspin. He quit his real estate job and went back to pulling scams, but even that work dried up. Most of the Bonannos were now in prison, including Bill, Joe Jr, Batts and Sal. Peter Licavoli had retired and Peter's son, Teddy, was also in jail. It was 1972 and Two Tonys was thirty-two years old. He had hit rock bottom, so when an opportunity came up to move to Alaska, he jumped at the chance of a fresh start. Little did he know that in the frozen north, things would get far heavier than they had ever been in Arizona.

Arriving in Alaska with his friend Sherman, Two Tonys got a job behind the bar at a Holiday Inn, where he met a woman called Linda. They fell in love and Two Tonys found he had fallen on his feet. Linda was a wealthy real estate investor who had just moved to Alaska. She bought a plush four-storey home and moved Two Tonys in alongside her son and daughter. They decided to get married and Linda helped Two Tonys buy a nightclub where business was soon booming, fuelled largely by workers building the Trans-Alaska oil pipeline.

Life was good again. As a club owner with a rich wife, Two Tonys enjoyed the high life and local popularity. He had a young family and enjoyed playing the part of the responsible partner. He was also seeing his daughter again, bringing her up for holidays in Alaska and eventually buying a house in Tucson so he could make regular trips to visit her. But, as ever when things were going well for Two Tonys, his dark side caught up with him and sent it all into a tailspin. This time it was something that would change his life forever – cocaine.

One night at Two Tonys' club, the bartender offered him a line of coke. He had always refused before but this night he decided to try it. The high he got made him feel so good about himself that he was left instantly wanting another line. Soon, Two Tonys was buying his own coke and using it regularly at work. His club played live rock 'n' roll music and attracted many oil workers, alongside native Inuits and bikers. It was a rough crowd, but Two Tonys had a strong team of bouncers, including Blake, who had moved up from Arizona to join him, along with his best friend, Sal. One night at 5 a.m. when it was time to close, six tough-looking bikers from a local gang called The Brothers refused to leave.

When Two Tonys asked the bikers to go, they started shouting abuse at him so he grabbed a gun from behind the bar and forced them out. Outside, one of the bikers came steaming at Two Tonys, who raised his gun and shot at the drunken man. He had intended to fire a warning shot between the feet, but after drinking and snorting coke all night, he missed and shot the biker in the foot.

The police and ambulance arrived and the biker was taken away. But the cops weren't too displeased to see a notorious gang member shot and agreed on a story with Two Tonys that the man had pulled a knife on him first. However, they warned that his life was now in danger. The biker was a psycho called Gunner, a Vietnam vet who had just been released from prison, and the biker gang weren't to be messed with either. Made up mostly of other Vietnam vets, The Brothers were known for violence and gang crimes. Two Tonys decided to call in their leader, Big Jim, for a sitdown. The chat was cordial and Two Tonys explained that if Gunner tried to hurt him or his family, he had a contract out to kill him. Big Jim seemed content to let the matter drop and Two Tonys breathed easier.

But The Brothers weren't finished with him yet. Gunner came round asking for help to pay for the medical bills for his foot. Two Tonys refused. A while later, two of the gang who were drinking at the club pissed in the waitress station. Another time, Two Tonys had to kick out the gang leader, Big Jim, and an associate, for wearing their biker jackets against club rules. After this incident more bikers came back when Two Tonys wasn't there and attacked one of his bouncers with nunchucks, splitting open his head.

The next night, at near closing time, six of the biker gang entered the club. Two Tonys was expecting trouble. He told the bikers to remove their jackets and they reluctantly complied. Later on, one of the bikers, named Koot, called Two Tonys over to their table and complained that the whisky was too weak. Two Tonys ordered him another but Koot soon called him back to complain again. Two Tonys had had enough and told Koot and his friends to get out but before he had a chance to call his bouncers together, another one of the bikers, a big man called Crash, started punching Toto, the same bouncer they had attacked with nunchucks the night before. Unfortunately for Crash, he picked the wrong man. Toto was a three hundred-pound strongman with no neck, whose body was solid muscle. The big man headbutted Crash, causing blood to spurt from his broken nose.

In the meantime, Koot pushed Two Tonys backwards into a table. Two Tonys put on the knuckle dusters he had prepared for such an occasion. He hit Koot square in the temple with the dusters and watched with satisfaction as the big biker hit the deck. Toto now had Crash in a headlock and was squeezing the breath out of him. Two Tonys managed to calm everyone down and stop the fight, calling off Toto before he killed Crash. The bikers left and the police arrived, wanting to make arrests, but Two Tonys refused to cooperate, saying the beef had been resolved.

With some respite from The Brothers, Two Tonys set about revamping the club. He borrowed $200,000 from the bank by remortgaging two of Linda's properties and set about rebuilding the place to an architect's plans. The new joint was to be called the Alaska Mining Company and was decked out with memorabilia from the pan handling and ore mining days of the Gold Rush. It was a swanky place that played disco music and was decidedly not aimed at biker gang members and their cronies.

In the meantime, The Brothers had done their own restructuring. They had merged with another gang and opened a gambling den from which they were selling coke; they had also started extorting club owners for protection money. One owner refused to pay. The gang broke into his house and shot his wife and son-in-law. The Brothers were soon back sniffing around Two Tonys' club again. One day he got a call from a waitress, telling him one of the bouncers, Jett, had shot one of the bikers five times outside the club. Two Tonys went down to the jail to bail Jett out. After the shooting Jett needed to make himself scarce so he holed up in a cabin in the woods with several friends, all armed to the teeth in case the bikers turned up.

Things were getting tense. Everything came to a head when Two Tonys found out that Gunner, the biker he had shot in the foot, was threatening to break into his house and mess with his wife and kids. His daughter was visiting at the time and this was the final straw: he decided that he had to take care of Gunner once and for all.

He got his opportunity one night when the owner of a gambling house called to tell him that Gunner and Happy Jack had stopped by. Gunner had got so messed up on drink and pills that Happy Jack had left him in a room out the back, where he had passed out on a beanbag. Seizing his chance, Two Tonys told the owner to leave, but to keep the back door open. He sped over there and found Gunner still comatose in the back room so he approached the biker carefully, placed his gun in the sleeping man's mouth, pointed it up and fired. Blood and brains spurted out through the top of Gunner's skull. Two Tonys put another bullet in the man's head behind the ear to make sure. Now he had to deal with the problem of the corpse.

Two Tonys called Jett to come and help, then he went to a hardware store and bought a sleeping bag, some blankets, a clothesline and some plastic sheeting. The two men put Gunner's body in the sleeping bag and wrapped the whole corpse in the plastic sheeting secured with the clothesline. They drove to a remote location in the woods three hundred miles away and dumped the body over a bridge into a river.

Somehow word got out that Gunner's body had been dumped. Two Tonys suspected Jett's big mouth. In any case, word got back to him that The Brothers suspected him of having some part in Gunner's murder and that Gunner's older brother, Koot, was looking for revenge.

Not long after, Big Jim, Happy Jack and Koot were seen queueing outside Two Tonys' club. He decided to let them in, thinking it might look suspicious if he turned them away. Inside, Toto seated them at a prime table without charging them entry. Furious, Two Tonys demanded Toto go back and get the money off them. This didn't go down well with the bikers. They approached the bar where Two Tonys was standing. After just a few words the exchange escalated into violence. Big Jim told the gang members to draw their weapons. Suddenly Koot was coming at Two Tonys with an ice pick. Sal grabbed Koot from behind. Two Tonys ended up wrestling with Big Jim. He heard shots being fired but couldn't throw Big Jim off until Toto jumped on him from behind, smashing the biker over the head with a heavy flashlight.

They eventually managed to throw the bikers out. When Two Tonys went back inside, he found Sal bleeding heavily from an ice-pick wound to the head. Even more worrying was Blake. The big man had been shot through the arm into the chest and was lying unconscious, bleeding heavily. Two Tonys accompanied Blake to the hospital, but he only lasted a few hours before dying.

After the violence at the club, Linda said she needed to live separately from Two Tonys to protect the kids. Two Tonys moved into a flat in Anchorage and went about planning how to take apart the biker gang. He didn't have long to wait. He was eating dinner at a friend's house when he got a call from Jett, telling him he had Crash's body in his basement – Jett had kidnapped the biker from a brothel and murdered him.

Two Tonys hurried over and helped Jett carry the heavy body up the stairs and outside into a camper van. He left Jett to dispose of the body and returned to his apartment. There were bloodstains all over his suit and he needed to clean everything up before going back to his friend's house.

After the murder Jett wanted to get out of Anchorage. He asked Two Tonys for help but when Two Tonys offered $5,000, Jett was none too pleased with the amount. They were at Jett's house with his friend, Fred, mixing up coke for a big deal, when Jett turned on Two Tonys, throwing him into a chair and taking his gun off him. Sensing that Jett was planning on killing him and taking the money from the safe in the club, Two Tonys offered to take them to the safe himself to get Jett all the cash he needed.

On their way to the club they stopped off at Fred's house. Two Tonys noticed that the bathroom window had an eight-foot drop that he could escape from. He excused himself by saying that he needed to use the bathroom and climbed through the window, ran to the car and drove off. Then he flew to Phoenix to lay low for a while and called his business partner to tell him to buy his half of the club. With so many enemies now in Alaska, Two Tonys needed to relocate but first he needed to go back to Alaska to claim the $50,000 he was owed for his half of the club. When he arrived back in Anchorage his partner told him he couldn't get the money for another week. Two Tonys went to the club to snort coke and have a drink with Sal and some of his other buddies; he wondered how long it would be before The Brothers turned up.

It wasn't long. The throaty roar of motorbikes outside alerted them to the gang's presence. By the time they got outside the bikers had gone, but they found a bomb planted behind the bins. Two Tonys stationed some guys with guns on the roof in case the bikers came back, then left with his friends in several cars, all carrying guns. They drove around until they saw some bikes up ahead, waiting to ambush them. When Two Tonys got out of his car and fired some shots up the road, the bikers fled.

The next day, Two Tonys went back to the club to check on the money – it still hadn't arrived. As he was driving away, he was followed by two bikers. He did a U-turn and headed back to the club but as soon as he got out of the car, Koot was running at him with an ice pick. Two Tonys managed to avoid Koot's blow and they ended up wrestling on the floor. Hearing the commotion, Toto ran outside. He clubbed Koot over the head with an iron bar, knocking him out.

A few days later, Two Tonys was able to leave Alaska with his money and not long after, in May 1977, Crash's body was found wrapped in a sleeping bag and clothesline. The police searched Jett's house and found that a section of his clothesline was missing, matching the clothesline tying the corpse. Jett was arrested. In the meantime, the bikers burned down his house. A sex worker had told them that Jett had killed Crash but he eventually managed to beat the murder rap and was released. Not long afterwards, he disappeared completely – Two Tonys assumed that the bikers must have got their revenge.

Back in Tucson, Two Tonys was forced to split up with Linda – he couldn't expose her and the kids to danger any longer. He stayed in a hotel and lay around all day snorting coke, drinking and eating good food. But if he thought he would be safe in Arizona, he was wrong. He soon found himself being tailed by a man in a yellow cab. When he pulled over and confronted him, the man told him he was a detective and that the police had received intelligence that a man recently released from prison called Jack Watson was planning on murdering him in revenge for some killings in Alaska. When Two Tonys asked to see a picture of the man, he recognised him immediately – Koot.

Two Tonys remained vigilant. In the meantime, another of the hotel guests called Dan offered him a drug deal from a supplier in Mexico. Two Tonys' own supplier had dried up so he decided to test the guy out, giving Dan's friend $5,000 upfront to take to Mexico. Dan told him the man would require just a few days to cross the border, get the drugs and come back to Tucson with the coke but when the appointed day arrived, the man didn't show. Nor the next day. High on coke and a night of drinking, Two Tonys went to Dan's bedroom.

The room was littered with guns, one of which, Two Tonys knew, he kept in his bedside drawer. Dan had been asleep and responded in a grumpy tone when Two Tonys started questioning him about the whereabouts of the drugs. Two Tonys was already suspicious that Dan's friend had pocketed his money and done a runner. Drunk and high on coke, Dan's attitude was making him angry. Then Dan did the worst thing he possibly could: as Two Tonys stood up to leave, he reached for his bedside drawer where Two Tonys knew his gun was stashed.

Two Tonys reacted quickly. He drew his own gun from its concealed holster in the small of his back and fired a shot straight into Dan's mouth, finishing him off with a second shot to the head.

Two Tonys quickly left, disposing of the remaining bullets before heading out to see Sal, who had moved back to Arizona. At Sal's house, he changed his clothes and drove out to the desert to bury the gun, then went back to clean the blood and brains from Dan's hotel room.

The next day, Two Tonys was walking outside the hotel when gunshots rang out around him. When he looked up, he saw Koot coming towards him, firing rounds. Two Tonys drew his gun and fired back, then heard shots coming from behind Koot. Suddenly Koot fell, shot through the leg. Cops came running up and arrested him. They had been monitoring the hotel, waiting for just such an attack. That same afternoon one of the chambermaids had found Dan's dead body in his room. The police questioned Two Tonys but they had nothing to link him with the crime.

With Koot in jail, Two Tonys felt like he had a new lease of life but all that ended when rumour reached him that The Brothers had hired a local biker gang, The Dirty Dozen, to whack Two Tonys for them. Two Tonys was sitting in a nice restaurant about to tuck into some prime ribs when the door flew open in and in strode a biker hefting a baseball cap. He knew instantly that the man was there for him. Of course he couldn't shoot him in front of so many witnesses so he turned a table over and fled out the back into the kitchen. The biker followed. At the end of the kitchen, Two Tonys spotted some rotisserie skewers as long as spears. Seizing one of them, he turned to face the biker. At just that moment the restaurant's owner and another man grabbed the biker from behind, pinning his arms back. Two Tonys raised the spear. He was about to stab it into the biker's heart when the owner shouted at him to stop. Coming to his senses, Two Tonys escaped out the back.

A few days later, Two Tonys took a crew down to the biker gang's headquarters in an auto repair shop. They were all tooled up and Two Tonys made his point that the gang should stay away from him in future. After that, he decided it would be a good idea to get out of Tucson for a while. He knew a guy who owned a club in San Diego who was moving away, so his friend allowed Two Tonys to run the club for him. For a while he cleaned up his act but it wasn't long before he was hitting the coke hard again, robbing the club's owner of much of his takings. He was promptly fired.

Soon after, Two Tonys was in a fight for his life. He was coming down the gangplank of a boat bar when he saw two guys waiting for him. Too late he realised it was Big Jim and Happy Jack from The Brothers and they were carrying weapons. Instantly flipping into survival mode, he flicked his arm down, causing his folding hunting knife to slip down into his hand from his sleeve. He went straight for Happy Jack, aiming the knife at his eye and causing the big biker to let out a howl of pain. While Happy Jack was incapacitated, Two Tonys slit his throat with the knife – blood gushed onto the ground.

Suddenly Two Tonys found himself on the ground as well. Big Jim had hit him with something, and hit him hard. He was seeing stars and bleeding badly from his face. Fighting to stay conscious, he rolled under a truck and out the other side, then ran and ran until he reached a shopping centre, where he called a friend to come and pick him up. Two Tonys didn't want to go to hospital but the cut on his face was so bad it needed stitches. Considering the situation, he had got off lightly.

Hearing that more Brothers were heading down to San Diego, Two Tonys decided it was time to return to Tucson. He knew a guy there called Zane who owned a construction company and sometimes needed help sorting out recalcitrant debtors or union men. Two Tonys had done some work for him before and Zane offered to front him $20,000 to purchase a bar. In return, Two Tonys and his crew would do odd jobs for Zane. One of these jobs was to put fear into three guys who owed Zane money.

It was St Patrick's Day 1978 and all the bars in downtown Tucson were packed. Two Tonys took a new friend, a six-foot-four Viking named Vic, and hit the town. They found one of the guys, Scott, drinking in a bar with his girlfriend. Two Tonys asked Scott to step outside for a word. Scott complied but once outside, tried to make a break for it. Vic and Scott started scuffling and Scott drew a gun. Vic managed to bear-hug him so that he couldn't raise his arms to shoot Two Tonys. Pulling out his hunting knife, Two Tonys stabbed Scott twelve times. Then Vic grabbed Scott's gun, spun him round and shot him in the back for good measure. Scott was rushed to hospital but got away with his life, barely.

Vic and Two Tonys headed to the second guy's apartment, where they found him at home. Two Tonys pistol-whipped him until his face was a bloodied mess. The third guy pleaded innocent so they took him to a payphone and called Zane, asking what he wanted them to do with the man. But Zane lost his nerve and told them to let him go.

Not long after the attacks, Two Tonys was arrested by two plain-clothes police officers. He was advised by his attorney to take a plea deal for the attacks on Scott and Carl. Despite this, he ended up receiving a maximum sentence of seven and a half years. He was sent to Florence Prison in the desert, where the temperature was so hot that the chains burned the prisoners' hands.

Unfortunately for Two Tonys, Koot – the biker who had tried to shoot him – was also incarcerated in Florence. On the plus side, so was Vic, the six-foot four Viking, who was also a high-ranking member of the Aryan Brotherhood prison gang, so he could offer Two Tonys protection. But Two Tonys had killed Koot's brother and the biker was thirsty for revenge. One day, Two Tonys happened to bump into Koot outside

144

the clerk's office. Koot went for Two Tonys immediately. Two Tonys managed to hit the biker with a set of punches before the guards broke up the fight.

Two Tonys was sent away and went back to his job in the kitchen, where he was stirring a huge pot of corn with a long aluminium ladle. It wasn't long before Koot came crashing in. Spotting him, Koot picked up an industrial can opener and went for Two Tonys. Two Tonys pulled out the aluminium ladle and swung it overhead like a broadsword. Koot raised the can opener to block the blow but the impact landed on his hand, almost severing a finger.

Koot was sent to hospital and Two Tonys to lockdown. When Two Tonys came out, he was told that Koot was planning on killing him with a shank. The time had come to do something about Koot once and for all. Together with Vic and Skull, another high-ranking Aryan Brother, Two Tonys paid a visit to Koot's cell, all tooled up with shanks. Once inside, Vic guarded the door while Two Tonys and Skull went for Koot. Koot backed away, realising straight away that he was in trouble.

Two Tonys feigned a punch with one hand then grabbed the side of Koot's neck and plunged the shank into his chest just below the breastbone. With the knife pointed upwards, Two Tonys was able to get the shank into Koot's heart and wiggle it around. A sound like escaping air rushed from Koot's chest. At the same time Skull approached from behind and cut Koot's throat. Blood gushed everywhere. Koot went down on his back and tried to kick his attackers away. Two Tonys stood on one of his legs and tried to get another stab at his heart while Skull hacked at his neck until Koot's writhing body finally stilled.

The two men quickly shoved Koot's body under the bed, then ran from the cell. They stripped out of their clothes, which were immediately washed with bleach. The shanks were taken away by two lower-ranking Aryan Brothers and buried in the recreation field. It was a professional hit by three professional killers and none of them were caught. With Vic and Skull's high standing in the Aryan Brotherhood, no one would dare rat them out.

Two Tonys served the rest of his time and was released in the early eighties. Feeling guilty for having missed so much time with his daughter, he decided to move to Phoenix to be closer to her. In an attempt to go straight, Two Tonys got a job at a car dealership. Things went really well for a year. He kept his head down and spent a lot of time with his daughter. But it didn't take long for the past to catch up with him again. Skull was released from prison and turned up at Two Tonys' house looking for help. Two Tonys gave him a room and some money and fixed him up with a job. At first things were okay, but soon Skull was snorting too much crystal meth and becoming a nuisance.

One day, Two Tonys came home to find Skull and a friend moving his stuff out so they could set up a crystal meth lab in his house. He flipped and told Skull to get out of his house. Skull reacted badly and Two Tonys had to de-escalate the situation. Skull was so dangerous that if things went further, he could kill Two Tonys on the spot. Two Tonys would have to think of another way of getting him out of the house.

Not long after, Two Tonys got a call from his daughter. She said that Skull had asked to talk to her and had taken her out to a bar. Once there, Skull had tried to give her some speed and had hit on her. Two Tonys was furious and his mind was now made up: he was going to have to kill Skull.

A few days later, he told Skull that he knew of a good store to rob in a nearby city, Prescott. Skull insisted that his new chemist friend accompany them and Two Tonys agreed. Now he would have to kill two people. Two Tonys insisted that there would be no guns on the journey – they would pick up the weapons in Prescott – but secretly, he was carrying a pistol in the back of his trousers.

The atmosphere in the car was tense. Two Tonys' survival senses were tingling like mad and he began to form the impression that Skull was also intending to kill him. His suspicions intensified when they pulled into a store to get some refreshments. Skull pulled a gun out and put it under his seat. Two Tonys asked why he had brought it and Skull pretended he had forgotten to leave it behind. Skull and the chemist went into the store and Two Tonys saw them arguing – something was definitely up. This was confirmed when they got back in the car and Two Tonys saw Skull hand the chemist a bag with the gun hidden under it. Two Tonys said he needed to use the toilet and left. He concealed himself behind a truck, where he could see them both and have some cover if a shootout started.

When Two Tonys saw the chemist pass the gun back to Skull, he knew it was about to happen. Taking the initiative, he moved towards the car and put a bullet in Skull's head at close range. Skull made eye contact with him for a split second before Two Tonys fired three more shots into his head, finishing him off. He then turned and fired at the chemist, but the gun jammed and the man ran off.

Skull was still highly respected among the Aryan Brotherhood so now Two Tonys would have not only the police and the Brothers after him, but the Aryan Brotherhood too. There was no choice but to flee Phoenix. He drove to Tucson and turned up at his old friend Sal's house. Sal took him in but Two Tonys' crime partner had become a born-again Christian. While he was staying at the house, Sal continually badgered Two Tonys into converting to Christianity, even taking him to an exorcism to rid him of his demons. Two Tonys soon tired of life at Sal's so he wasn't too disappointed when his story appeared on the TV show *America's Most Wanted* and he realised that he would need to get out of the country for a while. He spent some time in Mexico and then using a fake ID, flew to Hawaii, where he stayed in the wilderness on the back of a dormant volcano.

Every now and then, Two Tonys would fly back to Phoenix to see his daughter and to collect money from debtors to continue his lifestyle. His daughter, without knowing why, would drive him on these trips so that if they were pulled over, it would be her name that was taken by the police and it would come back clean. Two Tonys was on one of these visits when he received a call from Sal, asking him to come round urgently. He asked his daughter to drive him to Sal's house but told her to wait in the car while he went inside.

Walking up the drive, Two Tonys heard none of the familiar sounds of family life he was used to at Sal's. The hairs on his arms started to prick up. He approached more cautiously and knocked with one hand, his other hand on his gun.

When the door opened, Sal was standing there with a gun pointed at the back of his head. Behind him was a heavily tattooed Aryan Brother. Before the gang member could react, Two Tonys drew his gun and shot, hitting the man in the shoulder. The gang member and Sal both fell to the floor and Two Tonys moved forward to finish the man off, but just then more Aryan Brothers emerged from inside.

Two Tonys fired several shots at them and fled outside. He crouched down at the gate and fired some more shots. The Aryan Brothers fired back. Two Tonys sprinted down the road to the car and screamed at his daughter to get ready to drive. Shots rang out behind him. Two Tonys turned and fired back, then jumped in next to his daughter. More shots blew out the rear windscreen. His daughter was screaming and crying, almost hyperventilating with terror. She nearly flipped the car screeching round a corner. Two Tonys held the wheel and tried to calm her down at the same time. Incredibly, they managed to get all the way back to Phoenix without being pulled over by the cops or being overtaken by the Aryan Brotherhood.

His daughter had finally calmed down by the time they got back to her grandmother's house in Tucson, but when they entered the house late at night and found no one home, Two Tonys' survival senses again pricked up. The power went off and the police turned up, surrounding the house with SWAT teams. As he walked past the news cameras, Two Tonys delivered his warning to the Aryan Brotherhood, ensuring that he would be placed in isolation and safe from reprisals while in prison.

Two Tonys was housed in the Maricopa County Jail while waiting for his trial. It arrived over two years later in 1993 and he faced the death penalty for killing Skull. Convicted of first-degree murder, he was sentenced to ninety-one years plus life. He knew that he was never getting out of prison, which made it seem pointless when, in 1996, he was also tried for Dan's murder. Two Tonys decided to have some fun and represented himself in court, using the opportunity to wind up the homicide detective who had been on his case ever since he moved back from Alaska. Unsurprisingly, he was found guilty and sentenced to another life sentence, bringing his total to 141 years behind bars.

Many people would have crumbled but Two Tonys had an incredibly positive mental attitude which he maintained until the time I met him. He used his time in prison wisely, reading as many books as he could and learning what he could about life and the world. Reading authors like Aleksandr Solzhenitsyn, a political prisoner in Stalin's USSR, helped him to keep a positive outlook. Imprisoned in Siberia, Solzhenitsyn and his fellow prisoners had to fight every moment to stay alive in the harsh conditions, counting themselves lucky if they found a fish eye in the thin soup, and having to wrap old socks around their faces to prevent losing parts of their ears and noses to frostbite. Every time Two Tonys started to feel sorry for himself, he would remind himself how bad people like Solzhenitsyn had it and he would force himself to cheer up.

With this positive attitude, Two Tonys made the most of his time in prison. Incredibly, he also managed to stay alive, despite his beef with the Aryan Brotherhood. When I met him in 2005, he was a respected old-timer who could use his influence to save people's lives, and often did, including mine.

When I started my prison blog in 2004, I wrote a lot about Two Tonys – his story, his character and his philosophical attitude. He became an instant hit with my readers and they had hundreds of questions for him, all of which he tried his best to answer. He even solved a murder case for one reader whose father, Joe Hootner, had been murdered while mixed up in organised crime. Two Tonys knew Hootner and divulged that the Bonannos had whacked him to cover up the fact that they had been scamming Peter Licavoli out of money on a joint project while he was in jail.

During my time in the Arizona prison system, I must have spent hundreds of hours talking to Two Tonys, listening to his stories while frantically scribbling them down, discussing books, or giving each other advice on how to keep our heads straight. It was an immense privilege to hear him tell me that I was like the son he never had. When my release was confirmed in 2007, saying goodbye to Two Tonys was the hardest part of leaving. As we said goodbye at the chain-link fence we told each other we loved each other and I promised to write to him regularly, which I did, right up until his death in 2010.

Two Tonys never got out of prison but he managed to maintain a close relationship with his daughter, who was the most important person in his life. She visited regularly and her visits were always occasions looked forward to with immense pride and excitement. Eventually, she was married to a kind guy and had two lovely kids, who Two Tonys got to see regularly and who provided a new source of joy in his life.

After I left prison and returned to the UK, I stayed in touch with Two Tonys and he continued contributing to my blog. In 2008 he was diagnosed with cancer. As ever, he was philosophical about the possibility of death. He had lived an exciting life and enjoyed what he could. The only thing he would have changed was the drugs, which he blamed for most of the bad decisions in his life. Two Tonys didn't fear death, just the pain that could make life so debilitating towards the end. In the end, he was carried off quite quickly by an attack of pneumonia. He was to spend less than a week in Tucson's medical unit, a place he hated and dreaded spending his final hours in. He was sixty-nine years old, which he viewed as not too bad for someone in his line of business.

Like everything in life, Two Tonys took death on the chin. He knew who he was and what he was and he accepted it, just as he tried to accept whatever life threw at him. As he said in his last-ever blogpost just before the end:

Life is a book we live. My book was good. You're holding it in your hands. I tasted it all. Good and bad.

Death is a part of life. They go together like pork chops and apple sauce. True believers in the Pearly Gates can't wait to die.

Don't mourn for me 'cause I've lived a life.

6

Jon Watson

'In for a penny, in for a pound'

He is feeling stressed as he walks into the dorm.

He just wants to be away from other inmates, back in his single cell where he can be alone with his thoughts, and not be tempted by his propensity to violence. Making him share a room with child molesters is a ticket for carnage. He tried to warn them. They didn't listen.

What he sees when he enters the dorm is the worst possible thing that could happen.

One of the inmates, a known paedophile, has switched the TV to the PBS KIDS channel. The man is leering at the young children on the screen. He looks around at the other prisoners as if daring them to do anything about it. Then, turning back to the screen, he puts his hand down his pants.

Incredulous, the other inmates stare at each other. One of them asks if anyone is going to do something about it.

And that's enough.

'I got this,' he says and grabs a walking cane off another prisoner.

He strides up to the paedophile and beats him with the cane until the man's face is an unrecognisable pulp.

When the child molester is dead, he walks calmly out of the

room, intending to tell a guard. In the corridor, on the way to an office, he sees another known 'chomo' – a child molester. He hesitates for a second, then thinks, 'In for a penny, in for a pound.'

Gripping the cane tightly, he approaches the man and beats him to death with it, then strolls calmly to the office to report the two homicides.

Two dead bodies in as many minutes. Perhaps this time they'll listen when he asks not to be housed with paedophiles.

Jonathon (Jon) Henry Watson admitted to killing the two paedophiles in 2020 at Corcoran State Prison in California. He was already serving a life sentence for murdering a local drug dealer in 2008. Watson was classified as a violent and dangerous man and he had been used by prison guards to exact vigilante justice on other inmates in return for the privilege of a single cell in California's notoriously overcrowded prison system. But when Watson had refused to toe the line, he was transferred from his single cell. He warned that he would kill any paedophiles he was forced to house with. California's prison authority, the California Department of Corrections and Rehabilitation (CDCR), didn't listen and a bloodbath ensued.

Now in his mid-forties and serving three life sentences, Watson is currently incarcerated in Kern Valley, a maximum-security prison in Delano, California. Because of his high-security incarceration, I have not been able to interview him in the normal way, but gathered information from email exchanges and in the process of publishing his book.

Watson grew up in a healthy family environment which was, ironically, dominated by law enforcement. His uncles and cousins were all police officers, following in the steps of Watson's grandad, who had gone into law enforcement following his return from the Korean War. Grandpa Hank was a heroic figure to the young Watson. He could quick-draw his pistol and shoot the head off a rattlesnake. But despite his mastery of firearms, Hank never used his weapon during his entire career as a cop; instead, he used reason and common sense to resolve disputes.

Watson's father's side of the family was a different matter entirely. They were Teamsters, union agitators who ran the trucking union across California. His father made money through union corruption and often working with gangsters, bikers and criminals. The two sides of Watson's family were opposing influences on his growing character. He was more inclined towards his grandad's quiet dignified heroism, but when Hank died, he was left with the grittier reality of his father's approach to life.

Watson was always tough. While at school, he worked part-time as a ranch hand. His favourite pastime was play-fighting with one of the goats, with whom he would wrestle until the animal headbutted him. Undeterred, Watson would get straight back up and dive in for more.

Watson generally stayed on the right side of the law but got in trouble a few times, mostly for setting off incendiary devices and destroying property. Later in his youth, his crimes caught up with him and he was sent for a stint in the California Youth Authority. The CYA was a gladiator school for young offenders which was, according to Watson, much worse than anything you would read or hear about it. Rather than rehabilitating, the CYA brutalised and traumatised young offenders into career criminals and gangbangers, forced to affiliate with drug gangs to survive the harshness of life. The institution also left its mark on Watson, although gang affiliation would never be his thing.

Watson was a lone wolf.

After high school, Watson trained at a cosmetology school to become a tattoo artist. He then studied at Shasta College in northern California and trained as an emergency first responder. He also worked as a bartender in a club and as a mortgage organiser. In his spare time, he liked to work on motorbikes and was the lead singer in a punk band called Nation of Idiots. His band were well known on the northern California punk scene. Watson showed his dedication to his craft by getting a tattoo of a fifties-style microphone across his throat. Other fashion choices were a sign of the violence to come. He wore a T-shirt bearing the words 'Kill Your Local Drug Dealer'.

Watson did exactly what it said on the T-shirt when, in 2008, he and an accomplice, Jason Leon Belles, broke into the house of Garrett Benson in Cutten, northern California. Benson was a local dealer with a large amount of marijuana being grown and processed in his house. During the raid, Watson and Benson struggled and Benson was shot three times, dying hours later in hospital. The court made it out as a drug raid gone wrong but Watson says he entered the property with the intention of 'smoking' a drug dealer. Watson hated drugs and he felt that it was insufficiently 'punk' to wear a T-shirt with a slogan 'Kill Your Local Drug Dealer' without also 'walking the walk'.

Watson originally pleaded guilty to murder, but later tried to retract his plea. He had accepted a plea deal to serve a fifty-year-to-life sentence. When he found out that his co-defendant had pleaded guilty to voluntary manslaughter and was facing just seven years and eight months, Watson tried to withdraw his plea. He said that he had been confused under the influence of medication at the time and that his attorney hadn't effectively represented him. Watson's attorney argued against him, saying that she had asked him at the time if he felt able to make decisions and that he had answered yes. The judge denied Watson's appeal to change his plea, saying, 'I believe Mr Watson was in full possession of his faculties at the time of his plea.' He then sentenced Watson to life imprisonment with a minimum period of fifty years.

Watson was thirty years old at the time.

As a new lifer, Watson was immediately exposed to the chaos and inefficiency of California's prison system. He was transferred between various prisons like a pinball machine, shuttled between San Quentin, Mule Creek, Salinas Valley, High Desert, Corcoran, Folsom and Kern. When he did get to settle for a while at San Quentin, he tried to adapt to what would be the rest of his life as best he could. He got a job as a housing clerk, responsible for allocating cells to incoming prisoners but he soon found the role was more stressful than he bargained for. Between the needs of the guards and the desires of the inmates, Watson's job became a seven-day-a-week exercise in futile diplomacy. And there was a darker side, too. When a new busload of prisoners arrived, inmates would approach Watson offering him money to share a cell with a particular arrival who they had taken a fancy to.

Watson refrained from ever taking their cash.

All new prisoners in Californian face a crucial choice: whether to join a gang or go it alone. Becoming a gang member offers you some protection and security, but it also involves responsibilities and carries its own dangers, like being beaten or killed by rival gang members. Being a lone wolf affords you less protection, but leaves you the master of your own destiny. The choice of gangs to join is almost dizzying, including the Mexican Mafia, the Nuestra Familia, the Black Guerilla Family, the Aryan Brotherhood and the Nazi Lowriders. As noted earlier, Watson was a born loner so the choice for him wasn't difficult but that didn't prevent him from being falsely labelled by the guards as a member of the white-supremacist group, the Nazi Lowriders.

According to Watson, people like him are designated as belonging to gangs to serve the particular narrative the prison authorities are trying to push at that moment. If they want the Nazi Lowriders to look dangerous, people get added to their list. If the threat needs to move to another gang, names get transferred. The problem for inmates like Watson is that belonging only nominally to a gang brings all of the dangers but none of the protection.

One reason Watson kept away from gangs was that he didn't like drugs. According to him, most, if not all, of the drugs in prison were brought in by guards (a statement he backs up by pointing out that the drug supply never dwindled during the Covid lockdowns). These drugs were then passed on to the 'shot-callers', high-profile gang leaders who distributed them through their networks. The gangs had become rich from the drug money, which gave them another means of appealing to new prisoners. Many of the incoming inmates were penniless and couldn't afford even the basic necessities like toilet paper, toothpaste and deodorant. Joining a gang meant access to money, provided they did whatever dirty work the gang demanded.

The California prison system was so flooded with drugs that the high-up gang members could get wealthy while inside but it made for problems if the guards had to do a sweep of the prison. At such times, inmates would get short notice that a search was about to occur and so rather than lose their drugs, most would just take them all in one go. This would lead to overdoses and deaths in the run-up to major searches.

With gangs comes violence and the California prison system is no stranger to this. The first murder Watson witnessed was of a man called Ty Lopes who, with an accomplice, had raped and murdered an eighteen-year-old girl. Lopes was put in the cell next to Watson, where Lopes' cellmate beat him to death. It was the first time Watson had seen blunt force trauma to the extent where the victim's face was no longer recognisable. When the body was dragged away, some of the blood and fluids seeped into Watson's cell and he had to be pulled out while it was decontaminated.

Lopes' murder was the first of many Watson would be forced to witness. The worst killing was that of a man beaten to death with a bag full of rocks. The man took a very long time to die. His face gradually turned into an unrecognisable mush, but he kept breathing and muttering and whimpering pleas for help. Worst of all, he began to defecate. Watson watched in astonishment as the man's killer broke a broomstick and shoved the end up the victim's rectum. When the police arrived and asked about the broom, he told them calmly, 'Well, the dude's pooping everywhere and I just wanted him to stop pooping.'

Soon, Watson was more than just a witness to violence. As a lifer and a murderer, he had a ready-made reputation but soon built on this by showing that he could take care of himself and would take no nonsense from anyone. The guards took note and found him a role that he describes as a 'privateer', an enforcer who they would use to punish sex offenders or other prisoners they didn't like. They would cell Watson with sex offenders and paedophiles in the expectation that he would beat them up. In return, he would earn himself a single cell, the prize of all inmates in the CDCR's overcrowded prison system. Every year the guards would ask him, 'What are you going to do to earn your single cell this year?'

Being celled with a psychopath was just one way of punishing prisoners in the California Department of Corrections and Rehabilitation. Another method was what Watson and his fellow prisoners wryly referred to as 'the Flop'. The Flop was used to mess up the chances of a prisoner's upcoming parole. As their parole date approached, an unpopular inmate, who had perhaps written a complaint against a guard, would find a prison officer in his cell one day. Before the inmate had a chance to speak or move, that guard would perform 'the Flop', throwing himself theatrically to the floor and screaming in pain. He would then push his emergency button and a dozen other officers, standing conveniently nearby, would rush in and beat up the offending prisoner. This was a triple whammy for the poor inmate – they received a beating, were sent to the punishment block and had any chance of parole removed. Meanwhile, Watson and his fellow inmates would stand by, awarding points for the style and technique of the guard's 'Flop'.

An even worse form of punishment was the 'block gun'. This was a weapon that was designed to discharge plastic projectiles into a rioting crowd. The block gun was designed to be fired into the floor so the bullets bounced off the hard surface before impacting on inmates. However, when the guards particularly didn't like someone, the prisoner would be cuffed and held on their knees while the block gun was fired directly into their head. The results were horrendous – teeth knocked out, scalps peeled away from skulls and prisoners needing Frankenstein-style stitches to piece their heads back together. What was just as bad as this cruel treatment was the complicity of the doctors, who were aware of what had happened but covered for their colleagues by writing up false medical reports.

Another way of 'controlling' prisoners was through forced medication. Watson speaks of one inmate called Ryan, a reasonably pleasant, non-violent young man, who the guards deemed as a control risk. They had persuaded the doctors to advise that Ryan be placed on psychotropic drugs, which basically lobotomised him, leaving him a barely-walking zombie who would sleep for days on end.

Another prisoner the guards labelled a 'troublemaker' was called Fabian. His crime was that he had mental illness, exacerbated by his experiences in prison, which meant he required special treatment. This extra paperwork clearly annoyed the guards so he was labelled a control risk. One day, Fabian insulted the mental health staff and so, to teach him a lesson, the guards re-celled him with another prisoner who was clearly marked as having single-cell status. This would almost certainly mean a severe beating for Fabian. Sensibly, he refused to enter the cell and when the guards moved as if to force him, he ran. Fabian made it to the second tier and climbed onto the railing, shouting that he would jump if anyone came near him. One of the guards shouted, 'Jump then,' and Fabian did so. He fell more than twenty feet to the concrete floor below, injuring his hip and breaking his ankle. The guards rushed down and beat him severely while he lay injured on the floor. They then cuffed his wrists and his broken ankle and dragged him to a punishment cell instead of the hospital. Fabian later received medical treatment but while he was in a wheelchair the guards would always cuff his broken ankle as an extra form of punishment.

As well as the various forms of physical and mental abuse, good old-fashioned beatings were also still popular with the guards. The installation of CCTV cameras had made this more difficult, but there were still blind spots where the guards' justice could be meted out in privacy, such as the infamous eighth floor in Sacramento County Jail. Watson suffered the worst beating of his entire prison career on Sacramento's eighth floor in May 2008, six months before he murdered the drug dealer, as mentioned at the beginning of this chapter. He had got on the wrong side of the guards by refusing to share a cell with someone, so four of them took him on the express elevator ride to the floor marked eight.

Watson was a prison rookie at the time but he knew enough about the eighth floor to understand that if you took the beating placidly you would be – more or less – all right. If you tried to defend yourself or fight back in any way, then you were in for a beating that could leave permanent damage, or even lead to a coma or death. With this in mind he was determined to let the guards have their way with him. He kept his cuffed hands behind his back and took their blows as best he could. However, everything went wrong when he hit the floor and the guards started kicking him while he was down. This violated Watson's sense of fair play and that made him angry.

Watson did then what his Grandpa Hank had always advised against – he 'switched horses mid-stream'. In the heat of the moment, he changed his mind about passively accepting the beating and began kicking back at the guards as he struggled to pass his cuffed hands under his feet and get his hands out in front of him. Seeing their victim dare to struggle, the infuriated guards began to turn their kicks into stomps, seeking to do real damage to their prone victim.

The guards roughed Watson up so thoroughly that his clothes were beaten off him, along with two toenails. He was then dragged to another cell to share with an Asian man. This was another calculated move by the guards because sharing a cell with an Asian person would lead to Watson getting a beating from the racist Aryan Brotherhood. Fortunately, Watson's cellmate was a generous character who cooked him some ramen soup to make him feel better, while Watson picked off the remainder of his toenails. 'They beat you up hella bad,' the man observed and Watson replied, 'Yeah, I did not win.' At which they both broke down in hysterical laughter.

The many-faceted system of punishing inmates was just part of the larger machinery of corruption that oiled the gears of California's prison system. Not only were the prison officers providing most of the drugs, they would also make money off inmates by various other rackets, including selling them mobile phones for a whopping $3,000 each. Corruption was also endemic among the heavily unionised 'free staff', the workers attached to the prisons who weren't guards. One of Watson's friends told him about a trip to the dentist that was stretched out over two months. On the first visit, the dentist cleaned the teeth on the upper right side of his mouth. On the second visit, the upper left side was cleaned. A third visit was reserved for the lower right side and a fourth visit to finish the job. This was a typical grift in a unionised system where the longer a job took, the more money was paid – no questions asked.

Prison transfers suffered from similar 'delays'. The bus would leave one prison and half an hour later, would stop for a break. Similarly, guards would arrange for a bullet to get 'lost' whenever a nice overtime payout was required, usually in the run-up to Christmas. The scam worked by triggering an emergency situation in which the whole prison needed to be swept. The intensive work of searching every cell would require lots of overtime but the guards would also make sure they didn't have to work too hard. Large numbers of prisoners would be placed in the punishment block so they didn't have to supervise telephone calls or yard time.

Corruption was endemic. In response to the inmate gangs, many of the guards formed gangs of their own, the so-called 'Green Wall'. Just like the gangbangers they were supposedly guarding, these officers would wear green bandanas in their belts and take every possible opportunity to confront, punish or beat the prisoners under their care. It was all part of the tribal prison mentality that the officers had succumbed to.

Watson explained to me how corruption spreads throughout the staff in prisons. When a new prison officer comes in, they may have a moral sense of duty but it is almost immediately put to the test. They witness a beating or some other form of corruption and will be expected to toe the line in the way they write up the incident. If they go against what all the other guards say, they have immediately made themselves the enemy of the very people who should have their back. Invariably, they do toe the line and thus are instantly compromised. The path is now open to higher and higher levels of corruption. This means that the few good officers with strict moral principles are filtered out early. As Watson says, 'They leave in order to preserve their dignity and self-respect, or they get run out of town. What remains are the ones with the lowest personal morals and the highest thresholds for disgust. So, are they all bad? Not at first, but they sort themselves out and what remains is not good.'

The best of what remained was what Watson called the 'eight-and-the-gate' crew. These were the guards who just wanted to do their jobs and go home. They didn't join the Green Wall or get involved in the higher levels of corruption or organised violence. They were still compromised but at least they wouldn't pull a 'Flop' on you or falsely brand you a 'chomo' and cell you with a psychopath.

To negotiate the treacherous landscape of corruption, violence, drugs and gang warfare, inmates needed what Watson calls a high 'prison IQ'. Watson developed his own prison IQ through years of harsh experience. It amounted to a kind of sixth sense about the next stunt the guards were about to pull, along with a heightened sensory perception and intuition of danger. Watson compares it to the heightened senses of troops going into combat, who can tell the calibre of every artillery shell by sound alone. Similarly, a prisoner with a high prison IQ will be able to tell from the specific squeak of sneakers on the polished floor exactly what kind of activity the inmate is engaged in. Watson illustrated this with a story of when he was watching a friend's back while he sorted out a problem with another inmate. While on guard, Watson heard the squeak of sneakers and the sound of a punch bag being hit. From this, he was able to identify which inmate had punched the bag, what kind of punch he had used and that the man had a strong wrist.

Watson was safe from most of the worst forms of guard corruption while he was acting as their enforcer. This suited him well as he didn't have a problem with beating up sex offenders and in return, he was given a single cell for his troubles. He hated chomos and rapists and was happy to do the guards' dirty work. The problem came when they started placing him in cells with so-called 'weirdos' who weren't really sex offenders, just inmates they wanted to punish for some reason or other. Watson was a violent man but he still had a code of justice: he didn't beat up people who didn't deserve it.

Watson's career as an enforcer came to an end when he started refusing to beat up cellmates the guards placed with him. The first time was when the guards celled him with a man who had refused to take a tuberculosis test. They wanted

Watson to punish him and although he didn't like the man, refusing a medical procedure did not offend Watson's code. As punishment for refusing to beat the man, both Watson and his new cellmate weren't allowed to leave the cell or have visits. The guards were trying to ramp up the tension in the cell so they would fight but rather than succumb to their wishes, Watson negotiated a solution with the guards where the man was put on suicide watch and he could move out.

The second and final time was when Watson was celled with a fat child molester. This would normally be fair game for Watson but he quickly realised there was something not quite right about the situation. His new cellmate was clearly mentally ill and when Watson read his paperwork, he saw that the man was autistic. Watson refused to touch him.

In return for Watson's non-compliance, the guards sought to revoke his single-cell status. In 2018, the prison authorities began the process in earnest. Watson complained and stated clearly that he was a dangerous man, and that if he was housed with sex offenders or paedophiles, murders would be committed. Fortunately for Watson, the psychiatrist assigned to him – Dr Dreiss – was fully in accord with his opinion and told the housing officers there was no way Watson should be allowed back into the regular prison population. But the authorities were determined, so much so that they moved Dr Dreiss to a position where he could no longer make recommendations about single-cell-status prisoners. With Dreiss out of the way, Watson's new psychiatrist made it clear from the outset that they would be recommending he be housed with regular prisoners.

In return, Watson made it clear what would happen, so clear that he left a paper trail of his statement that included letters to the Centre for Clinical Interventions, the psychiatric division, the administrators in Sacramento and even the Governor of California, Gavin Newsom.

Dr Dreiss wrote a letter in support of his claim, which Watson attached to his correspondence with the various prison authorities. The letter stated: 'It is my opinion as a mental health professional that inmate Watson should remain on single cell status for the duration if [sic] his stay in the CDC-R.' It also said, 'Additionally, to force inmate Watson to double house would constitute an immediate threat to the safety and security of both himself and any/all inmates forced to house in a cell or dorm with him. It would be both negligent disregard and deliberate indifference to the safety of all concerned should inmate Watson's single cell status be revoked.'

Unfortunately, Dr Dreiss's recommendation no longer carried any weight now that he had been moved on.

Watson tried again. He sent a letter entitled 'Letter from a Concerned Citizen' to all the authorities he could think of, spelling out as plainly as possible what would happen if he were housed with paedophiles and sex offenders. The letter read:

Well, if someone is reading this, then all has went bad. Charles Bronson bad. In a world surrounded by pimps, drug dealers and baby rapists, the only surprise is that it took this long, but I get ahead of myself.

First things first, I warned that if my single cell was removed, that people would die. I put it on CDC-R Form 22s, and there is no plausible deniability as both signed and responded to the 22 forms . . .

So again, if you are reading this, then I have given you at least one dead body. If it happened in the cell, then it is likely that I made it to the yard to kill more. In for a penny, in for a pound, right? But what is important is what got me to this point. For a decade I have exhausted every tool a human being can fathom trying to negotiate a reasonable and diplomatic course through the bureaucratic shit-show that constitutes your administrations in this Orwellian quasi-commie prison industry, but reason and diplomacy are not the currency of prison. So it is clear to me that despite my greatest efforts (I've begged your staff and so-called 'mental health' clinicians ad nauseum to help me with this one thing, see Health Care Services 602# MCSP-HC-19001394, more on this later; additionally, I have written the wardens, the DRB, and even Governor Newsom), what you need from me is plain old fashion murder. The more horrific the better the odds that it will raise the questions that deserve answers. Why are murderous lifers being forced into medium custody dorm living with low-level offenders which we will no doubt kill, should the situation turn to violence?

Keep in mind that this is all simply just your chickens coming home to roost. For years I have allowed your C/Os to use me as a weapon, housing shit-bag after shit-bag with me, know that Ol' Watson would 'take out the trash'. You know it and I know it. So cut the shit. You want to pick who I harm. You want to be the architect of violence in prison. And you want to control the narrative. Well, I am no longer compliant. Should I ever have to disclose the violence I have rendered unto these shit-bag inmates on behalf of custody we'll all be in court for the next decade. So that is also not my M.O., but, should I somehow survive the upcoming storm, know this: I will never double-cell and bow down to your manufactured housing crisis. These cells are designed for one man, and while I do deserve to be in prison for the rest of my life, I do not intend to let my 8th Amendment be trodden upon. Sic Semper Tyrannis.

> If I shall miss some of the child rapists in my violence I
> then apologize to their victims as this is a missed opportu-
> nity to bring them closure . . .

Even this stark warning wasn't enough, however. Still the
authorities were pushing to have Watson's single-cell status
revoked. Watson realised what was coming one day when he
was waiting for a committee meeting to determine his threat
level. He had been escorted to the meeting room too early
and was forced to stand outside in the hallway while the
various experts discussed the imminent case. Watson heard
the entire conversation, including when his psychiatrist told
the gathering, 'His stepmom, father, and brother have all died
recently, so it's not like he has anyone to fight or litigate for
him if it does go wrong.'

Inevitably, Watson lost his fight and was moved into a
dorm with other prisoners, including sex offenders and child
molesters. The inevitable was imminent, particularly because
for the last year, Watson had been having a recurring dream.
In the dream he had been released on parole and was trying to
find a job but every time he tried to go out, a child would turn
up, telling him they wanted to stay with him. Watson would
trail around town, tracking down these lost kids' parents, but
every time he dropped one off, a new one would spring up.
He regarded the dream as a premonition that would come into
effect if he were housed with paedophiles – he would do what
he could to protect the children.

In 2020, he was transferred to Corcoran State Prison, a
lower-security facility where he would share a dorm room
with several other inmates. Watson was still on orientation,
the period when a new inmate is learning the ropes and can
notify the authorities of any potential threats, when he was

introduced to someone who set off an instinct that he calls 'the Howling'. As the man approached and offered to shake his hand, Watson felt a tingling sensation run up his spine, across his shoulders and down his arms and legs. The Howling was Watson's in-built paedophile detector, an instinct he says is accurate 80–90 per cent of the time, and one which fills him with a kind of divine purpose to exterminate paedophiles.

As Watson told Joshua Long, co-author with Jason Vukovich of the 2023 book, *Avenging Child Sex Abuse: Vigilante Violence in Prisons and the Community*, 'When I am in harmony with this Howling, when I am only a vessel of truth, I am my best me. And I am entirely more dangerous and stronger than I would be if I were serving my own interests.'

Acting on this instinct, Watson refused to shake the man's hand, saying, 'You don't want to know me, bud, I'm an asshole.'

Later, he checked up on his premonition with a guard and found out that the Howling instinct had been correct. The man was a child sex abuser who was soon to be released. From that moment on, Watson knew that he was going to kill this man.

The deal was sealed when Watson saw the man and another known paedophile leering at child actors on television. One of the men had his hands down his pants. Watson felt the rage overtake him but he tried one last time to save everybody from what was inevitably going to happen. He walked into a psychiatric counsellor's office and said, 'Last chance . . . If you don't get me off this yard and back to a higher level of custody, I'm going to fuck these dudes up.'

Again, he wasn't listened to and the deal was sealed. Later that day, Watson saw the man who he'd refused to shake hands with again watching TV. This time he was watching the PBS KIDS channel. As Watson looked on, the man put his hands down his pants and glanced around, as if challenging anyone to do anything. Several of the inmates looked at each other silently, then one of them voiced what they were all thinking, asking if anyone was going to do anything about this.

It was like a trigger that sent all of Watson's pent-up frustration and anger into motion: 'I got this.' He took a walking cane from another prisoner and beat the man to death. On the way to report his crime he spotted another known child trafficker and thought to himself, 'In for a penny, in for a pound.' He beat that man to death with the walking cane too, dragging the body in front of the other prisoners and shouting, 'You were eating with this paedo yesterday! You were buddies with him!'

According to Watson, the 'convict code' of killing or beating up paedophiles and sex offenders is a joke, at least in the Californian prison system. He says that so many sex offenders are constantly in and out of the system that if the inmates were to attack all of them, they would have a full-time job on their hands. Instead, people tolerate and even get friendly with them. The worst are the prison gangs who talk the loudest talk. These gangs often protect paedophiles and sex offenders who pay them protection money or who are good drug customers. Watson told me that often when a new inmate came in, he would be told by other prisoners that the new guy was just in for drugs or some other innocuous offence. He would double-check the paperwork and find out they were actually sex offenders, for whom the other inmates were covering.

With the double homicide over, Watson walked calmly to the office and turned himself in. He had brain matter on his shoes and the walking cane in his hand was covered in blood. Yet handing himself in was less straightforward than it should have been. There was a young guard in the office who was a nice guy and knew Watson's reputation for being a joker. When Watson said, 'Man, I got some bad news for you,' the officer replied, 'You're not going to hit me with that cane, are you?' Watson then started joking about how this little cane couldn't hurt anyone. He set the cane aside to ease the guard's worries and sat down. They talked for a while as if everything was normal. Eventually Watson decided he had to break the news to him. He said, 'Hey, just so you know, I just smashed two paedophiles with this cane and one of them is probably dead. I'm almost certain of it.' But still the guard didn't cotton on. He replied, 'Oh, man, Watson, you just you crack me up. You're a funny dude.'

Eventually Watson had to get the guard to look around the corner to where the carnage littered the floor. Suddenly the guard wasn't laughing anymore. Politely, he told Watson he would need to be handcuffed and, equally politely, Watson complied. The scene suddenly became one of panic and chaos with officers everywhere and no one knowing quite what to do. Watson should immediately have been removed from the crime scene but for some reason they just left him sitting there in handcuffs the whole time. Watson responded in the only way he knew how – by making bad jokes. When the body of the first paedophile was carried past him, he said, 'Oh, children everywhere pulling for you, but you're going to do all right, you know?' When the next man went past, he said, 'Well, his eyes were so blue that when I smashed his head, one blue left, one blue right.'

One of the officers present was a trauma specialist. She mistook Watson's jokes for temporary insanity brought on by trauma and had him placed on suicide watch. It took Watson three days to convince the guards that telling bad jokes was just what he did and that he had no suicidal feelings whatsoever. In fact, he felt no remorse and not the slightest hint of regret. As he says, 'Frankly, I don't feel bad. I didn't ask to be put in that dorm with paedophiles. If I regret anything, it's that I stopped after two. I should've at least got a hat-trick!'

Word soon got out of the double homicide in Corcoran Prison and a local journalist, Nate Gartrell from *The Mercury News*, requested a telephone interview. Watson was – finally – considered too high-risk for a phone interview so instead he wrote a letter to Gartrell, explaining what had happened. In the letter, Watson explained his motives for the killing:

Being a lifer, I'm in a unique position where I sometimes have access to these people and I have so little to lose . . . And trust me, we get it, these people are every parents' worst nightmare. These families spend years carefully and articulately planning how to give their children every opportunity that they never had, and one monster comes along and changes that child's trajectory forever.

The Mercury News published the story and it went viral. But first, according to Watson, it had to undergo censorship from the prison officers' union, the California Correctional Peace Officers Association (CCPOA). Gartrell had originally intended the piece to expose the California Department of Corrections and Rehabilitation (CDCR) as being complicit in Watson's crime by refusing to heed his many warnings. According to Watson, Gartrell had to sign a non-disclosure agreement in order to speak to the CDCR and, when the story was written up, it had to be passed to the CCPOA, who removed anything that implicated them in the crime. Gartrell tried to write Watson a letter in reply to thank him for his help with the article but this was blocked by the CDCR, who told Gartrell it was undeliverable.

After Gartrell's article was published and gained a lot of attention, Watson was inundated with letters, nearly all of them congratulating him and thanking him for his services to society by ridding it of two paedophiles. He also received lots of money paid on to his commissary tab by numerous well-wishers thanking him for the double homicide. Soon these payments were blocked by the CDCR, a move which was unprecedented except for gang leaders and high-up drug dealers who used such payments as a means of laundering money.

Watson pleaded guilty to the two murders and was sentenced to two life sentences without the chance of parole. It was now certain that he would spend the rest of his life in prison. In the short term, he was sent to Kern Valley, a maximum-security prison, where he languished in solitary confinement in the Secure Housing Unit (SHU) for over two years. Yet this suited him just fine. He hated prison guards and 98 per cent of inmates, and he didn't want to be put in another situation where he would be forced to kill a child molester.

In Kern, Watson was placed in a cell that was covered in blood. No one came to clean the room or even to give him any cleaning products to do it himself. He was forced to use his own socks, which he would wash out periodically in the sink. When he finally had the cell clean, the guards came and moved him to another cell that was also filthy. This process was repeated five times. Watson was used to these kinds of shenanigans and got on as best as he could. Doing DIY on cells was nothing new to him. He had once had a cell that leaked badly so he created his own recipe for mortar that he had learned from reading about the construction of the Great Wall of China. He used rice, soap and water to create a paste, which he smothered over the cracks. Once dried, it worked perfectly.

Watson says he is happy in Kern. To him, the SHU is like a holiday that keeps him away from other prisoners. His only concern is that the prison authorities will lower his threat status so that he will be forced to breathe the same air as paedophiles and sex offenders again. Now that he is out of solitary confinement, he asks the guards every evening to put a cap on his door – that means a marker to remind them not to open his door in the morning. This is usually used as a punishment but Watson chooses it voluntarily. He stays in his cell in the dark for days on end, not speaking to anybody – he prefers it that way.

Watson has used his time alone constructively to write a book about his experiences in prison and the corruption of the CDCR. He believes it was his divine mission to kill paedophiles. He hopes his book will act as a call to arms to others to do the same. Yet at the same time, he admits that he never would have gone down this path if it wasn't for the way the California prison system moulded him via its trauma, corruption and sheer bureaucratic pettiness.

Watson is a complicated man, a multiple murderer who had an ordinary happy childhood but lost himself somewhere along the way and became a victim of a monolithic system that has nothing to do with correction or rehabilitation. That system has transformed him unalterably – whether into a monster or an avenging angel depends upon your point of view. But leaving moral judgement aside, the transformation was forced upon him in a pressure cooker atmosphere that leaves very few unscarred or unchanged, and almost always for the worst. As Watson writes in his book:

I can go from laughing at a *Friends* re-run to two dead bodies in a millisecond. I didn't come to prison like that. I cut hair, tended bar, went to college, played in a band. Now I try to sit in my cell for days at a time in the dark because I can hardly not kill half the people I meet. That clock is ticking. I can go two weeks without saying a single word. This is rehabilitation?.

According to the California Department of Corrections and Rehabilitation, California's recidivism rate (the tendency of a prisoner to reoffend) has averaged around 50 per cent over the past ten years, versus Scandinavian countries, which have a recidivism rate of less than 20 per cent and actually offer the inmates meaningful education and life and job skills.*

'. . . The only thing that I think that I have to look forward to now is killing more scumbags,' Watson concludes.

---

* https://information.auditor.ca.gov/pdfs/reports/2018-113.pdf

7

Anthony Ruggiano Jr.

'They threw him in the ocean, and he's never been found'

'So what are we gonna do about this guy?' he asked his father. 'We're gonna kill him,' came the simple reply. And so the hit had been planned.

The man lured Frankie into the trap with the promise of planning a heist, to drive him to the location without spooking him. So far, everything was going to plan, but with the sudden flush of adrenaline in the man's system, there also came a rush of doubts.

Shaking them away, the man kept a poker face as he accompanied his father and Frankie inside the diner. His father grabbed Frankie's hand and said, 'I want to talk to you,' escorting him into a separate room. This was the cue for the hit. His heartbeat pounding in his ears, the man walked out into the diner and gave the nod to the soon-to-be made associate of theirs, who took a gun from under the counter and made his way calmly into the back of the diner. Several seconds later, the man heard the *pop pop pop* of several shots being fired. The mobster emerged from the back.

He looked at the man and said, 'This fucking guy don't wanna die.' He went to the counter, loaded more bullets into the gun and went out back again. Two more shots fired off before an eerie silence settled over the place.

Assuming the job had been done, the man popped his head into the back room to see his father and their associate standing over the body of Frankie. His father looked up and said, 'Go to work, make out nothing happened and then I'll come see you tonight.' So he did as he was told: he left the diner and jumped into his car, leaving the dead body of his brother-in-law lying in the back room.

It was just another day in the life of a Mob-affiliated gangster but little did he know, this day would have repercussions that would change the course of his life forever.

'My belief system is, if you want to be in the Mob, you want to be associated with the Mob, X Y and Z, A B C might happen to you,' Anthony Ruggiano Jr. told me about the murder of his brother-in-law more than thirty years after. 'You have to follow the rules, and the rules are, you don't beat up wise guys' wives or mothers.'

Now in his seventies, Anthony Ruggiano Jr. looks and sounds like the stereotypical Mob wise guy, the kind of character you would expect to see on *Goodfellas*, *The Godfather* or *The Sopranos*. Indeed, his life story reads much like a script. Ruggiano Jr. was born into the Mafia life. The son of Anthony 'Fat Andy' Ruggiano, a captain in the Gambino crime family and a Mob household name in New York, Ruggiano Jr. began his career as a gangster the moment he left school.

Ruggiano quickly put together his own crew and was soon making more money than he knew what to do with. He was involved in several Mafia hits, including on his own brother-in-law, and hung out with some of the most famous and notorious mobsters of the modern era, including John

Gotti, Sammy 'The Bull' Gravano and Paul Castellano. For his various misdemeanours, Ruggiano Jr. served fourteen years in prison and battled a decades-long cocaine addiction that almost killed him. But when he finally faced life in prison for murder in 2006, he had to grapple with the hardest decision of his life – whether to take the hit for a crime family who no longer looked out for him, to put his young family through even more misery, or to cooperate with the Feds and become the one thing that his beloved father hated more than anything else on earth – a rat.

'I spent fourteen years in prison,' Ruggiano Jr. told me. 'My daughter was three years old when I went to prison, she was eleven when I came out. My son was thirteen, when I came out he was twenty-one. My son has been visiting someone in prison his whole life. There's collateral damage to our lifestyles that you have to take into effect.'

Born in Brooklyn in October 1953, Ruggiano Jr. came into the world just a few months after his father, the legendary Fat Andy, became a made man in the Gambino crime family. Anthony Ruggiano Sr. was just twenty-six years old when he was initiated into the American branch of La Cosa Nostra. With the birth of his son closely following, it was to be what he would always call the best year of his life.

Born in 1926, Ruggiano Sr. had had a tough upbringing on the streets of East New York in Brooklyn. When he was just six years old, his father was struck by a streetcar and died there on the street. Ruggiano Sr. was left to be brought up by the Mob associates and gangsters that he hung around with.

Growing up, Ruggiano Sr.'s two best friends were called Larry and Lenny. Larry's father was Frank 'The Dasher' Abbandando and Lenny's uncle was Harry 'Happy' Maione, two legendary Mob hitmen who carried out contract killings for the infamous Murder Inc., the enforcement arm of Meyer Lansky's National Crime Syndicate, which represented the Italian and Jewish Mafia. Between them, Abbandando and Maione carried out dozens of hits for Murder Inc., Abbandando using his trademark technique of an ice pick through the heart. Both men were executed by electric chair at New York's Sing Sing Prison in 1942.

Growing up in this kind of company, there was only one way Ruggiano Sr. was headed and life on the streets of Brooklyn provided just the education he needed to get there. Ruggiano Sr.'s childhood coincided with The Great Depression and poor families in Brooklyn were having to survive by eating pigeons and squirrels. 'He was a tough kid,' Ruggiano Jr. told me. 'He learned how to fight because in Brooklyn, everybody was Brooklyn Dodger fans. My father was a Yankee fan. My father loved Joe DiMaggio, so he told me he learned how to fight really good because he just had to knock out all the Brooklyn Dodger fans because he was the only Yankee fan in the neighbourhood.'

When he was eighteen, Ruggiano Sr. was drafted to serve in the US army for the Second World War. During training, he had a drill sergeant who was abusive and regularly taunted Ruggiano Sr. with racial slurs about his Italian heritage. One day, Ruggiano Sr. waited for the sergeant to visit the latrines. He followed the man inside and stabbed him. He then fled the military base and hitchhiked back to New York. Back in Brooklyn, his mother forced him to surrender to the military police and he was imprisoned in Fort Leavenworth military prison in Kansas until the end of the war. Just six months after his release, Ruggiano Sr. was back in prison, this time in Sing Sing in New York, where he was taken under the wing and mentored by a wise guy who would later become the underboss of the Lucchese crime family. Back on the outside, Ruggiano Sr. hooked up with his old friend, Tony Lee, and the two began robbing poker and dice games around the Brooklyn area, including the games of some dangerous mobsters like Carmine 'Charley Wagons' Fatico, a powerful captain in the Gambino family.

When Charley Wagons found out the name of the young kid who had robbed his game, he sent for Albert Maione, brother of Happy Maione of Murder Inc., and asked him to get the money back. According to Ruggiano Jr., Maione replied, 'There's only two things you could do with this kid, either you kill him or give him a job.' Wagons decided to meet Ruggiano Sr. to decide for himself. Ruggiano Sr. went to the meeting while his partner, Tony Lee, waited outside in the car with two guns at the ready. Fortunately for the young Anthony, the weapons weren't required: the Mob capo took a liking to him and decided on the latter option, employing him as his driver.

Ruggiano Sr. was only twenty-three years old but his involvement with the Mob was soon to go much deeper. One day, Charley Wagons took him outside for a private chat and said, 'If I ask you to kill somebody, would you do it without asking any questions?' Ruggiano Sr. only thought for a moment before responding with a 'yes'. His first hit came not long after.

Ruggiano Jr. recounted the story as he remembers his father telling it: 'A couple of weeks later, they picked him up at his mom's because he still lived at home with his mother. They picked him up at my grandmother's house with Charley and another guy in the front seat, and there was another car following them, which Charlie's brother, Danny, was driving. And my father got in the back seat and they pulled out. My father told me, "When we pulled out and got away from grandma's house," he goes, "I whispered in the guy's ear.' I said, "You whispered in the guy's ear?" I didn't know what he was talking about. I said, "What do you mean, you whispered in the guy's ear?"'

Ruggiano Sr. made a gun shape with his hand, pointed to his son's ear and repeated the phrase, 'I whispered in his ear.' After that, Charley Wagons introduced Ruggiano Sr. to Albert Anastasia, who was at that time the head of the Gambino family. Ruggiano Sr. then did some hits for Anastasia and proved himself so worthy that Anastasia had him made just a couple of years later, when he was twenty-six years old. Ruggiano Sr. had made such an impression that he became a made man even though the books were currently closed, meaning no one was being made at that time.

Ruggiano Sr. went on to do a lot of work for the Gambino family. He became a captain or 'capo' and had his own large crew. He continued to be involved in Mob hits, seven of which Ruggiano Jr. is aware of, but there may have been many more. One of his hits was the murder of three hustlers who had robbed a crap game run by Gambino underboss Aniello 'Neil' Dellacroce.

As well as his own murders, Ruggiano Sr. gave the okay for many more, including that of his own son-in-law. And, of course, he had his fingers in countless pies, in and around New York. He was even involved in the infamous Lufthansa heist popularised in the 1990 movie *Goodfellas* which, at the time, was the largest cash robbery on American soil. Ruggiano Sr. was the man the robbers sought to fence their stolen gold and jewellery through the illegal gold and silver exchange he ran with his partner, Tony Lee.

Growing up in his father's house in Ozone Park in Queens, New York City, Ruggiano Jr. knew nothing of all this. 'I didn't know what he did,' Ruggiano Jr. told me. 'I knew something was different but I didn't know why . . . like, he was not home the same hours as my friends' fathers, and he would take me with him on the weekends to bars he owned. How he got treated when he walked in – he was like a celebrity and guys would stick money in my pocket.'

Ruggiano Jr. says the first time he realised what his father really did was hanging out with his friends in the neighbourhood after school. He would see some of the older guys glance at him and whisper, 'That's Fat Andy's son.' When he was in his early teens, Ruggiano Sr. began taking him round all the wise guy-owned clubs in Ozone Park, where he introduced him to faces like Charley Wagons and John Gotti. Fat Andy wanted everyone to know his son's face so they could look out for him if he got into trouble on the streets. With this introduction to the life, Ruggiano Jr. soon knew everything about his dad's occupation and wanted to emulate it himself. However, his ambitions didn't go down well with Ruggiano Sr., who wanted him to go straight and have a normal career.

Things came to a head when Ruggiano Jr. turned sixteen and was permanently suspended from high school. Turning his back on education, he asked his father for a job, but the response he got was not what he expected. Ruggiano Sr. was so disappointed, he wouldn't speak to his son and avoided him whenever he saw him. In desperation, Ruggiano Jr. called his uncle, Frank, who was also in the game. Frank came round for a sitdown in their kitchen and Ruggiano Jr. explained that he wanted to start working. Pretending to misunderstand, Ruggiano Sr. offered to get him a job with the bricklayers' union. But Ruggiano Jr. pressed his point until his uncle intervened on his behalf and finally, his father relented.

'He looked at me and I'll never forget, like it was yesterday,' Ruggiano Jr. told me. 'This was 1969. He sits back in the chair and he looks at me and then he leaned forward and with his finger, he went, "You want to work for me?" He says, "Well, remember one thing – going to jail is all part of the job."'

With his dad on board, Ruggiano Jr. began his Mob education in earnest. His dad took him out to all the favourite Mob hangouts, pointing out all the wise guys, telling him their stories and indicating those who had done 'work' – Mob slang for murders. But even now, Ruggiano Sr. was trying to dissuade his son from an interest in the life. One night, his father took him to a bar called the Five O'Clock Club on Church Avenue in Brooklyn. The club was packed and everyone was coming up to say hello and to introduce themselves to the infamous Fat Andy. Even though Ruggiano Jr. was only seventeen, he was served alcohol with no questions asked because he was Fat Andy's son. But after an hour or so, Ruggiano Jr. noticed that the atmosphere had changed.

'All of a sudden he says to me, "Look around,"' Ruggiano Jr. told me, 'So I look around. He goes, "You notice anything?" I go, "Yeah, the bar got kind of empty." He goes, "You know why?" I don't know why. He goes, "Because I'm here." I said, "For sure?" He goes, "Yeah, because they don't know if I'm here to kill somebody, smack somebody, shake somebody down." He goes, "This is how you want to live, that people don't even want to be in your company?"'

It had been intended as a salutary lesson in the life of a mobster, but it backfired. 'I fucking loved it,' Ruggiano Jr. told me. 'I was like, whoa, this is the greatest thing since ice cream.'

Having convinced his father of his desire to work for him, Ruggiano Jr. got his first job. It was working an illegal black-jack game for a man called Philly the Pimp at his club on

Long Island. Ruggiano Jr. loved it and was soon making more money than a teenager could dream of. He started getting arrested too, mostly for bar fights. Knowing who his father was, the cops would take him home, where they would shake down his father for several grand before letting him go without charges. He also started hanging out at the Ravenite Social Club in Little Italy, a Mob hangout owned by Neil Dellacroce, then underboss of the Gambino crime family. Ruggiano Jr. was living the high life, making $100 a day, crazy money for a teenager in 1970.

Ruggiano Jr.'s first involvement in murder came with a hit on a guy called Louis Baja, a Puerto Rican cocaine dealer with whom he did some business. According to Ruggiano Jr., murder was never presented to him as an option, like it was with his father. Instead, one day Ruggiano Sr. took him aside and explained that his associate, Louis Baja, had stepped out of line and had to go. Baja had been seeing Neal Dellacroce's daughter and had been warned off the relationship. Baja, however, had ignored the advice and continued dating the underboss's daughter. Now he had to pay the price for his lack of respect.

Another hit was on a man called Frankie Gish, who had done some work with Ruggiano Jr. 'John Gotti, my father, Pete Gotti, Angelo Quack Quack and Johnny Carneglia had a meeting in this bar,' Ruggiano Jr. told me, 'and they were talking at a table and then my father called me over and he said, "Sit down." I sat down and he looked at me and he goes, "Listen, Frankie Gish gotta go." I said, "All right." And then they told me the plan that he was going to meet me and Johnny Carneglia was going to shoot him. So I just got thrown into these conspiracies. Nobody asked me if it was okay.'

Ruggiano Sr. had made it clear from the outset that murder was part of the job description of a Mob associate – it was just work and to be treated as such. 'My father used to tell me when you get out of bed in the morning and go kill somebody and then come home and have dinner with your family,' Ruggiano Jr. told me, 'that's work. But if you're drunk and you do it, or you do it out of anger – that's murder.'

Soon, it became second nature to Ruggiano Jr. to sit having dinner, drinking and laughing with men who he knew were going to be assassinated a few days later. Ruggiano Jr. was young and took it all in his stride, and even got a buzz from the notoriety. He remembers the first time he saw his name in the newspaper connected with a crime and what a rush it was. After being arrested over a lottery racket, he was mentioned in the *New York Daily News*. That night, he went out clubbing and enjoyed celebrity status because of his mention in the news.

Another surreal moment of celebrity came in 1978, when Ruggiano Jr. received his first prison sentence for a liquor store robbery on Long Island. He and his crew had a strategy of renting empty lots next to drug or liquor stores, then drilling through the walls to rob their next-door neighbours. One such robbery went wrong and Ruggiano Jr. was arrested and convicted. He was out on appeal for two years but in 1978 was forced to surrender himself to the authorities. Before handing himself in, his associates threw him a huge party to say farewell.

'It was like in the movies, like in *Goodfellas*,' Ruggiano Jr. told me. 'Me and my father, we got all dressed up, suit and ties. We get in the car, we pick up Tony Lee, meet my father's crew . . . We go to Manhattan to the Ravenite. We walk in. Neil had a big spread for me and all. It was like I was going away to Harvard.'

Ruggiano Jr. was just twenty-three years old and had just married his first wife, Alice. It wasn't a great time to get a five-year prison sentence, but he took it all in his stride and his two-and-a-half years in prison flew by. 'It was different than it is today,' Ruggiano Jr. told me. 'All the cops, the COs were on the take. We'd have plenty of food. Wherever I went, there was someone waiting for me with a package with shower slippers and everything, and I was very comfortable. People looked out for me. I knew people everywhere, every jail I was in I knew somebody.'

Ruggiano Jr.'s father made sure to visit him wherever he was staying. The old man had such a reputation with the guards that, even when Ruggiano Jr.'s prison was put on lockdown, he still got a visit with his son. Fat Andy simply refused to leave until he saw him, so the guards quickly cuffed Ruggiano Jr., brought him down from the cells and let him have his visit.

Ruggiano Jr. was released in 1980 after serving two and a half years. When he came out, he found that the heat had transferred to his father. A district attorney from Suffolk County kept subpoenaing Ruggiano Sr. for small stretches in prison. Eventually getting fed up with it, Fat Andy told his son he was moving to Florida to avoid any further prison sentences. Ruggiano Sr. already had a crew down in Miami and several operations going, so it was a smooth enough transition. Meanwhile, Ruggiano Jr. moved back and forth between New York and Miami to help his dad and deal with his own operations.

Unfortunately, the heat had followed Ruggiano Sr. to Florida and a warrant was soon out for his arrest. Fortunately for him, the FBI raided his house in Ozone Park first, which gave his wife an opportunity to warn him. She called Ruggiano Jr. about the raid and he telephoned his dad in Miami to tell him the Feds were after him. Fat Andy went on the run in

Miami, growing his hair and beard and hanging out with a local biker gang.

But the disguise only worked for so long. In 1984, Ruggiano Sr. was found and arrested by the FBI. He was given a forty-year sentence for racketeering. Being in prison meant that Fat Andy would miss out on one of the biggest turning points in modern Mafia history. In 1985, the head of the Gambino family, Paul Castellano, was murdered, gunned down outside Sparks Steakhouse in midtown Manhattan. It had all the hallmarks of an inside job but came as a complete surprise to Ruggiano Jr.

'When it happened, I was home watching TV,' he told me, 'and it came on. They interrupted the show to say that Paul Castellano was just murdered in Manhattan. So I jumped up and I ran to the phone and I called up my father's partner, Tony Lee, and I said, "Paul just got shot." And he said, "I know."'

The way Lee said 'I know' made Ruggiano Jr. realise that his father's partner had been in on the hit.

Ruggiano Jr. went to see Tony Lee the next day. His father's partner told him about the planning of the hit, in which he had been involved, along with John Gotti, the new Gambino head, and Sammy 'The Bull' Gravano, his new underboss, along with several other high-ranking Gambino wise guys. The murder had come as a surprise to Ruggiano Sr. too and he was desperate to hear news about it. Ruggiano Jr. and Tony Lee travelled down to Florida to tell him the details in person and Fat Andy gave his professional seal of approval over the way the hit went down.

Castellano's murder was controversial, to say the least, as it was on the family's own boss and hadn't had the seal of approval of the other four New York crime families, but it was a popular move among the Gambino stalwarts like

Ruggiano Sr. and Tony Lee. They had never agreed with Carlo Gambino's choice of Castellano as the new head of the family, seeing him more as a businessman than a traditional gangster.

Ruggiano Jr. himself had nothing against Castellano. The Gambino head had come to his wedding in 1977 and given him $500 in a card. But the incident provided a salutary example of why Castellano wasn't respected by his soldiers. The day after the wedding, when Ruggiano Jr. and his dad were opening the cards and gifts, Ruggiano Sr. saw the card from Castellano and immediately took it off his son and ripped it into tiny pieces. The card contained Castellano's signature, a rooky mistake for anyone so high up in the lifestyle.

Despite some mixed feelings about the boss's death, Ruggiano Jr. did well out of it. His father and Tony Lee were tight with John Gotti, his father having been made at the same time as the new boss. Gotti and Ruggiano Sr.'s family had both come from the same region of Naples, so they had a connection through the motherland. Now, under Gotti's regime, Ruggiano Jr.'s money-making potential began to soar: 'It gave me some more prestige because of my relationship with him,' Ruggiano Jr. told me, 'so it opened up some doors for me because everybody knew I was close to him.'

Ruggiano Jr. had first met John Gotti when he was thirteen years old. Because of his father, Ruggiano Jr. had always enjoyed a close relationship with Gotti before he became the Gambino head. Gotti liked to talk to him about sport and respected the younger man for having served time in prison. Ruggiano Jr. said that Gotti used to goof on the other gangsters around them, saying, 'You think these guys ever ate a baloney sandwich? They never did a day in jail.' The superstitious Gotti also liked the fact that he shared a star sign with Ruggiano Jr., both being Scorpios. All in all, Ruggiano Jr. liked him and to

ANTHONY RUGGIANO JR.

this day speaks highly of him: 'People try to entice me into talking bad about the guy,' he told me. 'I don't have anything bad to say. He was always good to me. He always treated my family well. He always looked out for us. Was he a murderer, a drug dealer, a gangster? Yeah, he was definitely all of those things, but personally, he was always good to me.'

Ruggiano Jr.'s relationship with Gotti's underboss, Sammy 'The Bull' Gravano, was less warm, but still cordial. As with Gotti, Ruggiano Jr. had first met Gravano as a kid when his father had taken him to visit the older gangster at one of his construction businesses. Ruggiano Sr. had been in the same crew as the captain that made Gravano, so the family ties were tight. But Gravano was always more standoffish than Gotti: 'He was a very stern guy,' Ruggiano Jr. told me. 'When you would walk into the Ravenite, John would sit at the back table, and a lot of times Sammy would be standing up next to John like this with his arms crossed. If you walked up to the table and you went to shake Sammy's hand first, he would go like this to you,' Ruggiano Jr. made a nodding gesture to the side, to illustrate what Gravano would do, 'like you shake John's hand first.'

Ruggiano Jr.'s place in the new regime was cemented soon after Castellano's death, when he was invited to the Gambino Christmas party alongside all the made men and a few select others. Ruggiano Jr. and John Gotti shared a love of partying and after Gotti's takeover of the Gambino family, Ruggiano Jr. would often be seen drinking with the big man at the best clubs in New York, using Gotti as a way to attract women. 'He would go out to Pastels disco in Brooklyn,' Ruggiano Jr. told me. 'He'd sit in the back and everybody would be looking, and I'd come out and I'd say to the girls there, "You want to meet John Gotti?" And I would take them up to the table and sit there, because I liked women. And then he would lean over to me and he would say to me, "You think you got enough girls at the table? Stop bringing them."'

Gotti's habit of signing autographs for enthusiastic fans went down less well with Ruggiano Jr., who had been brought up in the strictly tight-lipped Mafia tradition of his father. Like everyone else, Ruggiano Jr. says he could see the writing on the wall for Gotti's celebrity-style gangsterism and what it would ultimately lead to. 'We were exposed,' he told me, 'and we all knew we were exposed and we all knew that eventually it was going to hurt us.'

In the meantime, however, Ruggiano Jr. was having too much fun and making too much money to care. He had his own crew, many of whom he had known since childhood. They were tight, and because his captain was also his father, Ruggiano Jr. never had to kick any of the money he earned upwards like the rest of the Gambino soldiers. This made him the target of jealousy among the other Mob associates and lower-level wise guys, but what could they do about it? His dad was Fat Andy.

Ruggiano Jr. was living the high life. He remembers the singer Frankie Valli eating dinner at his house. He remembers snorting cocaine with David Bowie. He even remembers walking into a bar to see his father drinking with Frank Sinatra. But not everything about the lifestyle was glitz and glamour. Ruggiano Jr. not only had to keep one eye open for police, but for rival gangsters as well. One time, coming out of a bar with his friend, a young guy who had a beef with them started shooting at them from across the road. The two friends had to duck behind a car to avoid getting shot. Another time in a club, the two guys he was with started arguing. One of them pulled out a gun and shot the other in the face, which not only covered Ruggiano Jr. in blood but led to a tense standoff: 'I was standing right there and the guy just was staring at me, and I'm staring at him and I'm going, "Oh, this fucking guy's gonna shoot me."'

Fortunately, the man put the gun away and ran out the door.

Another scary moment occurred when Ruggiano Jr.'s friend, Louie, got into a fight on Queen's Boulevard, in which he stabbed his assailant. The victim later got in touch with Ruggiano Jr. to tell him he wanted $2,000 or he would give Louie up to the cops. Ruggiano Jr. agreed to pay but the meeting with the victim and his friends was more than he had bargained for. The men took him down into some tunnels that run below the Lower East Side of Manhattan and which featured in the 2002 movie, *Gangs of New York*. As Ruggiano Jr. was led further underground he became convinced that he was about to be murdered. Fortunately, death wasn't on the cards that day and the transaction went down smoothly.

On another occasion Ruggiano Jr. was sitting in a bar in downtown Manhattan when Neal Dellacroce's son, Buddy, and his cousin, Sally, walked in. They had just committed a murder so when two cops entered the bar, they understandably panicked. Buddy handed his gun to Ruggiano Jr., who knew nothing about the killing. Fortunately, he wasn't searched, but his father was furious with him when he found out that he had taken such a hot weapon with the police around.

On another occasion, Ruggiano Jr. was saved from being stabbed by the quick thinking of one of his friends. His companion grabbed a ceramic ashtray and smashed it over the attacker's head. This incident led to a big sitdown with Ruggiano Jr., his father, his assailant and his wise guy boss, Black Phil. 'My father wanted to kill the kid that tried to stab me,' Ruggiano Jr. told me, 'and Philly, the guy that we was sitting down with, he said, "He wants to apologise." My father wouldn't accept the apology so I never really saw the kid anymore.'

Another big sitdown came after Ruggiano Jr.'s brother's best friend stabbed a connected guy in a fight. The Colombo family murdered the man in revenge right outside Ruggiano Jr.'s house. The case was so potentially incendiary that Paul Castellano himself was at the sitdown. The Gambino head told Ruggiano Sr. that the murder would have to go unavenged, perhaps creating another reason why Castellano was unpopular with Fat Andy. Another big sitdown was occasioned when Anthony Stabile, a wise guy from the Lucchese family, shot one of Ruggiano Jr.'s friends. Again, Ruggiano Sr. was called in to help find a solution that would avoid a bloody inter-family war.

One of the other dark sides of the Mob that Ruggiano Jr. witnessed was how they dealt with mental illness. A friend of his called Vitto Guzzo, who was the son of a wise guy from the Colombo family, suffered a nervous breakdown and was admitted to a psychiatric ward. After he was let out, Guzzo suffered another breakdown and was readmitted to hospital: 'He came out and he disappeared off the face of the earth,' Ruggiano Jr. told me. 'That's how the Mob deals with mental illness.'

Ruggiano Jr. was now struggling with an illness of his own: cocaine addiction. He had started experimenting with drugs in his early teens, smoking weed and dabbling with LSD. His first brush with cocaine happened when he was nineteen years old in Puerto Rico. His father had branched into the music business and became friends with a group called Jay and the Americans. Ruggiano Jr. went on tour with the band in the early seventies and in Puerto Rico he would drink wine and smoke weed with them while they warmed up before gigs. Then one night he walked in to find some of them snorting white powder through straws. When Ruggiano Jr. asked what it was, they offered him a straw and a line and he never looked back. Ruggiano Jr. was soon taking the drug regularly, but he had to keep his habit secret. Drug taking was strictly frowned upon by the Mafia although, according to Ruggiano Jr., everyone was doing coke behind closed doors, especially in the seventies and eighties. The problem was that by the eighties, Ruggiano Jr.'s cocaine habit had become so pervasive it was no longer on the down low. He was freebasing cocaine and had come to realise that if he didn't quit the drug soon, it would kill him.

Ruggiano Jr. checked himself into a rehab centre in Vermont in 1988, after seeing an advert on TV where a car, a plane and a house disappeared up a girl's nose. Tony Lee paid the treatment fees in cash as Ruggiano Jr. had no medical insurance. Ruggiano Jr. got out of treatment on a Wednesday night and flew back to New York. On the Saturday, he went with Tony Lee to see John Gotti at his regular haunt, the Bergin Hunt and Fish Club. After lunch, Gotti took Ruggiano Jr. aside for a private chat.

'We go outside and he looks at me, he goes, "How do you feel?"' Ruggiano Jr. told me. 'I said, "I feel good." He goes, "Do you think you got it beat?" So I look at him, I go, "Well, I'm not going to do any of it today." He goes, "Okay, what can I do for you? Do you need anything? I don't want you stressed out." Now this is the boss of the most powerful crime family in the country at the time. He's asking me what he could do for me because he doesn't want me stressed out.'

Ruggiano Jr. told the boss that he didn't have a car, so Gotti got on the phone and called a friend. Putting down the phone, he told Ruggiano Jr. to go to a car lot on Atlantic Avenue and ask for a guy called Anthony. Tony Lee drove him down to Atlantic Avenue, where the man was waiting for him. Ruggiano Jr. was told to look around the lot and take any vehicle he desired. He was first tempted by a Cadillac but then spotted a beautiful white-bodied, leather-trimmed Pontiac Bonneville, which he drove away with.

Ruggiano Jr. drove back to the Bergin Hunt and Fish Club, where Gotti handed him some cash. 'He says to me, "Here's two thousand dollars,"' Ruggiano Jr. told me. 'He says, "I want you to come here every Saturday with a hundred dollars," and he went, "and don't fucking disappoint." I said, "No, I'll be here every Saturday." So I went back the next Saturday, I gave him a hundred. I went back the second Saturday, I gave him a hundred. The third Saturday, I go back and we go for a walk and he tells me, "How you doing?" I go, "I'm doing good. I'm back to work. I feel great." I was looking better. I'd put on weight. I was dressed nice. I was starting to feel like my old self again and you could see it. He says, "Well, you look good." I go, "Thanks." He says, "How much more you owe me?" I said, "Well, this would make 1,700." He goes, "Okay, keep the rest for a gift."'

After his brush with addiction, Ruggiano Jr. could have been viewed as a liability. The gift of the car and the cash was a nice way of showing him that he was still a valued member of the family. But the message was clear – he had to keep his act clean and start making his own money again in order to prove himself. Little known to him at the time, it wouldn't be long before he would have the chance to show his worth to the family by helping out with a murder.

Ruggiano Jr.'s sister had recently married Frankie Boccia, an armed truck robber with Mob connections. Before they had tied the knot, a captain in the Gambino family, Danny Marino, had warned Ruggiano Jr. and Tony Lee that Boccia was bad news and not someone his sister should be hanging around with. Boccia, it seemed, had a penchant for dating Mob bosses' daughters. He had already been out with Sonny Franzese's daughter and also Danny Marino's niece, which was why the Gambino capo knew he was bad news. But Ruggiano Jr.'s sister had ignored the warnings and stayed with Boccia, and now the consequences were beginning to come to light. Frankie, it turned out, had been shaking Ruggiano Jr.'s mother down for money on a regular basis. She was so scared of the young gangster that she hadn't mentioned a word of this to her husband or sons, for fear that Boccia would hurt them. If it wasn't for one particular incident . . .

It was at Francine and Frankie's baby shower that the trouble had started. At the party, Frankie racked up an $800-dollar tab that Francine and Anthony's mother had to pay. When they got home later that night, Francine's mother confronted Frankie about the tab and the young man lost his temper. Anthony's wife, Alice, upon hearing screaming, had rushed downstairs to find Frankie grappling with her mother-in-law on the floor, trying to choke her. Alice had scratched Frankie's face until he released her mother-in-law and then called Anthony, who was away at drug rehab, to tell him the news.

By the time Anthony came out, plans were already underway to take revenge. Mob hits are never crimes of passion carried out in the heat of the moment. Murders bring down heat so they need to be carefully planned and okayed from the top. The first task for Ruggiano Jr. and Tony Lee was to get the okay from Fat Andy, who was still languishing in prison. Ruggiano Jr. flew down to Florida to see his father and tell him about Frankie's misdemeanour. On hearing about the attack on his wife, Ruggiano Sr. said, 'Does this guy think I'm dead?' Ruggiano Jr. explained the plan for the hit and his dad sanctioned it.

Back in New York, Tony Lee met with Gene Gotti to explain the situation. Gene reported back to his brother, John, and quickly came back with his blessing for the hit. John Gotti had a particular fondness for Ruggiano Jr.'s mother, having known her since he was a kid. Now everything was in place and the plans for the murder could be finalised and put into action.

Anthony was to lure Frankie into the trap at the diner with the promise of a safe house heist, then drive him to the location without spooking him. Tony Lee would then lure Frankie into the back and Skinny Dom, who had been proposed to become a made man, would carry out the hit. Frankie was an asshole who had attacked his mother, but to Anthony he was still his brother-in-law all the same, married to his sister and father to his baby niece. Anthony's sister knew nothing about the hit, let alone that her own brother was involved in the imminent murder of her husband.

Anthony drove his passenger to his death and getting Frankie to the location without spooking him was his number-one priority. He was surprised how easy it was. Anthony fabricated details about the job they had invented to lure Frankie into their trap. He and several of his Mob connections had created a story about a drug safe house they wanted to raid. They needed Frankie's expertise as a thief, so the story went, to break into the place and grab the loot. There was no safe house, of course, but Anthony and his Mob friends knew that the promise of riches would be too tempting for Frankie to turn down and would lure him into a meeting at a place of their choosing. It would be the last meeting Frankie would ever attend.

Anthony pulled up opposite Café Liberty, a diner in Ozone Park, Queens, owned by his dad's crime partner and fellow

196

Gambino wise guy, Anthony 'Tony Lee' Guerrieri. Anthony escorted Frankie across the road to where Tony Lee's brother, another Gambino soldier called Mikey, rose from his chair and greeted Frankie with a warm embrace and a kiss on the cheek. Mikey showed them into the diner then closed the door behind them.

Anthony hadn't felt nervous until this point, but when he heard the faint click as Mikey locked the door from the outside, adrenaline began to pump around his body. Frankie Boccia was a dangerous kid, notorious around the neighbourhood. He made his living as an armed robber, holding up armoured trucks; he was associated with several Mob guys and had been involved in a couple of homicides with his partner, Peter Sicario. Tony Lee and his associates were professionals, but with a dangerous guy like Frankie, things could still go badly wrong, especially if he got spooked.

Inside, two Gambino associates, Freddy, and Dominic 'Skinny Dom' Pizzoni, were sat at the bar alongside the owner, Tony Lee. They were eating bagels and laughing. When they saw Frankie, they all rose to hug him. Tony offered Frankie a bagel, which he declined.

Tony grabbed Frankie's hand and said, 'I want to talk to you,' escorting him into a separate room. This was the cue for the hit. His heartbeat pounding in his ears, Anthony gave the nod to Skinny Dom. The soon-to-be made man took a gun from under the counter and made his way calmly into the back of the diner. Several seconds later, Anthony heard the *pop pop pop* of several shots being fired. The hit went smoothly and Ruggiano Jr. went to work as usual that day. Later that night, he got a call from his sister. Francine sounded worried and said Frankie hadn't come home. Ruggiano Jr. told his sister he had dropped Frankie off at the corner after the meeting with

Tony Lee and that was the last he had seen of him. Later that evening, Ruggiano Jr. drove to his sister's house, where he had to keep up the pretence with Frankie's dad.

'This is how insane the mob is,' Ruggiano Jr. told me, 'I actually took his father that night to go look for him, knowing that he was in the trunk of the car.'

Boccia's body had been stuffed into a sleeping bag that Ruggiano Jr. had bought for the task a couple of days earlier. This unusual item probably gave the game away to Ruggiano Jr.'s wife, Alice, who commented on it one day, saying she'd noticed the sleeping bag in the trunk before Frankie's death, but that it had disappeared at the same time Frankie went missing. Ruggiano Jr. replied coolly that he didn't know what she was talking about and his wife never mentioned it again.

While Ruggiano Jr. was allaying the suspicions of family members, Tony Lee was disposing of the body. 'The next day they took him on this guy Tommy's boat,' Ruggiano Jr. told me, 'and they took him out into the Atlantic Ocean and they wrapped him up. And Tony Lee punctured his lungs and cut open his stomach because they don't want him to float up to the top. And they threw him in the ocean, and he's never been found.'

Ruggiano Jr.'s sister may have had her suspicions about her husband's fate, but she never let on. It was almost two decades later, when Ruggiano Jr. decided to cooperate with the Feds, that his sister found out the truth about her husband's disappearance. On the day that the police took Ruggiano Jr. in for questioning, he asked them to take him to see his mother and sister first. Ruggiano Jr. admitted to them about the murder. His sister screamed and shouted at him, but it was his mother's reaction that had the most chilling effect. She just shook her head in disappointment and said, 'I can't believe that your father made you do things like that.'

Ruggiano Jr.'s sister refused to speak to him for many years, but he says they have started talking again recently after the death of their mother and now their relationship is the best it could be, under the circumstances.

After the hit on Boccia, Ruggiano Jr. was proposed to become a made man. Unfortunately for him, he was arrested in 1989 before the ceremony could take place. Unbeknownst to him then, the same scenario would play out again and again in his Mob career. When he was released in 1992, he was due to be made again but was promptly re-arrested. Ruggiano Jr. came closest to being made in 2004. This time he was told that the ceremony was just a formality and that he could attend sitdowns like any other wise guy. The family was just waiting for the rubber stamp of the ceremony, which would take place around Christmas time. But once again, fate and the law intervened and Ruggiano Jr. found himself in custody again: 'I guess it was like divine intervention,' he told me.

In 1989, Ruggiano Jr. was arrested for a large illegal lottery operation. The money involved was so big, it made the front page of the New York newspapers, which had the unfortunate side effect of getting him in trouble with John Gotti. 'It was on the front page of the news,' Ruggiano Jr. told me, "John Gotti Crew 14 million a Year". Now, John had nothing to do with it. It was my father's business, so when I get out on bail, I go to the to the Bergen Fish Club. I walk in. He goes, "Hey, where's my money?" I go, "What money?" He goes, "We made 14 million last year. I didn't get 10 cents."'

Fortunately for Ruggiano Jr., Gotti was only joking.

The 1989 arrest was the start of a decade which Ruggiano Jr. would spend mostly behind bars. For much of the early nineties he was in and out of prison on short stretches, but in 1996, while still serving time, he was indicted by the FBI in Florida on a big RICO (Racketeer Influenced and Corrupt Organizations) case with several other mobsters that included a murder conspiracy charge. Ruggiano took a plea and was sentenced to a further ten years but the jail time didn't stop his operations or his money-making potential. He had stayed off cocaine and had a wide range of operations running, including two chop shops, a vending machine business and a fraudulent credit card operation.

The nineties saw the death of Tony Lee, as well as Ruggiano Jr.'s second marriage and the birth of his daughter. In 1997, Ruggiano Sr. was released from prison, having served thirteen years of his forty-year sentence. In 1999, Ruggiano Jr. was still inside, working with his attorney on a plea to get fourteen months removed from his sentence, when he received a call from his mother, saying his dad was feeling dizzy but refused to go to the doctor. Ruggiano Jr. spoke to his father and tried to convince him to get medical advice, but Ruggiano Sr. was more interested in talking about his son's legal case. The call finished with Ruggiano Sr. agreeing to see the doctor the next day if he still felt dizzy. It was the last time Ruggiano Jr. would speak to him. Not long after, Ruggiano Sr. died. He was seventy-two years old and had been all but abandoned by the family that he had served loyally all his life.

'My father died in the street alone and broke after doing thirteen years in prison,' Ruggiano Jr. told me. 'He got out, he had no family, no friends. He was all alone.'

Even Ruggiano Jr. wasn't at his father's funeral – the authorities had refused to let him out of prison to attend.

His father's death was a watershed moment in Ruggiano Jr.'s life in more ways than one. It marked the time when he began to question how much he wanted to remain in the Mob life. These doubts were precipitated in 2000 when he was still in prison. He received a visit from one of his associates telling him they had a problem with the Gottis. John Gotti's brother, Pete Gotti, had paid the man a visit, saying that now Fat Andy was dead, Ruggiano Jr. owed him $1,800 in his father's stead.

Apparently, while Ruggiano Sr. had been in jail, his daughter had crashed her car into a limousine belonging to a company owned by Pete Gotti. Fat Andy had called Gotti about the incident and had been told not to worry about it, Pete had dealt with it. However, when Ruggiano Sr. got out of prison, he was paid a visit by one of Pete Gotti's partners, asking for the $1,800 to cover the crash. Fat Andy was fuming with rage at this news. He had just got out of prison and Gotti was expecting him to pay all this money, especially after he'd assured him he'd dealt with it.

According to Ruggiano Jr., his father shoved the invoice back in the man's hands and told him that if Pete Gotti wanted the money, he could meet Fat Andy on a corner of his choice and Ruggiano Sr. would hand the money over in person. Needless to say, he never received a call from Gotti. However, the Gambino man clearly hadn't forgotten the debt, or the insult, and on Fat Andy's death, he was calling on Ruggiano Jr. to cough up the cash.

The whole scenario left a bad taste in Ruggiano Jr.'s mouth and when released from prison in 2004, he found that his attitude to life had changed. He was on the 12-step addiction recovery programme, had found spirituality and started praying regularly and, in his own words, had 'developed a conscience'.

On his release in 2004, Ruggiano Jr. decided to go straight. He found himself a job as a truck driver and was surprised to discover that he loved it. Every day, he would drive into

Manhattan and relish the feeling of freedom and the comfort of not having to look over his shoulder every five minutes. But life has a habit of catching up with people, and in 2005 it did so. Ruggiano Jr. was sitting outside his son's house, enjoying the sun, when he suddenly found himself surrounded by armed FBI officers. He was arrested and charged with the murder of his brother-in-law: Frankie Boccia.

Ruggiano Jr. managed to get out on bail but as his trial approached, he began to struggle with finances to fight the case. He had only just got of prison and was broke. His father had spent most of the last part of his life in prison and had died penniless, leaving his children nothing. Ruggiano Jr. reached out to some people who his father had supported in the past, but no one was prepared to help him, not even guys whose lives his father had saved. The same thing had happened to Ruggiano Sr. in the last few years of his life and the feeling of being left out in the cold added another sour note to the unpleasant taste in Ruggiano Jr.'s mouth.

These negative experiences were gradually leading Ruggiano Jr. towards the most momentous decision of his life. For a year, he toyed with the decision of cooperating with the Feds. He faced life in prison for a so-called family who had left him out in the cold, yet still he couldn't bring himself to do the one thing that his father hated more than anything in the world – ratting. He would pick up the phone to make the call then put it down again. In the end, he called one of his father's former lawyers for help. The man made some phone calls to Ruggiano Jr.'s co-defendants' attorneys and a couple of days later, came back to Ruggiano Jr. with news he could hardly believe. His co-defendants, according to the lawyer, were preparing to sacrifice him at the trial to mitigate their own sentences.

That night, Ruggiano Jr. kept fingering a business card given to him by an FBI agent. He never usually kept Feds' details, but this one he had pocketed because the man had been kind to him, allowing him out of a holding cell to use the toilet and buying him a sandwich. Ruggiano Jr. played with the card for several minutes but still he couldn't bring himself to make the call. The next morning, he passed the card to his wife and asked her to ring the agent when she got to work.

Ruggiano Jr. ended up testifying against his co-defendants in the trial over the murder of his brother-in-law. Due to his testimony, Skinny Dom, the man who had pulled the trigger, received a sentence of eighteen years. Ruggiano Jr. himself pleaded guilty to his part in the murder. At sentencing, his niece, the daughter of Frankie Boccia whose baby shower had indirectly led to the murder of her father, pleaded that Ruggiano Jr. receive a life sentence. Ruggiano Jr. was in court to hear his niece's plea, as was his own daughter and his ex-wife, Alice, and he broke down in tears when he heard her statement. 'The anger you have left with me is indescribable,' Boccia's daughter told the court, explaining how her family had told her for years that her father wasn't dead but had abandoned her. 'I can't tell you what that did to me as a child,' she added.

With a record of testifying, Ruggiano Jr.'s life was obviously in danger. He was put under an FBI witness protection programme and went into hiding after being sentenced to time served and a supervised release term of five years. But his time under witness protection only lasted a year and a half. After this time, Ruggiano said family matters intervened and he decided he needed more freedom, so he signed himself out of the protection programme and now lives openly under his own name. Ruggiano Jr. admits there is probably still a hit out on him, but he doesn't live in fear. One reason is that the Mob is not what it used to be and he doubts the organisation now has the will, or the teeth, to carry out such a murder.

'Nobody's coming after me,' Ruggiano Jr. told me. 'I'm not saying there's nobody out there that's capable of it. There's people capable of committing murders, don't get me wrong, but who's going to send them? I think it's pretty much over,' he added about the power of the modern-day Italian-American Mafia, going on to explain the reasons for its demise.

'I think it started probably after the books were opened in the seventies. I mean, they started straightening out a lot of guys that weren't even criminals. You're straightening out guys that never went to prison. They weren't legitimate guys, they were just big earners. Then they developed the witness protection programme where now you're going to be protected, you're going to get supported, you're going to get paid. So now the world started changing. And then John [Gotti] put everybody on front street so that started a lot of Investigations. The Gambino family had captains that they didn't even know who they were, and John made them come to the Ravenite once a week. So he put everybody on front street, so that was that was the end of it. He put it on the front page, but I think it started to crumble before John. He just was the final straw.'

It turned out that Ruggiano Jr.'s father, one of the last of the traditional Mob legends, had already seen the writing on the wall back in 1998 after his release from prison. Ruggiano Jr. remembers one of his last meetings with his father when Ruggiano Sr. had visited him in prison: '[I] was sitting in the visiting room,' Ruggiano Jr. told me, 'and he comes to visit me. He goes, "Listen, I'm opening up an import-export with a big warehouse. We're going to sell fruit and vegetables and it's for you when you come home." I said, "It's for me when

I come home? What are you talking about?" He goes, "Our life is over." I said, "What are you talking about? Why is it over?" He goes, "Because the two things we had going for us are finished – everybody feared us and nobody cooperated." He goes, "Nobody fears us anymore and people are cooperating, because it's over." And he was right.'

With his Mafia life behind him, Ruggiano Jr. was living in Michigan when he got the call that would move his life onto a new track. A friend asked if he would like to become a counsellor in the drug treatment centre where he worked. With Ruggiano Jr.'s experience of beating addiction, the friend thought he would make an excellent advisor for some of the younger people who came into the centre. Ruggiano Jr. decided to give it a go. He went back to college to obtain the necessary qualifications and began working to help recovering addicts, a job he still does to this day.

'I try to help people change their lives, stay clean,' Ruggiano Jr. told me. 'I'm trying to get some forgiveness, make up for my past sins.'

There are things Ruggiano Jr. still misses about the life. 'I miss the money,' he told me. 'I miss the action. I miss the respect. I go to concerts; I used to sit in the front row, now I gotta sit in the back.'

But he also has regrets about the life he lived, including what he did to his sister, not getting an education, and the amount of time he was forced to spend inside, especially missing out on the childhoods of his children. He sometimes regrets ratting on his former colleagues, but he maintains that he would never have done it if his father, Tony Lee and John Gotti were still alive. When he cooperated, a new generation was in control. Ruggiano Jr. felt he owed nothing to these people. Most of all, he regrets the way the life destroyed his family. His mother had to be hospitalised through depression and he, his sister and brother all became drug addicts.

One day, while his father was still in prison, Ruggiano Jr. went to visit and confront him with the mess the family was in. He asked his dad what role he felt he had played in the family's self-destruction. In a moment of rare self-reflection, Fat Andy told his son, 'I stopped paying attention.' For Fat Andy, the Mob came first and Ruggiano Jr. had made the same mistakes as his father before him, missing out on most of the first decade of his children's lives. But it is a mistake he is now determined to put right. He spends as much time with his now grown-up daughter as possible, going to concerts with her and bringing her to interviews.

Weighing his former and current life, Ruggiano Jr. has realised that although he may no longer be wealthy or powerful, he is much more content now than he has ever been. For three decades, he has been clean and never has to look over his shoulder for flashing lights and whirring sirens. He has realised that the Mob life, while exhilarating for a short period, is ultimately a destructive path that ruins the lives not just of gangsters themselves, but of everyone around them. It is a message he is determined to get across to young people today who may find themselves attracted by the lifestyle.

'All that glitters isn't gold,' Ruggiano Jr. told me, 'I knew John Gotti and my father – to me, they were the two biggest gangsters in the world. John Gotti died chained to a bed in prison and my father died in the street alone and broke after doing thirteen years in prison. He got out, he had no family, no friends, he was all alone. At the end of the day, it's your family that suffers.'

8

Nick Yarris

'I can't stop throwing up from the shock of almost getting my face blown off'

The prisoner waits in his cell. He knows what is coming.

Today is Gladiator Day, when the staff try to disperse the racial tensions among the prisoners by pitting white against black, white against Hispanics, Hispanics against black.

The prisoner is on death row so he's fair game for the guards' sadistic entertainment. He faces the death penalty for the rape and murder of a wife and mother of three. But with a price on his head among the other inmates and a five-year life expectancy in Huntingdon State Prison, a supermax correctional facility in the state of Pennsylvania, he is unlikely to live long enough to face the electric chair.

He steels himself as he hears the footsteps of the guards along the corridor and the scrape of metal as the door of his cell slides open. The guards motion impatiently for him to move.

'Yarris, you're up,' one of them tells him.

He is escorted down the corridors to the exercise area, a series of dog-kennel-like cages, nineteen feet long by ten feet wide. Inside one of the cages his opponent is waiting for him, a big black man, while a crowd of guards stands impatiently around. They will be cheering on their fighter and taking bets over the winner.

He already knows the rules – three to five minutes inside the cage. Once the doors are closed, anything goes. He has seen men have their eyes gouged out; he has seen them beaten to death. He knows there is no point refusing to fight. If the prisoners won't fight, they both get beaten by the guards. Better to take your chances with the man opposite you.

As he is thrust into the cage, he gets a better look at his opponent. The man is so big, most men wouldn't stand a chance. But the prisoner has a reputation as a psychopath, an angry man who beats his head against the wall of his cell until he has to be taken to the medical ward to be patched up. He can see the fear in the other man's eyes. Then the gate clangs shut, the roaring of the guards rises to a crescendo and the fight is on.

His opponent is so big, the prisoner can hardly get a hold of him. But the other man is so scared he can hear him making strange guttural noises, sounds of primitive terror. He feels a brief stab of pity then quickly buries it. There is no room for pity inside the cage.

That only gets you killed.

Nick Yarris's story is not only one of the most interesting and powerful I have ever come across, but one that is close to my heart. It was this story that first inspired me to try and make a success out of what I do now, writing and podcasting. When I saw an interview with him in 2016, I found the experience so powerful and inspirational, I knew that this was what I wanted to do with my life.

It's not just the tribulations that Yarris went through that made his tale so engaging, but the way he dealt with and ultimately overcame them. Sentenced to death in 1982 for a rape and murder he didn't commit, Yarris spent twenty-three years in solitary confinement on death row. Escaping, largely by accident, he was top of the FBIs most-wanted list before being recaptured. He was beaten, tortured, stabbed and made to fight like an animal in gladiator bouts with other inmates. He became the first prisoner in the US to seek DNA testing for his case, a decade-and-a-half-long process that ultimately exonerated him, only after wearing him down so much he requested his own execution.

Despite the unfairness with which he had been treated and the many tragedies and suffering life threw at him, Yarris went on to find a new kind of strength which he teaches to this day – the power of kindness. His story is a true inspiration.

Born in 1961, Yarris was raised in a working-class family in Philadelphia. His father was a roofer and his mother a cashier at the nearby airport. His grandmother, an Irish émigré, was the housekeeper, staying at home while Yarris's parents worked hard to provide for him and his five siblings. Yarris's early childhood was happy, and growing up in the Philadelphia of the sixties was a pleasant, almost idyllic experience. 'Philadelphia was beautiful when I started off,' he told me when I interviewed him. 'I remember that we used to have these competitions in the neighbourhood for beautification, and we used to have parties where we'd block off the street in the summertime and have food and music.'

Yarris's area of south-west Philly was on the outskirts of the city near the airport, so there were wide tracts of nature where the young boy would go swimming in the rivers and walk with his dog, Jocko, in the woods. But when Yarris was seven years old, two things happened that would change everything and turn his life upside down.

He was walking with Jocko in the woods one day when he came across an older boy in his late teens, who he recognised from the neighbourhood. The young man was a tough guy with a reputation, who Yarris had even seen beat up adults. As soon as the boy spotted him, Yarris knew he was in trouble. 'He wore a T-shirt with a pack of cigarettes in the sleeve like they used to do, back in the greaser days,' Yarris told me, 'and he had his hobnail boots and blue jeans and he wanted to look tough. In my head, he looked enormous.'

Yarris tried to escape but the older boy was too quick. He made Yarris take a drag of the cigarette he was smoking and Yarris's head went dizzy with the nicotine rush. The next thing he knew, the boy had picked up a rock and smashed it into his head. Yarris hit the ground and soon the older boy twisted him around and was on top of him, raping him. Yarris began to whimper and the boy shouted, 'Shut the fuck up! I'll kill Jocko and your whole family if you say anything!'

When it was done, the boy told Yarris to say he had fallen off a wall to explain the head injury. Yarris went home and did as he was told. From then on, the older boy would often see Yarris around the neighbourhood and silently taunt him with their secret, often making as if to punch him so that the younger boy would flinch. Yarris would run home and sit in the basement of his family home, punching himself repeatedly in the thigh to try and rid himself of the fear. But that wouldn't truly happen until he discovered alcohol and drugs.

The second momentous event that happened to Yarris in 1968 was the death of Martin Luther King Jr. The murder of the civil rights activist changed everything in Philadelphia, transforming the city from an idyllic place to grow up in to a seething cauldron of hatred and violence. Following the murder, racial tensions set the once-peaceful city on fire and gang warfare took over, as did drug abuse. Yarris's area was particularly affected, as it was a small white district sandwiched between black and Italian neighbourhoods. 'It was the *Gangs of New York* on steroids back then,' Yarris told me. 'You had to come out and stand on the corner. There was no internet and you didn't have anywhere to go so right after dinner, you had to stand on the corner of 74th Street with, like, fifteen other kids and hope nobody attacked that night.'

Drugs were everywhere, with people taking methamphetamine, cannabis and prescription drugs like quaaludes. Yarris had his own first drug experience at the age of eleven. His brother dropped a tab of acid on his bedroom floor by mistake. The young Yarris bent over and picked it up while his brother searched in vain. He took the drug and went outside to Elmwood Park. It was a hot sunny day and Yarris wanted to cool his feet, so he took off his trainers and slung them round his neck while he bathed. 'The next thing I know, there was a giant pair of shoes trying to stomp me to death,' Yarris told me, 'and I was running from these shoes up the middle of the street, screaming my head off, and everybody thought I'd lost my mind.'

Yarris was soon drinking alcohol regularly and this, along with his early trauma, negatively affected his behaviour. He became, in his own words, 'ultra-violent', and was soon kicked out of school for his troublemaking behaviour. One day, another student stabbed Yarris with a pencil so he took it out and tried to stab the other boy back, unfortunately stabbing his teacher instead in the ensuing fracas.

With education no longer holding him back, Yarris was soon making money by jacking cars. In the seventies there were no alarms or steering locks, so vehicles were relatively easy to steal and the young car thief could earn between $500–$1,000 per vehicle. 'We would flip through three, four cars a night sometimes, on a rotation,' Yarris told me. 'You and three mates go out and you get a car and the three of you get in and you get two more cars, then you take those three, drop those two off, go back and get two more cars, so you have five-car nights.'

The proceeds from Yarris's crimes would all go on alcohol and drugs. His favourite was methamphetamine, which he would inject directly into his arm. Under the influence of the drug he no longer felt like the scared little boy who would run back to his basement and punch himself in the thigh. He no longer looked like that kid, either. At first, Yarris had thought he was going to be short like his dad, but at fourteen, he suddenly shot up and by sixteen, he was six foot two and almost two hundred pounds. At the same time he was training at a boxing gym and had become a talented boxer.

His fighting skills would come in useful at the juvenile detention centre where he was spending more and more time. He was first incarcerated at the age of fifteen after being arrested for robbery. Gang warfare reigned in the juvenile detention centre and kids from south-west Philly weren't numerous, so Yarris had to stick up for himself from the moment he stepped inside. 'After you get processed into the unit, someone's gonna ask you where you're from,' he told me, 'and you don't say shit, you just punch him in his face.' On one occasion Yarris and his friend found themselves fighting against eight other detainees, with Yarris having to rip a lamp off the wall to hold his attackers at bay.

All this time, Yarris had dreamed about getting revenge on the man who had raped him when he was a boy. He finally got his chance when he was nineteen years old. Yarris was walking along by some train tracks when he saw his tormentor coming the other way. 'He recognised in that moment that I wasn't a child,' Yarris told me, 'and he was shitting himself, and he had a quart of beer – I'll never forget – in his hand, and he dropped it and it broke. And then he started this pathetic pleading with me: "Nick, you know I got all kinds of problems, you gotta understand." And then as he was standing there, I'm like, damn this dude ain't no more than five foot nine, 175 pounds maybe, and in my head, he was this monster. And the more he pleaded with me and became pathetic, this horrible milk toast version of a human being, I freaked out and told him to get away from me. And then I actually jumped down off of this concrete table thing and I ran off, man, like I was sickened by him.'

In fact, Yarris was so sickened by the encounter that he fled Philadelphia entirely and ran away to Florida. He went on a drugs binge and wrecked his hotel room so badly, he was placed in a mental institution. There, he was diagnosed with aphasia, a kind of brain damage that affects the language centres of the brain. It caused Yarris to stutter and have problems expressing himself, and it also impaired his self-control, causing him to fly off the handle quickly and easily. Aphasia can be brought on by blunt force trauma so it was probably the attack with the rock preceding his rape that had caused the damage. The doctors told him his use of methamphetamine had exacerbated the condition as well.

Yarris spent eight months inside the mental institution before being released. He decided to try again and moved back in with his parents. He got a job and was going straight with a girl, then in 1981 he was stopped by the Philadelphia highway patrol. He made the mistake of trying to flee and they chased him for ten blocks before running him down. Once he was caught, one of the cops hit him in the mouth with his baton so hard that Yarris needed eighteen stitches, his wounds requiring cauterisation.

Yarris was so angered and traumatised by the attack that he started taking drugs again. Three weeks later, he was pulled over by the cops again and the trauma of the previous attack, combined with his aphasia, caused him to freeze with panic. 'I can't move,' Yarris told me. 'I look up at the dude and he's right there and I know he's saying stuff. He rips the door open, starts yelling at me, grabs me, pushes me backwards against the car roof and he put his forearm against my throat.'

Shocked into action, Yarris grabbed the policeman's arm and forced it downwards, shoving the man backwards. The cop then reached for his baton but, with the strength of panic, Yarris yanked it out of his hand. The cop then unholstered his gun and pointed it at Yarris. Yarris grabbed the weapon and pushed it downwards, at which point the gun went off. Stunned by the blast, Yarris tried to get the fuming cop to calm down. The man shoved the weapon into Yarris's neck and forced him into the car. Then with Yarris in the back, cuffed and subdued, the policeman did something that would change the young man's life forever. 'He composed himself,' Yarris told me, 'got in the car, looked in that mirror, looking at me, checking himself out, then he just got on the phone and he starts yelling, "Officer assist! Shots fired! I'm being attacked!"'

That night in the Chester County Jail, the officer who had arrested him wanted his vengeance, but Yarris was saved by the sergeant on duty, an African-American who wouldn't let the other cop into his cell. But things were only going to get worse for Yarris. Instead of being charged with resisting arrest, he faced trumped-up charges of kidnapping, reckless endangerment, possession of a firearm of a police officer and attempted murder. The full scope of his predicament came crashing home when his acting attorney told him he was facing a life sentence if found guilty.

Yarris was stewing in his cell, going through a drug with-drawal, when he saw a headline in the newspaper about the rape and murder of a thirty-two-year-old woman called Linda Craig. In December 1981, Craig had been abducted and driven in her own car to an abandoned area behind a church, just twenty miles away from where Yarris lived. She was dragged out of the car and raped before being stabbed to death. The story gave Yarris a desperate idea to save himself from his charges. It would turn out to be the worst mistake of his life.

Yarris decided if he pretended to know the identity of Linda Craig's murderer, he could bargain his charges down. He stewed on the idea for a while, trying to think who he could blame for the crime, until he settled on the name of an old drug-addict friend called Jimmy Bridge. Some time ago, Yarris had stolen a car from the airport and was showing Jimmy and his friend a big bag of coins that had been stashed inside the vehicle. Suddenly Jimmy's friend smashed Yarris across the head with a Magnum revolver. Yarris had woken up rolled up in an old carpet in the back of a pick-up truck. Jimmy and his friend drove him to the back of a warehouse, where they fired two shots into the carpet roll and left him for dead. Unfortunately for them, they had aimed too high and completely missed Yarris. Blaming Jimmy for the rape and murder of Linda Craig would be the perfect revenge and, moreover, Jimmy would be unable to deny the crime because, as one of Jimmy's friends had informed Yarris, he had recently died from a drug overdose.

As soon as Yarris told the police he knew the identity of Craig's murderer, their attitude towards him changed. Sud-denly he was being treated with kindness and respect and commended for his bravery. 'They even said they got off the phone with Officer Wright and he was willing to reduce the charges to reckless endangerment and resisting arrest,' Yarris told me, 'and I would get out in three days and that was it. And I was like, "What?" And they were like, "Yeah, you can get probation. If this is all true, you're doing a huge service to this community, thank you, and we want you to know you're going to go on with your life."'

Spurred on by the cops' encouragement, Yarris went on with his testimony. But there was one inconvenient problem with his story – Jimmy, the dead drug addict who had supposedly committed the crime, wasn't dead. He had survived the overdose, gone straight and could prove that he wasn't at the scene of the crime at the time of Linda Craig's murder.

Now the cops were angry and their suspicion turned on Yarris. Why was he so keen on pinning Craig's murder on someone else? And how did he know so many details about the crime? Yarris underwent a thirteen-hour interrogation in which they twisted his words to extract a 'confession' that he never made. There was no evidence connecting Yarris to Craig's death but the prosecutors concocted a story that Craig looked like Yarris's ex-girlfriend and that the murder had been a twisted kind of revenge killing. They also produced a prisoner who had been in a neighbouring cell to Yarris, who swore that Yarris had confessed to the murder.

In the meantime, Yarris had to go on trial for the concocted charges of kidnap and attempted murder of the police officer. He was represented by a lawyer named Samuel Stretton, who had agreed to defend him in both cases for just $1,500, the sum total of Yarris's savings. Stretton proved his mettle in the first trial when he exposed a glaring hole in the prosecution's case. The trial took place in April 1982. The police officer concerned, Benjamin Wright, testified that when he had pulled Yarris over, the young drug addict had got out of the car, punched him in the face, forcibly taken his gun, hit him in the face with it and then pointed it at his face, before Wright had heroically wrestled the gun off Yarris as it discharged next to him. The prosecution case relied on a photograph of the police officer's hand showing injuries which, they claimed, proved that Yarris had forcibly removed the gun from Wright's hand. But the story didn't hold water, as Yarris's lawyer pointed out.

'Samuel Stretton asked him to explain one thing,' Yarris told me. 'If I had assaulted this officer, punched him in his face, broke his eyeglasses and hit him with the gun that he said that I took out of his hand, why didn't he photograph his face?'

At that moment the prosecution's case fell to pieces. The jury found Yarris not guilty on all counts. It was a remarkable result, especially considering Yarris had already been charged with the murder of Linda Craig. But the success was soon to backfire. Incensed at the humiliation of his loss, the prosecuting lawyer was furious.

'The prosecutor took the file and threw it against the wall,' Yarris told me, 'turned around and said, "Motherfucker, you'll never leave this county alive, I swear to God!"'

The next week, the same prosecutor took over Yarris's murder case and began seeking the death penalty.

In June of the same year, Yarris went on trial for the murder of Linda Craig. There was no physical evidence linking him to the crime, except that he had the same blood type as the murderer. Instead, the prosecution case rested on emotionally influencing the jury. They showed the court pictures of thir-ty-two-year-old Mrs Craig alongside her husband and three adopted children, followed by pictures of her corpse on the autopsy table with her face smashed and body punctured with knife wounds. Then came the clincher: 'They showed two children's footprints in the snow,' Yarris told me, 'after they had found the victim in the snow, and it looked like angels' wings. The jury couldn't look at me after they had seen that, man, and I knew right then and there, they were going to take my life.'

The trial lasted just three days. The jury were so swayed against Yarris that when they went out for dinner after delivering their verdict, they put their dessert on hold so they could eat it after he had received his sentence.

As if to emphasise the injustice of Yarris's conviction, that day the courthouse was struck by lightning. Yarris was taken upstairs to stew in a holding cell while he awaited sentencing. When the judge sentenced him to death by electric chair, the young man's reaction wasn't one of shock or tears but pure rage. 'I was beside myself because no one could look me in the eye,' Yarris told me. 'Like they all were ashamed. So I was asking them, "How could you possibly sentence me to death and you don't even have the courage to look at me in the face?" And [the judge] got frustrated and he asked me, was I finished, and I told him no, that he could go to hell.'

Yarris's righteous anger did him no favours. By insulting the judge, he ensured he was sent to Huntingdon State Prison, a Level 5 supermax facility with the worst reputation in the state of Pennsylvania. At Huntingdon, according to Yarris, the inmates had an average life expectancy of five years. 'Huntington State Prison is the only prison in America ever condemned by the United Nations for its active practices of torture,' Yarris told me, 'so serious business. They were of a mindset early on that they needed a prison to break you if you stabbed a prisoner, murdered a staff member, raped a staff member, or you raped another prisoner. They had to send you somewhere that was so hard, or make it mentally so hard, you wouldn't do these things.'

Yarris was only twenty-one years old, the second-youngest man in US history to be sentenced to death. He was convicted of raping and murdering a woman with a young family. To say he was in for a tough time would be an understatement.

The first thing that struck him about Huntingdon was the lack of noise. There was a rule of silence among the inmates which, if broken, would lead to a vicious beating by the guards, followed by a jab of Thorazine which would, according to Yarris, knock you out for a week. Yarris was introduced to the rule when he first arrived at Huntingdon. The warden explained the procedure in a calm, quiet voice. When he asked Yarris if he understood, Yarris instinctively went to answer and got a quick backhand blow to the face. He also discovered the consequences of speaking first-hand when he dared to sing 'Happy Birthday' to himself on his birthday. The guards' beating ensured that his birthday was anything but happy.

The other thing that defined Huntingdon was the gladiator fights. Whenever the strict lieutenant was away, the guards would set about having some fun. Sometimes they would put two inmates who had beef into the same exercise cage, knowing that as soon as they walked away, the men would set on each other. Another favourite was interracial fights, often between death rowers. These fights originated, ironically, in order to keep racial tensions down among the guards themselves. 'A lot of the prison guards that were originally in Huntington State Prison were white,' Yarris explained. 'When the epidemic of crack and the housing of mentally ill people was changed, the prison system swelled to almost two million people and they kept bringing Spanish-speaking guards and black officers up into the mountains. When they saw these white officers beating the shit out of everything black and brown, they were disgusted by it. But you can't have staff-on-staff fighting, so in a crazy cockamamie way, they came up with a scheme that a black prisoner and a white prisoner could fight, and the black guards would pick out one and the white guards would pick out the other.'

Meanwhile, on the outside, Yarris's lawyers were busy arranging an appeal. When this came up in 1985, he was transferred out of Huntingdon for his appearance at the Pennsylvania Supreme Court in Philadelphia. Yarris was transported by two guards who were both in their sixties. After five hours of driving, the guards pulled into a petrol station to use the toilet. It was February and the coldest day of the year, and as he trudged through the snow to the toilet, Yarris's glasses began to fog up. It was tricky to manoeuvre to try and use the toilet while in handcuffs and with steamed-up glasses but he managed as best he could. He turned to leave the toilet and the guard indicated for him to duck under his arm. What happened next was pure chance.

'I started heading back to the car,' Yarris told me. 'It's night time, I've got foggy eyeglasses. I see the silhouette of the officer standing there at the front of the car. He turns around and faces me, hearing me in the snow coming towards him, but he doesn't see his partner behind me because the officer standing there holding the cubicle door had to go urinate so badly, he left me on my own. And that's what blew it, because this guy now thinks I overpowered his partner. He pulls the gun out, fires a shot.'

Shocked and panicked, Yarris turned and began to run. The guard fired a second shot and Yarris fell to the ground. Thinking he had hit him, the guard lowered his weapon and approached the prone figure. But Yarris had just stumbled. He got back on his feet and began running again, this time straight towards the plate glass window of the petrol station diner in the hope that the guard wouldn't shoot again for fear of hitting someone inside.

It worked and Yarris got around to the back of the building without another shot being fired. Once behind the building, he sprinted through the snow for a hundred yards before doubling back on himself until he was lying behind the same vehicle they had brought him in, figuring this was the last place they would look. 'I was laying there in the grass and I started vomiting,' Yarris told me. 'I've just now escaped from death row custody and all these sirens are coming, and I'm hyperventilating and I can't stop throwing up from the shock and trauma of almost getting my face blown off.'

The night was now filled with sirens as police cars came rushing in from all directions. Yarris managed to remove his glasses and used one of the plastic arms to pick the lock on his handcuffs. Looking up, he noticed that the building to his right was a police station so he got up and crept behind the building, where he lay in the freezing snow unmoving for the next two hours. He became so cold that his legs began to cramp up and his torso was convulsing so hard, his ribs hurt. He soon realised he would have to move, so he sprang up and started to run. Almost immediately a police helicopter seemed to emerge out of nowhere, its conical beam of light pointing in Yarris's direction.

Yarris continued to run with the helicopter chasing him. The chase went on for three hours with Yarris plunging through undergrowth that ripped his clothes and tore his skin to shreds. His feet became torn and bloodied and his hamstrings were pulled, but still he kept running with the helicopter following him. Towards the end he found himself in the open space of a car park, where ploughs had cleared the tarmac of snow. Ahead of him was a ten-foot-high metal fence that he had no hope of scaling before the helicopter caught him. It looked like the end of the road, but still Yarris refused to give up. He ran straight for the fence and once again, fate intervened.

'This helicopter is down on me,' Yarris explained, 'kicking up snow so much it's like I'm in a tunnel of snow, being shot forward as I'm running full on at this giant chain-link fence. And I stumbled, I went down on my face, and I slalomed. I didn't know the snow ploughs had pushed the fence to a gap, and as I slalomed over the edge, I went right under the fence, down a railroad track embankment that was like sixty feet high, and all the way down face first in the snow, and stood up, and I couldn't believe I wasn't injured, and I looked up and the bird went back over me, back to the parking lot.'

Free of the helicopter at last, Yarris walked down the train track for five miles until he found a 1965 Ford Mustang. Using his car-jacking skills, he got in the Mustang and drove to the house of a family member, who gave him a hundred dollars, some new clothes and some bandages to cover his wounds. From there, Yarris drove all the way to New York City.

In New York, Yarris booked himself into a seven-dollar-a-night hotel room in the Bowery, paying for a week upfront. He bought some Epsom salts and treated his wounded feet, pulling out sock threads that had been forced into the soft tissue of his flesh. For three days he stayed inside, unable to walk. When he finally ventured out, he passed a department store displaying TVs in the window. On some of the screens was footage of the night of his escape. It viscerally brought home that he was still far from free.

Yarris decided he needed to get out of New York but first he needed money. He went to a high-class restaurant and waited near the toilets until one of the diners got up to use the restroom. Yarris nipped over and took the man's jacket where he had left it on his chair, along with his wallet. On the way out, he went to the cloakroom and stole an expensive-looking fur coat.

Using the stolen credit card and a false name, Yarris booked a last-minute flight to Orlando, Florida, where he hired a taxi to take him straight to a pawn shop. In the shop he traded the fur coat for a hundred dollars and a gun. He got chatting to the man behind the counter, who Yarris had rightly identified as another criminal, and the man told him about another guy he knew who Yarris could rob for some easy money. Yarris took the gun and went to the man's house on the pretext of selling him some drugs. The man drove Yarris to where he had told him the drugs were stashed. Once there, Yarris pulled the gun on him and took his money and Rolex watch. He told the man to drive him back to his house to get the rest of his money but the man refused, so Yarris bound his wrists and threw him in the trunk. Unfortunately, he couldn't have shut the trunk properly because a few blocks later at some traffic lights the man jumped out and began screaming that Yarris had kidnapped him.

Yarris put his foot down on the accelerator and sped away. He drove to Daytona Beach, where spring break meant all the hotels were full. Exhausted, he eventually decided to sleep in the car. He was woken while it was still dark by three sharp raps on his window. Waking up with a start, he saw a police officer motioning him to wind his window down. The policeman had been called out to deal with a domestic dispute and asked Yarris if he had heard a woman screaming. Still sleepy and confused, Yarris said no, but then suddenly the cop drew his gun and pointed it at Yarris's face. While he was talking, his partner had come round the other side of the car and spotted Yarris's gun poking out from under a blanket on the passenger seat.

The police took Yarris to the local station, where he gave a false name. He was waiting to post bail of just $500 when he suddenly had a change of heart. He no longer wanted to be on the run, he no longer wanted to put his family through any more pain and torture. At first, he decided that after he had posted bail, he would have one last party in a dinghy off the coast before slashing his wrists, puncturing the dinghy and letting the sharks finish him off. Then he changed his mind and decided to face the music. He used his telephone call to phone his dad in Pennsylvania; he asked him to call the FBI and tell them where he was.

Within minutes of the phone call, Yarris's cell was flooded with officers and he was hauled off to a local maximum-security facility. He was still only twenty-four years old but for the twenty-five-day duration of his escape, Yarris had been top of the FBI's most-wanted list. The repercussions of his escape were swift and unyielding. He had thirty-five years added to his sentence, which now amounted to 105 years plus the death penalty. But the repercussions when he was transferred back to Pennsylvania were even worse.

'The prison officers lured me from my cell to go to my legal work boxes that were in storage,' Yarris told me. 'They took me up a set of metal stairs opposite death row, that was like a warehouse building with big open windows and lights inside. And then they brought me in and they flung me on the floor, and they were standing on me at first, and they got the cuffs off. They stepped on my shoulders, stepped on my knees and everything, held me down, took the cuffs off, then they stood me up and the two officers who got suspended for my escape, for not properly searching me, walked up. As soon as they started coming at me I tried to attack them – I knew they were going to just lay into me. So they knocked me unconscious and a guy named Murphy told me that they beat me for four minutes. Man, I pissed blood for a month. I thought I'd never stop peeing blood. So they beat me primarily on the backs of my legs, on my butt, beat me over my head and face. I have a detached retina in my left eye. They blew my eye out so bad, I thought I'd never see out of the eye again.'

It wasn't only the guards who were after Yarris. As someone who had supposedly committed a horrendous crime, he had a bounty on his head, which meant any inmate who killed him would get money put on their books. In Yarris's case the bounty was rumoured to be $10,000. Unsurprisingly, the attacks quickly started coming. On one occasion, he was struck with a pool ball inside a sock. The implement struck him so hard in the head that Yarris saw stars. From this and subsequent attacks, he estimates he has suffered severe concussion on no less than ten occasions. One of these he accidentally did to himself after being stabbed in the stomach by another inmate. 'I didn't think he had a knife, but he did,' Yarris told me, 'and he got it in me pretty good so I had to hold his hand and keep headbutting him to get him off me. And one point I went to headbutt him and I hit the metal railing really hard.'

With a large bounty on his head, Yarris had to be on his toes at all times. On one occasion he was almost caught on the landing by a noose lowered from a higher tier. Someone had called his name in an official-sounding voice so that he turned his head to see who it was. While he was distracted, another inmate lowered a noose from the tier above, trying to get it around Yarris's neck without him noticing so that they could garrote him to death.

To avoid danger, Yarris had to become a dangerous man himself. He learned the dark arts of how to maim and kill another man using the objects to hand. These included shanks (slicing instruments often made from the sides of prison boots) and shivs (round, pointed objects used to gouge out eyes or target arteries). He learned how to make weapons deadlier by smearing them with poisons concocted out of faeces, urine and tobacco, or by placing the poison inside a milk-carton bomb. He even learned exotic techniques for crafting catapults. 'I could kill you with a pair of underwear and a magazine and never leave my cell,' Yarris told me. 'I could take the underwear apart and use the elasticity from the waistband, along with that magazine, to create a catapult complete with a dart system so strong, it'll penetrate your neck and go through your artery or your optic nerve into your brain.'

The showers were the most dangerous place in the prison, where inmates were exposed and defenceless, and hence saw some of the worst violence. On death row, six inmates were allowed to shower together at one time. They were given exactly four minutes and if anybody attacked anyone else, all six inmates would receive a severe beating by the guards. This didn't prevent incidents happening, however. One time, Yarris watched as a young Puerto Rican man stabbed another inmate in the liver using a sharpened pork bone. The water was instantly turned off and the other prisoners were beaten by the guards while the victim was dragged away, his body flopping wildly as he died.

He wasn't the only man Yarris saw die. The first death he witnessed was early on in his incarceration, when he was just twenty-one years old. A man had been stabbed in the top of the head with a screwdriver. As he sat on his bed waiting for assistance, he asked Yarris if he was going to die. As Yarris went to comfort him, the man flopped over and passed away.

As a death row prisoner, Yarris lived alongside some truly dangerous men. One was the infamous serial killer Ted Bundy, whose cell was near Yarris's on death row in Florida after he was caught, following his escape. Bundy and Yarris could communicate through the vents in their cells but Yarris wanted nothing to do with the murderer, who he described as 'disgusting'. Bundy boasted about getting all the inmates' visitations removed because he had got one of his visitors pregnant. On another occasion he tried to get Yarris interested in the Bible. 'I told him I didn't get off on killing my mom, by killing little girls,' Yarris told me, 'and he went off on me and started shouting up in this stupid biblical voice.'

Another monster was Gary Heidnik, the original inspiration for Buffalo Bill in *Silence of the Lambs*. Heidnik had abducted several prostitutes and kept them chained in his basement, where he tortured and eventually murdered them, even feeding one of his victims to the others in ground-up dog food. Yarris lived next door to Heidnik for two years on death row in Pennsylvania and, whenever there was a power cut, Heidnik would put on a re-enactment of his crimes, reliving the torture and murder of the women and even recreating their high-pitched voices as they pleaded for mercy.

As well as the inmate-on-inmate violence, there were regular suicides, usually by jumping off the top tier of the landing. It was one of these self-killings that led to Yarris's life turning a corner. Up until then, he had focused on maintaining a sense of righteous anger about the injustice he had received, which helped him to keep fighting. To fuel the anger, he would beat his head against the walls of his cell until he had to be taken to the nurses' station to have it patched up. On one of these occasions, the guard was walking Yarris back to his cell when they passed an empty cell where another inmate had committed suicide. The guard stopped Yarris outside the cell and told him to go inside and take the man's books. Yarris salvaged as many of the books as he could and took them to his cell.

Yarris had never been a reader and indeed could barely read at all, thanks to his lack of education growing up. Now he decided to teach himself. He was shocked by how many words he came across that he didn't understand, so he got himself a dictionary and began using a technique he read about called the 'Rule of 10'. This involved taking a new word and spelling it ten times, then writing out its definition ten times and finally using it in ten different sentences. With this technique his vocabulary began to expand quickly and he became an increasingly voracious reader. 'I became so fluid that I quit counting books at 9,400 books,' Yarris told me. 'I fell in love with language, even that word, I just love the word language.'

As well as reading, Yarris taught himself to use language, practising writing long ten-page letters to his family and loved ones. He also taught himself to speak well, overcoming the stutter he had developed through the aphasia brought on by his childhood attack. He used his newfound skills to study law and with his knowledge, he began to help other inmates by writing letters to their legal representatives. He helped two inmates get off death row and helped another to seek voluntary execution. His legal and writing services became so valuable to the other death row inmates that they went on hunger strike when he was going through a period of mistreatment by the guards.

Yarris had found a purpose in life and, astonishingly, he realised that he felt happy on death row. But there was one purpose that lay beneath all the others, the one motivating reason that kept him studying and honing his language skills. 'On the day that they wanted to put me to death, I wanted to have a beautiful speech,' Yarris told me. 'Somehow I didn't want to embarrass myself. I kept thinking, I want to have something beautiful to say. I don't want to go to my death without meaning. But I didn't know how to get there without learning. So everything that I've shared about my life I never expected to share. I just simply learned how to speak beautifully to myself so that I could master my last moments.'

To help keep up his motivation, Yarris kept just one photo on his cell wall. It was a picture of himself as a seventeen-year-old boy fishing on the Susquehanna River. He had just caught a giant carp and was holding it up to the camera with a big smile on his face. 'I set one photograph of myself up there so that I could learn how to speak beautifully to that person,' Yarris told me, 'because he was the one that needed to get me out of there. There weren't many days I smiled as a kid, so I wanted that photograph to be the representation of the person I needed to get me out of there.'

Along with his new sense of purpose came a zest for life, which included setting up his own business. As a lifer, Yarris was allowed twenty-four doughnuts a month. He would pay another inmate a doughnut to be a runner and deliver his other doughnuts for ten postage-paid envelopes a piece. He used the stamps to send letters to penfriends all around the world. In each of his letters he would include a snippet of his hair for a specific purpose. 'All of my penpals all over the world, I would just ask them one thing,' Yarris told me. 'Do me a favour and throw my hair into the ocean because it's my DNA and I want to be free . . . so that I circumnavigated the whole globe while I was on death row.'

Yarris also learned to play chess and would go through bouts of playing it for ten or twelve hours a day, calling out his moves to an opponent in another cell who had a similarly marked board. He also taught himself yoga and meditation, and strengthened his body by combining resistance training with cleaning his cell of the fine film of dust that accumulated each day.

After six years on death row, Yarris's life took another sharp turn when he fell in love. Jackie was a volunteer working for the Pennsylvania Prison Society, a social justice organisation that was campaigning to get Huntingdon Prison closed down due to the gladiator fights and other mistreatment of prisoners. Yarris had been corresponding with Jackie's colleague, Pamela, and Pamela asked Jackie to interview Yarris about any complaints he had. 'I told her I didn't have any,' Yarris told me. 'So she's like, "So what, you like it here? You think you deserve to be here?" She was really struck oddly by my response. But I was like, "Look, the truth is I can't get a really good cup of coffee to save my life, other than that I'm okay.' And she's like, "How can you be like this? How can nothing bother you?" I said, "You gotta understand something – this is really sincere – I have to live here. I can't let this bother me, I'm trying to live."'

Fascinated by Yarris's attitude, Jackie returned the next week to see him again, and soon she was visiting regularly. Yarris could feel that Jackie was developing feelings for him and didn't want to string her along, knowing that they could never be together outside prison. But soon everything changed. Four months after he'd first met Jackie, Yarris saw a headline in a newspaper about the science of DNA testing and suddenly he realised – this was his ticket to being proved innocent. He sent the newspaper clipping to Jackie and when she arrived for her next visit he told her, 'I've got two things to tell you – one, I didn't kill Mrs Craig, and two, I think I'm in love with you.'

The two were married on 1 July 1988, six years to the day after Yarris was sentenced to death. Now, he had everything to live for. In February of that year, Yarris had written requesting to be the first prisoner in US history to undergo DNA testing to prove his innocence. In 1989, he attended a court hearing which he remembers as one of the proudest moments of his life. Thanks to his research, Yarris was the most knowledgeable person in the court about DNA testing and for those present, he broke down the details of mitochondrial DNA (used in cases when testing with standard nuclear DNA isn't possible) and how it could be used in forensic testing. His request was turned down by the court but he walked out of the courtroom with his head held high. In his murder trial he had been a stuttering wreck who people could easily talk over. Now, he was a powerful speaker who everyone listened to.

The denial of his request for DNA testing wasn't to be Yarris's only setback by a long shot. When the courts did eventually agree to allow DNA testing, it turned out that all the material from Linda Craig's autopsy had mysteriously disappeared. Undeterred, Yarris pushed on. He remembered that at his trial the prosecution had said that biological samples had been sent out for testing to a serology lab. Ironically, this was what had helped find him guilty, because testing on the samples had shown that Yarris had the same blood type as the killer. Yarris now called the lab and asked the head scientists if they still had any of the biological samples. The doctor soon came back with good news – they still had some well-preserved spermatozoa from the murderer. Overjoyed, Yarris requested that the samples be used for DNA testing. But again, he was to be disappointed. 'I was jumping up and down, believing it's on,' Yarris told me, 'and then a detective from the Delaware County District Attorney's office went and took those slides and put them in his desk for three years and let them sit there.'

It took five years before the biological sample was DNA tested and by that time, the results came back as inconclusive due to degradation of the samples. Those three years sat in the detective's desk drawer had done their job.

Still, Yarris didn't give up. After his sentence his mother had been told to pick up a box of his belongings from the courthouse. She had been horrified to be presented with a box of the victim's belongings by mistake, but she had noted that a pair of gloves had been part of the box, which might have belonged to the killer. Yarris had been campaigning to get the gloves tested for fingerprint evidence. Now he switched tack, trying to get them DNA tested instead. It took until 1995 before the authorities agreed to finance the testing of the gloves. The items were packaged up ready for shipment to California to be tested by Dr Edward Blake, one of the foremost forensic scientists in the country, who had worked on the O. J. Simpson trial.

What happened next was almost predictable. The package broke open during shipment to California, leaving the sample open to possible contamination, meaning it wouldn't stand up as evidence in a court of law. Yarris was devastated, especially when the latest setback caused another blow. 'Jackie at that time walked in,' Yarris told me, 'and said, "Look, Nick, I've been here doing this for nine years, my mom just died, I got a house full of legal boxes, and I just met somebody. I gotta go." So she left.'

Yarris was devastated, but part of him was happy for Jackie that she was finally free of this ongoing torment. 'It was a relief because I was sucking the life out of somebody through this miserable experience that was going nowhere,' Yarris told me, 'and I felt guilty and I felt happy and I tried to be really beautifully sweet, and I wrote her a really lovely letter, and I thanked her for teaching me how to be genteel and lovable, and I reminded her of how she made me smile and laugh.'

Things weren't going to get any easier for Yarris, though. In 1995 the authorities transferred the Huntingdon inmates to Greene County Prison, another supermax facility in Pennsylvania, where the prisoners would be allowed out of their cells for eight hours a day. Yarris had survived twelve years of solitary confinement in the country's most brutal jail, where the average life expectancy was just five years. He was entitled to hope for something better, but that hope would soon be dashed. The death rowers like himself and other prisoners deemed too dangerous were transferred to a special unit in Pittsburgh Prison, where the free time rule didn't apply. A total of forty-eight 'monsters and madmen', as Yarris referred to them in the title of his 2018 book, were squeezed into the special unit, where they were watched over by a handpicked selection of guards who were deemed too violent for lower-security prisons. It was here that Yarris was forced to inhabit a cell next door to the serial killer Gary Heidnik and forced to listen to the grotesque re-enactments of his murders.

The guards in the special unit soon instigated a regime of psychological and physical torture on the inmates. Yarris was targeted particularly badly because one of the guards thought he had stolen a photograph from his work folder. This guard tormented Yarris and ended up crushing his hand in a metal door. Yarris was then transferred out of the Pittsburgh special unit to Greene County supermax. But still things got worse. At Greene County, Yarris discovered he, along with fifteen other inmates, had been infected with the potentially fatal disease hepatitis C. Yarris had been beaten so badly by the guards that he had needed dental work to extract the roots from the teeth that had been broken. Unfortunately, a batch of prisoners had been infected by unclean instruments at the prison dentists.

Yarris listened as three other inmates slowly died of the disease in the cells around him, tormented by the guards the whole time. Not wanting to share their fate, Yarris signed up for chemotherapy to fight the infection, but a mistake in the dosage made the treatment worse than the disease. 'I was getting three injections a week initially,' he told me, 'and taking three giant horse tablets a day with each meal. And then it became six pills a day by accident, and they were giving me six injections a week towards the end. And I went out in the yard one day and I looked up on a beautiful bright sunny day, and I couldn't see a thing.'

The drugs had caused Yarris to go blind. The guards were unsympathetic, thinking it was a bluff to get special treatment, so he was sent back to his cell to stew. He spent the next three days in total blackness before his sight gradually began to return. But Yarris had finally had enough. It was 2002, he had survived twenty years in solitary confinement and finally his will to go on had deserted him. The first thing he did the evening his sight returned was to sit down in front of a bright light and pen what he hoped would be one of his final letters. 'I didn't want to die in agony,' he told me, 'and have them torment me and laugh in my face, and I wasn't going to have a beautiful speech, so I asked to die. I wrote a letter to the federal court and I asked that my lawyers be dismissed and that I be allowed to be executed. I would rather go out like that, as a man.'

The appeal judge who read Yarris's letter summoned Yarris's legal team and asked them why a prisoner who had been asking for DNA testing for fifteen years was now requesting execution. They didn't have a satisfactory answer so the judge decided to act. He demanded that any remaining DNA testing in the case be carried out immediately. The gloves that Dr

Blake had originally refused to test due to possible contamination were now tested in February 2003. They were found to contain the DNA of an unknown man as well as the DNA of the victim. Further DNA from the victim's underwear also matched the DNA of the man found in the gloves. None of the DNA profiles found matched Yarris's own.

The instant he received the news from his lawyer, Yarris realised he was a free man. He immediately called his mum to tell her the good news. But even in his moment of triumph, fate played him a rotten hand. 'I called my mother,' Yarris told me, 'and I said, "Mom, the DNA finally came back proving me innocent, do you hear me?" She's like, "Great, Nicky, that's so wonderful but I can't take this call right now. Your brother Mikey's having a seizure and he's laying on the ground at my feet and I'm waiting for the ambulance. I gotta keep something in his mouth so he doesn't choke to death."'

When the guard came back to collect Yarris from his phone call, he found him huddled up by the phone in the foetal position. The guard escorted Yarris to the shower, put a chair out for him, sat Yarris on the chair and pushed the button to make the water flow. It was the smallest act of kindness but it set something off in the already emotional Yarris. In the duration of the shower, he cried fifteen years' worth of tears.

Despite being proved innocent, Yarris's journey was far from over. He was forced to spend another seven months in solitary confinement, this time on the mental ward where all his possessions, all his precious books, all his little comforts, had been taken from him. He was left with just a plastic milk carton and a bed. When he asked one of the guards why this was being done to him, he received the reply that the prison authorities were worried that he would take revenge on one of the guards for everything they had done to him. With his usual attitude, Yarris decided to see the positive side of the situation. With no clutter or books to distract him, he was free to sit back and dream of the life he was going to live when he got out of prison. It was a dream he'd never dared to entertain before, but now he was free to indulge it at will.

When Yarris's release date finally came around, after he'd spent over twenty-one years behind bars, the authorities managed to botch that too. At 8.30 a.m. on the day of his release, Yarris was told he was free to go. The prison van drove him through the first barrier then up to the second barrier, but there it was stopped and told to go back. His paperwork wasn't ready. He had to wait in an empty room for another five hours before he was eventually let out.

Outside, the press were waiting, alongside his parents and other family and friends, including Jackie. Yarris walked up to the microphone and, in typical style, made not a single comment about his own unfair treatment. Instead, he named two prisoners who were still inside who he believed to be innocent and asked for someone to help fight their cases. Then he turned around and walked away.

One of the first things his mother did after Yarris's release was to sit him down and say something important to him. She told him all the years that he had struggled and suffered would be a waste of time if he didn't now become a really kind man. She asked him to promise her that every day he would try his best to be a polite and kind man, doing his best to help others. The conversation inspired the rest of Yarris's life and became the building block of his philosophy, based on the science of neuroplasticity. Yarris's practice focused on alleviating his own trauma and bypassing his anger issues by focusing on transformative acts of kindness towards others. 'You have a built-in reward system in your brain,' Yarris explained, 'and going out and doing the correct thing of interacting with other people with meticulous politeness actually rewards your brain, to the point you start erasing PTSD. The more you're involved in doing this, the more your brain doesn't have time to be involved with the destructive cycle of negativity.'

Yarris began putting theory into action and soon his life was filled with the practice of kindness in action. But still not everything was plain sailing. The hepatitis C, combined with the chemotherapy and the years of drug abuse, had ruined his liver and he was given only three years to live. He was put on the liver transplant list. His mother refused to wait. She encouraged him to go out every day and exercise until he could hardly go on, then he would come home and she would make him a healthy meal. They stuck to this regime every day until Yarris was back to full health.

With his new healthy body and approach to life, Yarris went out and started to make waves. He used his speaking ability to campaign for several causes, including fighting for other innocent prisoners on death row. His public speaking took him all over the world, including the Colosseum in Rome and the Houses of Parliament in London. He even spoke at the end of each performance of Shakespeare's *Titus Andronicus* at London's Globe Theatre for a whole season. Fusing his philosophy of kindness with the science of neuroplasticity, Yarris came up with a system called the 'Kindness Approach'. He wrote a book about it (titled *The Kindness Approach*) and claims he has saved thousands of people from suicide and addiction using this method. Yarris has written three other books covering different stages of his life, and in 2015, his story became a hit documentary film on Netflix called *The Fear of 13*. In it, he speaks directly to the camera for ninety minutes and the power of his storytelling carries the viewer through the mad rollercoaster of his life.

In 2023, Yarris settled in the UK and he is currently working on a documentary about his friend Alex, who has cancer. When we had dinner together, he told me, 'I am not in any way having any regrets. I think about this – I shouldn't even be here. I shouldn't be sane. I'm so proud of myself that I have never given away my kindness.'

9

Joey Torres

'Shut up, I'll send Joey after you'

The man hears screaming coming from down the corridor and, like all the other inmates, scurries to see what is happening.

Inside the guards' office there is a group of around twenty inmates all staring and shouting at something happening on the floor. He pushes his way through and what he sees makes him reel in disgust. On the floor is a female guard. One of the inmates stands hitting her in the face while another is ripping at her top, exposing her breasts.

He recognises the guard. She is new to the wing, having just one day's experience working on the psychiatric ward at Vacaville Prison, where some of California's most dangerous inmates are housed. The guard was scared because one of the inmates had been acting threateningly towards her. Her sergeant asked the man to keep an eye out for her and now here she is, being beaten and potentially raped.

Without any more thought, he throws himself on one of the men, beating him with his fists. But the big man is so out of it on psychiatric meds he hardly even feels his punches. In desperation, he turns around and looks for a weapon. He sees the guards' heavy landline phone and beats the man around the head with it until, at last, he falls limply to the floor.

The terrified female guard is finally able to find the panic button on her uniform and presses it, alerting the other prison officers. Meanwhile, the man helps pull her clothes together. He picks her up and begins carrying her down the corridor.

Just before the stairs, he sees the guards rushing towards him. They scream and gesticulate wildly. Suddenly he realises what this must look like. He tries to explain what has happened but it's too late. The guards take the now-unconscious officer from him and begin beating him with a wild fervour driven by rage. They throw him down the stairs and beat him so badly, both his knees pop out. Then they throw him in a punishment cell to stew on his bad luck.

Little does he know, but this is just the start of a brutal beating that will last ten hours.

Joey Torres has seen the best and worst of the US prison system. Incarcerated for more than thirty years, he was an amateur boxing champion who killed his manager during an altercation when the man pulled a gun on him. At just nineteen years old, Torres was persuaded to accept a plea deal that would see him incarcerated in a youth detention centre with a guarantee of release when he reached twenty-five years of age. Torres accepted the deal, but the authorities reneged on their end of the bargain and re-sentenced him to a life sentence when he turned twenty-five.

Torres became a co-founder of 18th Street Gang, one of the most notorious gangs in the US and across Central America. As an inmate, he was immersed in violence and brutality, being forced to take part in 'gladiator fights' in which two prisoners were forced to fight for the guards' entertainment under threat of being shot. Torres was so out of control that he was sent to a psychiatric facility where the most dangerous and unstable criminals in California were housed. But it was here that he turned his life around after he saved a female guard from being raped.

Torres went on to face another thirty years in prison, but his journey was transformed from one of violence and brutality to self-improvement and helping others, all while rubbing shoulders with the likes of Charles Manson and Sirhan Sirhan. He finally won his own release in 2017 after almost forty years behind bars. I've interviewed many lifers before, but few have had a rollercoaster ride to match Joey Torres'.

Born in 1960, Torres grew up in Panorama City, then a violent and impoverished area of LA, where gangs ruled the streets and racial tensions routinely led to bloodshed. At school, Torres didn't fit in. His mother was Sicilian and his father Puerto Rican. The white kids didn't accept him because of his Hispanic name and the Hispanic kids didn't like him because he looked white. This left him out in the cold until he reached the age of twelve. That was when he realised that he could fight and when everyone started to accept him.

Torres took up boxing and soon proved himself to be a major upcoming talent. He earned the nickname 'Boxer', an apt name for a boy who had already won two Amateur Athletic Union boxing championships by the age of sixteen. He also honed his fighting skills on the streets when he dropped out of school at fourteen and co-founded a local gang. This gang later became known as '18th Street' because its co-founders, Torres and his crime partner, also known as 'Boxer', lived on 18th Street. The 18th Street gang is now one of the largest in North America, spanning the US, Mexico and much of Central America. Torres puts its popularity down to his and his partner's mixed roots and its original inclusive nature: 'Sicilian and Mexican gangs weren't accepting anybody,' Torres told me, 'but because he was Salvadorian and I was Puerto Rican and Sicilian, we're the only gang in LA that has blacks, Chinese . . . That's why our gang is so big.'

Apart from his gang-affiliated activities, Torres would compete in street fights against anyone – and usually win. 'We'd go to an empty pool,' Torres told me, 'and whoever came out of the empty pool was the winner. My sister would take me, the family would come and they'd bet, and then I'd take on all comers.'

Torres was so confident in his boxing skills that when he heard about a legendary local karate fighter and trainer called Benny 'The Jet' Urquidez, he strode into his gym and challenged him to a fight, claiming that boxing was superior to karate. Torres was soon taught a lesson in the wider world of martial arts. 'He knocked me out in maybe the first minute,' Torres told me, 'with a spinning back kick, his trademark.'

Despite his humiliating defeat, Torres rose from the floor and asked Urquidez if he thought he had fallen with style. Urquidez liked the young kid's spirit and offered to train him in karate. Torres accepted and was soon excelling at this new system. Urquidez would put him in the ring with older fighters to try and knock some of the arrogance out of the young boy, but the trouble was, more often than not, Torres would win.

It wasn't just local street fights that Torres was soon engaged in. Through his mother, he was related to the Genovese crime family from New York and he remembers regular trips to the Big Apple to visit his uncle, Frank Genovese. Some of his most formative childhood memories involve these ties to the Italian Mafia. 'I remember 1973, being thirteen years old,' Torres told me. 'Me and my brother driving to Chino Prison to pick up Jimmy "the Weasel" Fratianno, who took me straight to the gym with Ruggiero Russo and Billy Bonanno, and he's trying to show me how to throw a left hook.'

Torres' older brother, Luigi, worked for the Bonanno crime family via two local club owners and gangsters, the Sika brothers, who ran the show for the Bonannos in LA. Luigi owned a pizza parlour, from where he based his hustles, until he was arrested in possession of an oil tanker full of marijuana and imprisoned in Arizona. Torres would collect debts for his older brother, a role his fighting abilities aptly suited him for: 'Frank and Joe [Sika] would tell Luigi, "Hey, send your brother,"' Torres told me. 'And I'd go do what I got to do, and they blessed me with a lot of money, a lot of money for a kid.'

Through Luigi, Torres got to work for gangsters, including Jimmy 'The Weasel' Fratianno, one of the Mob bosses who ran the Los Angeles crime family. Fratianno had been a boxer and he would spar with Torres and pay him to stand outside and whistle if the Feds turned up. Another was Jimmy 'Mac' McElroy, also known as 'The Meat Wagon'. Jimmy Mac was a member of the 'Westies' Irish gang but he would also carry out hits for the Italian Mob. He earned his moniker 'The Meat Wagon' because of the van he drove around in, full of corpses and body parts.

The respect Torres got from these legendary Mafia figures gave him the sense of pride and acceptance he had always craved and led to him at a young age being part of scenes that could have come from *The Godfather* movie itself. 'Russo had a salvage yard in Hayward, California,' Torres told me, 'and it was Jimmy, all his boys, my brother, Louie, Russo, Bill Bonanno and Joe Bonanno, and we're all in the salvage yard, talking shit to each other, and they're all saying, "Shut up, I'll send Joey after you." But when you're growing up with those people at the time and you're a kid, it was living the life.'

Meanwhile, Torres' fights in the ring were drawing increasing attention. He soon caught the eye of a man called José Ramirez, who was always on the lookout for the next up-and-coming talent. Ramirez took Torres under his wing and promised he would make him a world champion if Torres stuck with him. With Ramirez as his manager, Torres started making some good money from his fights, but he also picked up some bad habits from the man he looked up to. One day, when Torres was boxing with a broken nose, Ramirez offered him some cocaine. Torres tried it and found that it numbed the pain in his nose completely. But the feeling of invincibility was addictive. He continued to use the drug in all his fights because he could take any punch thrown at him without feeling the pain. The drug also made him arrogant and his manner became so cocky, the crowds would often boo him. But Torres had a right to be cocky: by the time he was incarcerated, he had an amateur boxing record of 103 wins, just two defeats and seventy-six knockouts.

Cocaine also made its way into Torres' social life. He would go out partying and stay up for three or four nights in a row. He was just sixteen years of age. But despite his youth, the partying soon began to take its toll. He would turn up to fights drunk and high and began to lose his edge. He got knocked out in one fight and soon his career began to nose-dive. To add insult to injury, Torres found out that Ramirez had been spending the winnings from the fights that he was supposed to be saving for Torres, who had a confrontation with Ramirez in his office.

As the argument got heated, Ramirez opened a drawer on his desk and Torres saw a gun. According to Torres' version of events, Ramirez picked up the gun. Torres grabbed his manager by the arms and smashed him back against the wall. Torres heard the gun go off. He let go of Ramirez and the older man slumped to the floor. Torres got scared and ran out of the office. It wasn't until later that he received news that his manager was dead. Although the shot had fired into Ramirez's shoulder, the bullet had ricocheted through his body, killing him.

Even though there was no evidence to tie Torres to the murder, his attorney advised him to accept a plea deal which would see him incarcerated in a youth detention facility for six years, after which he would be released. Torres was nineteen years old at the time, he would only be twenty-five when he was released. He figured it would be a good opportunity to get off cocaine and get his life back on track, so agreed to the plea deal and pleaded guilty to first-degree murder.

But once inside, Torres' life didn't turn around. Instead, he got involved in the incessant gang warfare that wracked California's youth detention system. He was gang-affiliated and his gang was at war. He was expected to do his part. His life became one long round of doling out violence and trying to avoid it being inflicted upon him. 'When you go to bed at night and you hear "shhhhh" on the floor,' Torres told me, 'and you know they're sharpening knives and you don't know if it's coming for you, and when you have to live with that every day, it's unimaginable. It's very taxing on one's soul.'

He was sent to Preston, a youth correctional facility in northern California, where the most violent juveniles were detained. After stabbing someone in the dining hall, he spent a year in the so-called 'Dungeon' but, again, this was nothing more than a gladiator school that inured him even further to violence and brutality.

In 1982, when he was just twenty-two years old and still serving time in youth detention, Torres made a mistake that would change his life forever. His girlfriend had been telling him how scared she was about the neighbourhood she was living in, so he wrote her a letter instructing her to buy a gun. The prisoners' mail was routinely read by the guards and after they saw the line about the gun, Torres was sent back to court where, without a trial, a judge re-sentenced him. 'The judge refused to withdraw the plea bargain,' Torres told me. 'He said, "You pled guilty to murder one, that's what I'm sentencing you to." He resentenced me to twenty-five to life.'

Torres was just eight months away from his release date at the time. He was on work release, travelling to the Port of Stockton each day to work as a bus boy at the local Denny's restaurant, planning for his future: he was going to resurrect his boxing career and still felt he had a shot at a world title. When he heard the sentence, all his hopes and dreams collapsed around his ears. 'The gavel hit and he said twenty-five to life,' Torres told me. 'My knees went like I got hit with a left hook right on the button and I couldn't even move. Time seemed to stay. The clock seemed to freeze. It's just like life stood still for that moment.'

Torres was sent back behind bars, but this time not to a youth detention facility but an adult prison in Chino. Because of his gang affiliations he was immediately put on lockdown and kept on strict watch. But that didn't stop him getting into trouble. He met a man called 'Gypsy' who, at the time, was high up in the Hells Angels. Torres made an alliance with Gypsy and was soon, as he puts it, 'taking care of business'. 'The honest way to put it,' he told me, 'is if you wanted somebody taken care of, you gave me a call. I was that guy. I'm embarrassed and ashamed of it but at that time it was either you did that or you were the victim.'

In 1984, Torres was transferred to Tracy, another tough prison then known as 'Gladiator School'. At Tracy, he was involved in a gang murder. He continued to get his hands on cocaine while inside and with his drug intake and violence, he was soon deemed so out of control he was sent to a psychiatric ward in Vacaville, where some of the most dangerous inmates in California were housed, including the infamous Charles Manson. Torres was diagnosed with Organic Brain syndrome, which caused chronic impairment of mood and behaviour, brought on by all the blows he had received to his head as a teenage boxer. He was classified by the prison authorities as 'volatile'.

That didn't stop him from fighting, of course. At the time, the California Department of Corrections hosted an inter-prison boxing competition which drew a lot of attention. As an ex-amateur champion, he was much sought after by the prisons and now he was fighting for Vacaville. He was in training for a fight when one of the guards asked him to keep an eye on a new female prison officer who was undergoing her first week on the job. Apparently, the guard had already got spooked over the threatening behaviour of one of the inmates. Torres agreed to look out for the guard, then went off for his fight. He won the ten-round match and returned to prison in the early evening, sporting a swollen eye.

Torres introduced himself to the female guard and she told him that she felt uncomfortable because two of the inmates had been continually staring and flashing their penises at her. Joey asked if she had told her sergeant about it. She said she had and the guard had spoken to the men but their behaviour was still intimidating. Torres tried to reassure her, then went for a shower. What happened next was the incident that changed his life.

'In the middle of the shower, I hear the screams,' Torres told me. 'I ran out of the shower and Charlie [Manson] has got his hands up and telling me do something about it. I just went in and extended round ten and picked up the phone. Back then there were phones that weighed about twenty, thirty pounds . . . and I proceeded to beat him with the phone handle and knocked them both out. In her pocket was her alarm. I hit the alarm. The bells went off. She was about a hundred pounds, a little girl. I carried her to the door, closed it to keep everybody inside and then I saw them running up the stairs at me and before I could say anything, they just proceeded to beat me because they thought I was the one who did it to her.'

The guards threw Torres down the stairs. His knees got caught between the steps and both knees were popped out, later requiring a double-knee replacement operation. In agony, he was hauled to a punishment cell, where he was regularly beaten for the next ten hours. 'They beat me so much and kicked me so much that it didn't hurt anymore,' he told me. 'It was just the thud and after a while I just accepted the punishment I was getting. I had never been beat that vicious.'

In the meantime, the female guard was in a semi-conscious state, unable to communicate. It wasn't until the early hours of the next morning that the guards found out the truth. They took Torres from the punishment cell and sent him to the infirmary, where he spent two months recuperating and receiving his knee operations. When he had recovered enough to be returned to the prison population, the guards said he needed to be housed in the hole for his own protection. By fighting on the side of a guard – never mind that she was a female about to be raped – Torres had broken the prisoner code and his life would now be forfeit. He spent a year in the hole, where the conditions finally got to him. He demanded to be transferred out. 'I refused protective custody,' Torres told me. 'I'm not a rat, I'm not a child molester, I'm a grown-ass man and if I have to pay the price for saving the life of an officer then I'll die on the mainline.'

He was transferred to California Men's Colony (CMC) in San Luis Obispo. In the cell opposite was Larry Singleton, a psychopath who had raped a fifteen-year-old girl, then chopped off both her arms and left her in a ditch to die. The girl went on to survive and was awarded two and a half million dollars in compensation. One day, when Torres confronted Singleton with his crime and mentioned the money his victim had been awarded, Singleton's response was chilling. 'He was rolling a cigarette,' Torres told me, 'and he looked up to me and said, "Yeah, but the bitch can't count it."' Singleton was coming up for parole while Torres was at CMC, but Torres and some other inmates managed to attack him a week before his parole was due, injuring him badly but not managing to kill him.

In CMC, Torres had to fight every day because of his reputation for standing up for a guard. Luckily, three of the main shot-callers at CMC were understanding men who gave Torres a certain amount of protection, calling off their own gang members. One of these was Lyle Hood, a shot-caller from the Aryan Brotherhood, another was Donald 'Big D' Garcia from the Mexican Mafia and the third was Rick Stevens, a former singer and shot-caller for the Black Guerrilla Family (BGF). But despite being off limits from gang reprisals, Torres still had to deal with lower-level violence from the non-affiliated prison population.

His 'crime' of protecting the female guard caught up with him when one of the female guard's attackers, known as 'TM', was transferred to CMC. One day, Torres was coming out of the gym while training for a boxing match. He was just passing through the turnstile outside the gym when one of TM's cronies came up from behind him and hit him over the back of the head with a metal weights bar. At the same time another man approached from the front and stabbed him in the neck with a knife forged from a welding rod. Torres pulled the knife from his neck and fought the two men until he blacked out and fell to the ground, unconscious.

He was taken to the hospital in a coma. A steel plate was fitted into the back of his skull to repair the damage caused and he needed surgery on his vocal cords where the welding rod had partially severed them. He woke up after a week in hospital and spent another two weeks in care before being transferred back to the prison with only some aspirin to keep the pain at bay. Stronger medication would be too sought after by the rest of the prison population seeking to get high.

Back in prison, Torres was transferred to the hole again for his own protection. It seemed doubly unfair to him that he was having to suffer punishment as well as daily attacks for saving a woman from being raped. That's when another inmate advised him to file a writ stating that he had saved the life of a correctional officer and demanded an appeal. The appeal was granted and an investigation was launched. This was in 1986 and only then was it discovered that the female guard had written a report about the original incident, praising and thanking Torres for his role in saving her. The report had never been placed in his file. Now the female officer wrote an affidavit in support of Torres and his appeal was successful.

The California Department of Corrections was now in a predicament. Torres had grounds to sue them for a lot of money. Instead, they offered to transfer him to any prison in the country. 'I chose Jean, Nevada,' Torres told me, 'because they had a golf course. I went from maximum prison to playing golf.'

It was in Nevada that Torres' life changed around. Compared to Californian jails, Jean was like a five-star hotel. 'There was a nice bed, TV, real porcelain toilet, wall-to-wall carpeting,' he told me. 'Every night at six the donut truck came in – newspapers, donuts, you want to go do eight holes on the golf course?'

On top of the luxury, his reputation as someone who had saved a guard's life preceded him and he was treated like a king by the staff, who gave him all sorts of privileges. This was the kind of acceptance he had always craved. He gave up drugs and used his newfound freedom to set up a charity, Boxers Against Drugs (BAD). Through his activities, he received a visit from former welterweight boxing world champion, Carlos Palomino, and the two became firm friends. Torres began giving anti-drugs talks to groups of schoolchildren, which he would do from a line in the warden's office, a process which he said truly turned his life around. Through his charity he started to raise funds to give some of these kids special experiences, like paying for 200 inner-city children to visit the Magic Mountain theme park.

Torres was still only twenty-six years old. He started training again and got back into boxing. He also began promoting boxing matches and selling boxing memorabilia. He got famous boxers to visit the prison, including Ray 'Boom Boom' Mancini, Ruben Castillo, Sugar Ray Leonard and Muhammad Ali. Torres even got Ali to visit his mother when she was dying of cancer. 'Ali takes my mother to the hotel room,' Torres told me, 'and he's showing her magic tricks because he loved magic, and my mother starts crying. She dies a week later, but Ali stood in my life for all those years. He was a great man.'

Through BAD, other sports stars started to join the fold, such as baseball players Darryl Strawberry, Eric Davis and Paul Molitor. With so many famous sporting names in his address book, Torres decided to start making some business deals of his own, hooking players up with sponsors and other side hustles. 'I had the top athletes in the world coming to the prison to see me and asking me to represent them,' he told me. 'I told them, I can make you a million dollars if you can make me a million . . . So then I started contacting Mercedes-Benz. You're a player, you're playing in Cincinnati. Mercedes-Benz will give you and your wife two Mercedes, give you $250,000 a year to promote Mercedes. I'd get my finder's fee, five-ten thousand, and then I'd move on to do the next deal – baseball card deals, memorabilia deals, and it got to the point where I needed to find places to put the money because I was making so much in prison.'

Torres was earning so much, he was giving tens of thousands of dollars to people outside of prison to hold for him and then forgetting he'd even given it to them. With all this wheeling and dealing on top of his charity and fundraising work, he was racking up a phone bill of $3,000 a month in the 1980s. He even got into the music business, paying for an up-and-coming LA rapper to record a song in a top recording studio. He helped organise a live event called 'Rapper Mania', where rappers from LA performed a concert that was broadcast live around the country. TV sports and news shows became interested in him and several pieces were aired about his life story.

Torres was unstoppable. His next move was to set up a radio sports chat show, where he would chew the cud with some of his famous friends and which was broadcast on an Albuquerque radio station. 'They gave me an hour between six and seven every evening,' he told me, 'and I would bring on my celebrity friends and I'd do it from the prison phone, three-way all over the world.'

All this was only possible with the permission of the prison authorities of course, which he had twisted around his little finger. In fact, many of the guards were working for him and would periodically drop by his cell to check if there was anything he needed. 'I had the guards that I would send five grand to their house,' he told me, 'and every day I wake up to go to the yard and come back to a bottle of vodka under my pillow, or the Rolex I wanted to wear, or my pinky rings. I paid the guards to do what I wanted.'

But in the midst of all this success there was sadness too. His mother was dying of cancer then and the end was near. Torres, who was now used to getting his own way, decided to call the director of the CDC to ask if he could be released for the day to see her. At the time of his call to the director, he had Carlos Palomino on hold on the same call. When the CDC head found out about this, he asked Torres to hang up while he spoke to Palomino privately. When the conversation was done, Torres received the news that he'd been granted a day's release to visit his mother in LA, an unprecedented step for a convicted murderer in California.

Torres also used his contacts to help his father, who was also dying of cancer. He got a boxing promoter he knew well to arrange for his dad to have a ringside seat at George Foreman's comeback fight, as well as getting him a seat on the bench for an LA Dodgers baseball game. 'I showed my father at the end who I really was,' he told me, 'so I'll never have no fear because my mother and father passed on knowing that they had a good boy.'

The same sports stars who worked with Torres on his fund-raising and business projects also began campaigning for his release. But it soon became apparent that only Torres himself would be able to do that. On top of all his other work, he had been busy schooling himself in law so that he could find a legal way out of prison. Someone pointed out that the law books he was reading weren't applicable to California law, being out of state. The only way he was going to gain access to the material he needed to fight his case was by asking for a transfer back to a California prison. He knew what that would entail: his life of luxury, leisure and business affairs would be over, traded in for one of discomfort, privation and constant danger. Still, he made the decision to go back – if it was the only way to win his freedom, he was willing to do anything.

Although he was prepared for the move back to California, even he couldn't have known what he was letting himself in for. He was transferred to Corcoran, a closed prison where all inmates were kept in constant lockdown conditions, shut in their cells for twenty-three hours a day. It was the early nineties and Corcoran had an infamous warden, George Smith, who had implemented a brutal regime. Under Smith's watch, prisoners were being shot and killed in alarming numbers.

Smith's regime also included 'Gladiator Days', where prisoners would be paired off to fight against each other while the guards watched and took bets on the outcome. The fights were treated as real entertainment events in which all the staff would gather around the prison yard, eating pizza and swigging pop. Torres, being a renowned boxer, was of course fair game for these fights, especially as the guards knew he could win them some money. There was no option not to partake. Some prisoners were shot dead for refusing, others faced an even more horrific punishment – the 'Booty Bandit'. 'If the cops didn't like you,' Torres told me, 'they would send this six-five, three-hundred-pound black man into your cell.'

Torres fought in two of the gladiator fights before a sympathetic lieutenant extricated him by giving him a job as his office clerk. This was a definite step up, but it also gave Torres a behind-the-scenes insight into the institutionalised brutality and corruption at Corcoran. It was Torres' duty to write up all the incident reports, which included all the fake notes that were used to cover guards' brutality, including beatings, shootings and even murders. An even more sinister phenomenon was the creeping ambulance that Torres and the lieutenant would walk alongside towards the yard. 'When I would get off work or they knew something was happening,' Torres told me, 'me and the lieutenant and the nurse and the doctor and an ambulance would slowly go across the yard, and before we even got to the unit, you would hear the gunfire. They knew ahead of time that they were going to kill somebody.'

Then, of course, there were the gangs, not least of which was the guards' own called 'The Sharks', due to the shark tattoos they sported. Some of these guards had it in for Torres because of his reputation and rank as a high-profile prisoner. That meant he had a target on his back. 'I've had situations where they would open my cell door,' he told me, 'and orchestrate a fight in front of my cell, just so they could shoot under the pretence that they were quelling the disturbance in front.'

It was while he was at Corcoran that Torres' father died. Warden Smith refused to let him out to attend the funeral, even though the Director of Corrections in Sacramento, James Gomez, had approved it. Much to Smith's chagrin, Torres managed to use his influence to go over the man's head. 'Jim Gomez said, "Fuck you," and sent five cars on the yard to come right to the unit and take me,' he told me, 'and as soon as I left the facility, they parked, took all the chains off me and said, "We don't know who you know or who the fuck you are, but damn."'

The brutality at Corcoran eventually came to a head with the murder of Preston Tate, who was shot by the guards supposedly for being involved in a violent incident but, according to Torres, was set up by the guards, who wanted revenge after Tate had lost a fight they had bet a lot of money on. Tate's shooting was a murder too far. It gathered publicity and soon there was a *60 Minutes* programme on CBS, investigating the incident. The FBI was called in.

But Torres had different battles to fight. If he was going to free himself, he needed to start researching California law to look for a loophole that could get him out. The problem was he was still acting like the old 'Boxer' from 18th Street and tackling the authorities head-on. It was a fellow lifer who changed Torres' path and put him on the right track. Michael Thompson (who we met in Chapter 2) was a former Aryan Brotherhood leader. He was a big, six-foot-four, well-built man with long blond hair and a beard. But as well as being incredibly tough, Thompson was intelligent and articulate, and he understood the system. He told Torres to stop fighting it like a boxer, head-on, and instead to beat them at their own game. He reminded him that he was not that guy anymore and pointed out how intelligent he was. Torres learned a lot from Thompson and credits him as 'Seventy per cent the reason why I'm here today.'

Under Thompson's guidance, Torres started fighting the prison authorities using legal arguments and loopholes. When it transpired that Torres and several other inmates had caught hepatitis C from sharing tattoo needles, the authorities wouldn't give the prisoners the drug they needed to fight the disease. With Thompson's help, Torres filed a legal appeal and it was successful. Torres obtained the correct drug for all the infected prisoners. It was his first taste of what the law could do, even in the hands of a lowly prisoner.

Another influential figure in Torres' development was Sirhan Sirhan, the infamous man convicted of killing Robert

Kennedy. Sirhan was a quiet and intelligent man who kept himself to himself, but he saw something in Torres beyond the brash gangbanger and tried to help coax it out. Sirhan helped improve Torres' vocabulary by giving him a new word each day. The next morning, stopping by Sirhan's cell, Torres would have to provide three sentences illustrating the meaning of the word. 'Sirhan was my mentor,' Torres told me. 'He told me that I was intelligent and I should stay away from the gangs and start educating myself.' Interestingly, Sirhan always maintained his innocence over the Kennedy assassination, pointing out that the gun he supposedly used to kill Kennedy wasn't actually his.

With Thompson and Sirhan's encouragement, Torres began spending a large portion of his days in the law library, reading up on case law, trying to find a loophole that would secure his release. To fund his legal work, he was selling pornographic pictures to fellow inmates that he'd had smuggled in by various girlfriends on the outside. With his studies amply funded, he would stay up late at night studying law books he had taken from the library. It was on one of these late lonely nights in his cell, at 3 a.m., that he finally made the discovery he had been looking for. 'I found this writ, 38th page of the Federal Reporter from 1943,' he told me. 'A writ of *coram nobis*. It's a United States law that says at any time during your sentence, if an error was made that wasn't the fault of you or the court, you could file back to your remaining court for a remedy. I went crazy, I knew I was going home.'

But it wasn't to be quite that simple. Torres filed his appeal no fewer than eighteen times before it was finally accepted. Fortunately for him, there was no limit to the amount of times such an appeal could be filed, so he just kept on going. His lucky break came when a bored judge was looking for something to read during his lunch break. Scanning through the files on his desk, he picked the shortest one, which was just six pages long, and it happened to be Torres'. The judge agreed with what he read and ruled that Torres' sentence should be vacated, meaning that he would go free, despite the district attorney's vehement protests.

When Torres found out the good news, it was 3 a.m. on 13 September 2001, just two days after 9/11. A few months and several legal wrangles later, he was allowed to be released, but only if he could post bail of $100,000. He made some calls to a few of his famous friends and Paul Molitor came through for him, not only posting his bail but also buying him a $20,000 car.

When Torres was released from prison twenty-four years after his incarceration, he was giddy with happiness and relief. Little details of the real world kept shocking him, like how heavy a proper knife and fork felt after two decades of using plastic cutlery.

Immediately after his release, he lived in a Holiday Inn in Beverly Hills, then went to stay with his sister in Santa Clarita for a while. He soon received the news that the DA was appealing his release, but for a while nothing could touch him – he was enjoying his freedom too much. He would enjoy it even more when he was made an offer to go to Las Vegas to stage a series of five comeback fights for a quarter of a million dollars. In his forties now and out of shape, he was told not to bother training, as all his fights would be fixed. The deal was through a boxing promotion organisation which operated out of Vegas. This organisation had some shady practices, such as bringing in Mexican fighters with poor records, then changing those records to look good so that the fighters they really wanted to promote could get lots of easy wins under their belts. In this way, the promoters could build up fighters

258

for a title shot, which would make the boxer – and them – a lot of money.

Torres did some work promoting fights for this organisation and was appalled at some of the fighters he saw used as fodder for the guys they were promoting. 'I was in Austin, Texas, for a fight,' he told me, 'and I would bring the opponents to the corner. I would bring the opponents, some poor kid that had duct tape and somebody else's name on his trunks – taxi drivers, they're in there for five hundred dollars. And after a while it got to the point where I would tell the people in the audience, "What round you want them to go down in? What round? Two? Okay, you buy me a beer."'

Torres was waiting for his big comeback, enjoying the swimming pool in a San Diego hotel, when he was approached by two men wearing garish Hawaiian shirts and looking so out of place, they could only be FBI agents. They said they had an offer for him: they were investigating fixed boxing matches and they were operating under the authorisation of Senator John McCain, who was trying to pass a bill against fight fixing. The agents said they knew about the DA's appeal to get Torres re-imprisoned. They told him they could make the appeal disappear if he helped them; they offered him $10,000 a month to work undercover to expose fight fixing in Vegas. He said he would think about it and took their card.

In Vegas, he contacted the FBI agents and was put in touch with an agent called 'Big' Frankie Manzione, a now-legendary undercover agent who had helped bring down the Gambino crime family. Torres agreed to work for the FBI and started to receive his $10,000-a-month salary, which he spent mostly on cars, women and cocaine. Freedom had gone to his head. But Torres maintains that he never ratted on anyone during his time working with the FBI. 'I never told on anyone,' he told me. 'Let me reiterate that to this day, as I sit here, no one has ever been arrested or charged with anything. I played the FBI like a violin.'

Meanwhile, the time for Torres' first comeback fight came around. He spent the night before the event in a hotel room rehearsing how his opponent would go down, but turned up to the fight drunk and high on cocaine. He went down heavily in the first round but miraculously came back to knock out his opponent later in the match. Some people in the crowd were shouting 'fix'. If only they knew . . .

With his comeback in full swing and his undercover FBI money rolling in, Torres was living the high life. 'For two years we ran Vegas,' he told me, referring to him and Big Frankie Manzione. 'There wasn't a casino we couldn't go in, there wasn't a club we couldn't get in. Frankie and the FBI had set up a company called YGJ, "You're Going to Jail", and nobody knew what it stood for, but me and Frankie knew what it meant. And we did fights, that's what we did.'

He told Torres that the FBI had no intention of helping him beat the DA's appeal, so Torres was well aware that he was living on borrowed time before he was re-imprisoned. Torres managed to take the FBI for a total of $1 million before he was arrested again. He claims he even made the Las Vegas gangster Hall of Fame for his two years of running wild in the city. The FBI later dropped its investigation into the promoter.

On top of the high life in Vegas, he was flying to Costa Rica regularly, where he knew a member of the Gambino crime family, who ran an international gambling operation out of the Central American country. Torres would take the information about the promoter's upcoming fixed fights to him and both of them would make money on the bets. The DA was furious that Torres was able to leave the country whenever he chose and tried to get his passport removed, but the judge ruled in Torres' favour. Torres could, of course, have fled the country at any time, especially as he knew he would be going back to jail at some point. But he owed his friend Paul Molitor $100,000 and wasn't about to run away on that kind of debt.

The inevitable happened in 2004, just two years after his release. Torres was in his hotel room at the MGM Grand awaiting an Oscar De La Hoya fight when the phone rang. As he picked up the phone, a group of armed FBI men burst into the room and arrested him. His bail had been revoked and he was returned to prison. He still held out half a hope that in court, he would see someone from the FBI, but not one turned up – he was on his own. The judge told him he would be re-sentenced for his original crime, a new sentence of twenty-five to life without any consideration of the twenty-four years he had already served. Part of the DA's case against him were statements taken from his parents, saying that he was a compulsive liar who couldn't be trusted to tell you the correct day of the week. Torres tried to point out that his parents had been dead for nearly twenty years but it didn't seem to matter: everyone in court seemed determined to send him down.

He was devastated. His life, it seemed, was over. And to add insult to injury, he was given a new prisoner number which meant any inmates who didn't already know him would assume he was a newcomer, or 'fish' in prison slang, and treat him accordingly.

Fortunately, he had one bit of luck. The head of the prison, Warden Sallas, remembered Torres from his early days in Tracy in the mid-eighties. In those days, the warden had been a guard and Torres had invited him to take off his badge and step into his cell to fight out their differences man to man. Sallas had agreed and received a sound beating. Warden Sallas was old school and respected Torres as a straight-up guy. He agreed to try and get Torres his old prisoner number back.

After a while Torres decided to give up feeling sorry for himself and go back to doing the only thing he knew how to do – fight. 'No matter what you're going through,' he told me, 'if you do not put your foot down and say this is enough, I'm gonna fight the fight, then you're going to stay in a cell forever. I've left many men back there that are going to die in there because they didn't have the fortitude or the balls to fight like I fought. If you know that it's right and you're right, then fight the fight at all costs.'

Torres went back to the law library and started researching again, looking for new ways to secure his release. By now he had a bachelor's degree in law and was doing legal work for fellow inmates, such as immigration and divorce cases. 'The guys would be getting deported to Mexico and they didn't want to go,' he told me, 'so I filed a writ to the court saying that their life would be in jeopardy and using the constitutional law to substantiate why they should be given a ninety-day hearing and not transferred out of the country, and for that, it would be three hundred dollars.'

One day, another inmate was moved into Torres' cell and offered him $500 to work on his case. Torres started reading the man's file and saw that he had received a 200-year sentence for repeatedly molesting his stepdaughter over a period of five years. He tried to hold himself together but one particular detail drove him over the edge: 'There was so much scar tissue that they couldn't tell how long she had been molested,' Torres told me, 'and when I read that, I pulled him off the top bunk and proceeded to . . . He was my rag doll till the next morning – I did things to him that no man should have done to him.'

After that, he was given single-cell status to protect other sex offenders from him. Throughout his prison career, Torres had been a prolific beater of sex offenders – a total of twenty-seven, which, he says with pride, he thinks should be added to his boxing tally.

Warden Sallas stayed true to his word and helped Torres in his legal fight, getting his counsellor to contact all kinds of officials, including the attorney general, to point out the unfairness of Torres' sentence. In 2009, this bore some fruit when his case was taken to the appeal court. However, the judge dismissed his appeal out of hand and re-emphasised that his new sentence started in 2004.

It took ten years for Torres to have his original prison number returned and his years served recognised. This was a starting point. From there, he launched a specific kind of appeal called an 'Order to Show Cause' to try and secure his release. An Order to Show Cause requires one or more parties in a case to prove or justify something to the court. In his case, it was to force the state to justify the legitimacy of re-sentencing him to life in 2004. In 2017, this eventually bore fruit when the appeal was granted and the California Supreme Court ordered the CDC's parole board to release Torres. When he appeared before the parole board, it was to face good news, but it still wasn't necessarily the end of his incarceration.

'What Governor Jerry Brown did in the state of California was, he brought in ex-captains, lieutenants,' Torres told me. 'And I went in front of them, and I loved it when they didn't say "Joey", when they said "Boxer". I remember: "You, Boxer, you shouldn't be here. We're granting your parole. But now it's up to the governor in ninety days to either grant it or deny it."'

They were the longest days of Torres' life, but fortunately for him, the Governor of California, Jerry Brown, granted his parole and for the second time, he was free. He was overjoyed with his release. But the thirty-plus years behind bars had left their mark. Torres was diagnosed shortly after his release with PTSD from the many traumatic events that he had experienced in jail. On the positive side though, this diagnosis meant that he received a monthly benefit payment from the state of California and that the state also paid his rent.

Living back in LA now, Torres' life has gone full circle. He lives in a run-down neighbourhood where violence is endemic, where gangs rule and shootings are an almost daily occurrence. 'When you hear gunfire every day,' he told me, 'and you're so used to it that your wife says, "Oh, that's a 45." And I go, "No, that's an AK-47." So, we make comments on the gunfire that we hear and then we look on TV to find out who died. That's the life I lead.'

But Joey Torres is still a fighter. His fight nowadays is to educate children about the dangers of drugs, gangs and violence. In 2023, Torres told his story on my podcast for the first time since his release and hopes his message will spread far and wide, helping children to make better choices than he did.

'I'm haunted,' Torres told me. 'I'm haunted by the men that I hurt. I'm haunted at the destruction I caused. And at the end of the day, I am only trying to better myself, that's all I can do, and give something back. Let my story be a story that someone can grow from.'

Afterword

I hope that I've left you, the reader, with a unique insight into the workings of the homicidal mind. Most often, we judge people on appearance or by our own standards. Yet there are people who, on the surface, may appear normal, but when they see red there are no limits to what they are capable of. Having lived with and interviewed so many killers, I always try to remain polite and cautious when dealing with situations with strangers. When I lived in Arizona, the news would periodically report road-rage murders, many of which I'm sure could have been avoided if people better understood the rage of potential killers, especially those with hair-pin triggers.

Re-reading the interviews included in this book, I was particularly fascinated by the back stories and contributory factors that led to the crimes committed, like Two Tonys being whipped and tortured by his parents. Exploring the minds of killers hopefully enables us to reflect on the different routes that lead to crime and prison. The recurring theme of childhood trauma should motivate society to better protect our kids to address this important root cause.

The USA seems to be harder on crime than the UK, and the UK homicide rate is approximately one-sixth of the USA's rate. Two Tonys told me that the death penalty wasn't a deterrent because killers like him assume that they won't get caught.

265

I was aware of people entering the brutal American prison system for lesser crimes and becoming murderers inside in order to survive gang warfare, or sexual assault. It seems the system breeds harder criminals and, in some circumstances, murder is respected and rewarded – an observation that allows me to bring you one final horror story.

In the maximum-security Madison Street jail in 2004, my cellmate Squeegee told me about Arizona's most dangerous prisoner, Bonzai, who became a killer inside.

'Throughout the jail, I've heard so many people talk about Bonzai,' I said. 'Is he the bogeyman of the Arizona prison system or what?'

'I served time with Bonzai at Florence,' Squeegee said.

'You knew him?'

'Yeah. Robert Wayne Vickers.'

'What's his story?'

'He was just some tall skinny kid arrested for doing burglaries in Tempe. He was only sentenced to do a few years. He came in in the late seventies. He was real quiet, not considered a threat at all, so they housed him with the general population at CB4, all two-man cells. He snapped 'cause his celly drank his Kool-Aid and didn't wake him up for chow. He waited for his celly to go sleep and killed him with a shank made from a toothbrush. He carved the word Bonzai on his celly's back. To show the guards his celly was really dead, he put a cigarette out on the corpse's foot. After that they called him Bonzai or Bonzai Bob.

'They charged him with murder and moved him to a single cell in CB6 – super-max housing for death row, gang leaders and the most violent prisoners. In CB6 they were locked down all day except to come out for showers. They said you couldn't escape from it but Bonzai managed to get on the roof.

'Another time, he picked his cell-door lock, waited for one of his neighbours to come out for a shower, came out and almost shanked the guy to death, but the guards stopped it. So he got attempted-murder charges for that one.

'Back then, the cells had power outlets, and you could heat up food in your cell, like plug-in hotpots from the store. In '82, Bonzai boiled up some hair gel and took it with him when they let him out of his cell. He told his neighbour to come to the front of the cell and threw it on him. He used toilet paper to set him on fire. His neighbour died and a bunch more nearly died from the smoke.'

'Why'd he kill that guy?'

'He'd talked some shit about Bonzai's niece. They transported him to Florence for a court appearance. In the holding cell, he picked the lock on his handcuffs, but made it look like he was still cuffed when they took him into the courtroom. He waited for the judge to start, then jumped up and attacked the people in the gallery. It was on the news. When the guards were about to cuff him for another court appearance, he pulled out a shank and stabbed one in the stomach and the other in the shoulder and armpit. He was so dangerous, the warden had a shower installed in Bonzai's cell and had the door welded shut. They considered him the most dangerous inmate ever in Arizona. In '99, they finally let him out of his cell – to give him a lethal injection. The guards said in his last years his crazy eyes made him look like he was possessed by the devil.'

My hope is that this book is not only a cautionary tale for us, but also for governments, too, when it comes to the policies they choose for their institutions. When politicians are posing for tough-on-crime soundbites to gain votes, they might want to consider the mindset of the prisoners due to be released – who could one day be any of our neighbours.

Acknowledgements

A huge thanks to our podcast team: James Esposito of Underground Films, Joe Adams of Audio Avalanche, Jen Hopkins of Gadfly Media, David James Wood and James Power at Material Studios in Liverpool, Liam Galvin of Liam Galvin Film and Freddie of Spiral Studios in Guildford.

Thanks to Lee Williams for the extra research and editing, and to Derick Attwood for proofreading.

Thanks to Sarah, Beth and the team at Orion.

Acknowledgements

Credits

Seven Dials would like to thank everyone at Orion who worked on the publication of *Sitdowns with Serial Killers & Murderers*.

Agent
Robert Kirby

Editor
Beth Eynon

Copy-editor
Jane Donovan

Proofreader
Clare Wallis

Editorial Management
Sarah Fortune
Kayleigh McKnight
Jane Hughes
Charlie Panayiotou
Lucy Bilton
Patrice Nelson

Audio
Paul Stark
Louise Richardson
Georgina Cutler-Ross

Contracts
Rachel Monte
Ellie Bowker
Tabitha Gresty

Design
Tomás Almeida
Nick Shah
Deborah Francois
Helen Ewing

Photo Shoots & Image Research
Natalie Dawkins

Finance
Nick Gibson
Jasdip Nandra
Sue Baker
Tom Costello

Inventory
Jo Jacobs
Dan Stevens

Production
Hannah Cox
Katie Horrocks

Publicity
Louis Patel

Sales
Dave Murphy
Victoria Laws
Group Sales teams across Digital, Field, International and Non-Trade

Operations
Group Sales Operations team

Rights
Rebecca Folland
Tara Hiatt
Ben Fowler
Maddie Stephens
Ruth Blakemore
Marie Henckel

Killers. Traffickers. Thieves.

Shaun Attwood is the man who talks to gangsters, drug lords and Mafia bosses. Infamously known for his time as the head of an international ecstasy ring in Arizona, Shaun has since turned to gaining the trust of some of the world's most dangerous people, interviewing and questioning them about their stories.

Collated from the many hours of interview material, and containing additional content exclusive to the book, Shaun brings together ten powerful conversations with the most gruesome and deadly gangsters of recent years.

Filled with truthful, brutal and often redemptive stories, Shaun's interviews feature international smugglers, Mafia enforcers and a man who escaped from Thailand's most notorious prison. *Sitdowns with Gangsters* is an unputdownable read that offers a glimpse into the lives and inner workings of some of the world's most fearsome gangsters.

Featuring a foreword from the UK's bestselling true-crime author, Christopher Berry-Dee.

Available now in paperback, eBook and audio

Bosses. Criminals. Killers.

Shaun Attwood, former ecstasy kingpin in Arizona turned author and podcast-host, has gained a reputation for earning the trust of some of the world's most dangerous people, including gangsters, serial killers and Mafia enforcers.

Drawing on his many hours of interview material, along with new content exclusive to the book, Shaun collates a collection of hard-hitting conversations with the most dangerous female gangsters he's met. With fascinating insights and gripping narratives, it includes interviews with Black Widow, a female gangster who previously worked for the Krays, a gang member turned prison rights activist, and the criminal mastermind at the heart of one of the UK's most sprawling county lines operations. *Sitdowns with Female Gangsters* is a pulsating, edge-of-your-seat read that exposes the most fearsome women working in the criminal underworld today.

Available now in paperback, eBook and audio